CHAUCERIAN FICTION

Robert B.
Burlin

CHAUCERIAN
FICTION

PRINCETON UNIVERSITY PRESS
PRINCETON, NEW JERSEY

Copyright © 1977 by Princeton
University Press
Published by Princeton University
Press, Princeton, New Jersey
In the United Kingdom: Princeton
University Press, Guildford, Surrey
All Rights Reserved
Library of Congress Cataloging in
Publication Data will be found on the
last printed page of this book
Publication of this book has been aided
by a grant from The Andrew W. Mellon
Foundation
This book has been composed in
Linotype Granjon
Designed by Frank Mahood
Printed in the United States of America
by Princeton University Press,
Princeton, New Jersey

CONTENTS

PREFACE

THIS STUDY of Chaucer might well be entertained as a "reading" of his major poetic fictions. Indeed, my method relies heavily on close reading or *explication de texte*, though I prefer the term "formal analysis," or even R. S. Crane's "semantic criticism." I have not, however, sought to recapitulate all that has already been well expressed, nor do I pretend to have something new to say on every issue. At this point in the history of literary studies, all Chaucerian critics are necessarily, like the theologians of his era, dwarfs standing on the shoulders of giants. I have, therefore, tried to negotiate a course between economical summary of what has oft been said and more expansive discussion of what seems to me to have been insufficiently explored, particularly in the context of Chaucer's career as a conscious maker of fictions. Consequently, my emphasis may not fall on what appears to be the primary concern, or "grete mateere," of many of these poems, specifically the early ones. Instead, I have singled out those aspects of the fiction, the thematic undercurrents, that relate more to the process of composition than to its ostensible occasion or purport. Thus, while I have tried to extend or reaffirm those interpretations I believe to be well considered, I have also sought to reinforce my convictions by placing the individual analyses in the larger perspective of Chaucer's own view of himself as a maker of poetic fictions.

The attitude of a medieval poet toward his art is notoriously difficult to ascertain. Dante alone has left explicit indications of what he was trying to do. In England there is hardly a serious attempt before Sidney to defend the poet's status. Inferences drawn from medieval and classical rhetorical manuals, from the other arts, or from the analogy of scriptural exegesis, while incidentally useful or corrective, when rigidly applied have been misleading if not self-defeating. Internal evidence, consequently, remains our primary resource: we must scrutinize imaginatively what the poet's own work implies about his understanding of the uses of fiction. Despite the perilousness of such an undertaking with a master ironist such as Chaucer, there is in his progress through various modes of fiction a strong underlying logic to his aesthetic assumptions, a logic that compels by its simplicity and the inevitability of its imaginative configuration.

The titles by which I have designated the three groups of poems in this inquiry indicate roughly the logical pattern I have in mind. The sections by no means reflect chronological progression, still less a spiritual or creative autobiography. By intentionally upsetting the generally accepted order of composition I have attempted to dissociate myself from theories dependent exclusively on external forces. Historical events and foreign literary influences may well have affected the kind of poem Chaucer embarked upon at one time or another and may have contributed to a reorientation of his concept of what he was doing. But the sequence of my analyses follows the inner logic of his development, which is essentially independent of, though it may be roughly coincidental with, the kind of tidy chronology literary historians exact.

The poems I call "poetic fictions" are those in which

Chaucer speculates, more or less explicitly, on the poet's relation to his audience, on the value (beyond incidental entertainment) of poetic activity, on the sources of its *affekt*, and on its validity as a means of apprehending anything that approximates an authentic estimate of the human condition. The "philosophic fictions" concentrate on this epistemological aspect of literary activity. They reproduce within the fiction something like the creative process, bringing to the fore the narrative persona as representative of the shaping imagination. Ambivalence in the narrator's authority and response affects significantly the kind of "philosophic" proposition a literary fiction can justly claim. Experimentation of this sort inevitably prompts a curiosity about the fiction-maker himself. Hence, I call the final group of poems, chosen from the *Canterbury Tales*, "psychological fictions" in as much as they reckon with the unspoken motives for telling a tale as well as the teller's pronounced intentions.

The logical coherence of Chaucerian fiction lies primarily in the dramatic use of the narrator and can be described as an oscillation of emphasis between the poles of Chaucer's favorite antinomy, "experience and auctoritee." Whereas the first group of poems promotes the illusion of authorial experience, the second works from the premise of authoritativeness. In the Canterbury group a multiplicity of narrators makes possible an anatomy of the kinds of experience that hide behind the fiction-maker's mask. Consequently, the opposition usually implied in the yoking of these terms acquires a characteristically Chaucerian elusiveness. Even the precise universe of discourse from which the antinomy is drawn has slipped past most of his critics, attracting little notice. An investigation into the origin of the terms may help to determine their linguistic status and supply a constructive guide to the elusive ways of Chaucerian fiction.

A word of acknowledgment is in order. I have tried to keep annotation to a minimum; Chaucerian bibliographies are more than adequate, and I see no need to reproduce them. My indebtedness to previous scholarship is, however, difficult to assess; I have tried to mention works of particular influence, but not all instances of shared insight. I share with many Chaucerians a more general and profound debt to Muscatine and Donaldson as well as to the editors, Robinson, Root, and Pratt, and other important critics such as Owen, Howard, Payne, Brewer, and Robertson. If I have slighted others in favor of works that appeared during the writing of this study, I hope they will appreciate the difficulties of doing justice to a literature that has grown astronomically during the past fifteen years.

Many friends have read my manuscript and made invaluable suggestions and corrections. I would like to thank especially Isabel MacCaffrey, Marie Borroff, Joseph Kramer, Jeannette Hume, Mara Maizitis, and Sandra Berwind. My wife, Katrin Ristkok Burlin, has also shared generously her time and counsel.

The Madge Miller Fund of Bryn Mawr College contributed to the preparation of the manuscript, and I am indebted particularly to Cornelia Seidel and Aida O'Connell for their careful efforts above and beyond the call of duty.

I am grateful to the editors of *Neophilologus* for permission to use portions of my article on the Franklin and to Middlebury College for the opportunity to try out some of my ideas on the Nun's Priest as the Samuel S. Stratton Lecture for 1972. Permission to quote from the second edition of F. N. Robinson's *Works of Geoffrey Chaucer* (1957) has been given by the Houghton Mifflin Company and Oxford University Press.

R.B.B.

CHAUCERIAN FICTION

EXPERIENCE AND AUTHORITY

"IN SCOLE IS GREET
ALTERCACIOUN"

*The only method of freeing
learning, at once, from
these abstruse questions,
is to enquire seriously
into the nature of human
understanding, and show,
from an exact analysis of
its powers and capacity,
that it is by no means
fitted for such remote and
abstruse subjects.*

HUME

CHAUCER'S thoughts a-
bout what we would call
literary theory are, like
most of his personal beliefs and
judgments, difficult to isolate and
interpret. Such clues as we have
appear in tantalizing disguises—
tossed off in a casual phrase, en-
tangled in a dramatic encounter,
or enthusiastically averred by a
patently fictive narrator. The in-
direction of fragmentary "internal
evidence" undoubtedly presents
severe problems to the theoretician
but is not without its virtues. The
critic may be left sounding ten-
dentious by comparison, but inso-
far as the poet's "definitions" are
implicated in the very process of
his fictions, they share in its ironic
cover, in the semantic relativity of
its dramatic occasions. The terms
that assume importance in Chau-
cer's poetry are—or are made to
seem—remote from technical dis-
course. By varying the context—
verbal, narrative, or generic—
Chaucer is, however, capable of
investing the most casual word or
phrase with dimensions of mean-
ing that, while they clearly mark
out the range of his thinking, pre-
clude simplistic abstraction.

Words for Chaucer, as for some

3

more recent schools of linguistic philosophy, mean what they mean when spoken on a particular occasion and cannot (to the frustration of editors) be glossed once and for all by a single modern equivalent. *Worthy* and *a good felawe* notoriously slip and slide through the *General Prologue*, as if condensing centuries of popular usage. Compressed into a single work, however, their semantic adjustments simulate that unthinking reliance on ready-made standards, the basic stuff of ordinary discourse. Apparently casual language produces more than the obvious local effects, satirically directed at the individual pilgrim. Cumulatively, such linguistic acts reproduce habits of judgment; we are forced into an awareness of our social propensity for unconsidered, *ad hoc* evaluation. Inconsistency and illogicality in the verbal pattern awaken a sense of the absent absolutes that in the pressure of everyday life we prefer to keep comfortably anaesthetized.[1]

The Chaucerian habit of drawing complex moral implications from simple, familiar words also characterizes what might be called his aesthetic pronouncements. In particular, when he yokes a pair of antithetical terms in this innocent colloquial manner, Chaucer appears to be offering some purchase on his theoretical conception of literature. The ubiquitous "ernest and game,"[2] for example, which generally masks a tangle of unspoken motives, carries over this psychologically acquired ambiguity when it is used to designate the formal (rather than the tonal) possibilities for any kind of spoken exchange. So convincing is their Chaucerian deployment that such antinomies have often been taken as proverbial, a dramatic poet's attempt to evoke the platitudinous, or at best a conditioned response of the medieval mind, conceiving reality in patterns of opposing extremes. The polarities by which Christian myth affixed the temporal to the eternal—Creation and Judgment, good and evil, heaven and hell—provide an analogue for the aesthetic habit of considering stories as either serious (in earnest) or comic (in game). Indeed, when Chaucer uses such phrases as "lust and lore" or "sentence and solaas," he seems to be considering the functions of art merely as incompatible alternatives. Harry Bailly, like many masters of ceremonies before and since, would undoubtedly be content to stop there, with a sure-fire formula for keeping things going, tragedy followed by comedy, a pious legend followed by a fabliau. But the terms are obviously no more satisfactorily polarized than the classical ideal they so closely resemble.[3]

As Chaucerian usage, and the articulation of the *Canterbury Tales* in particular, makes clear, such opposing terms may be both antithetical and interpenetrating. "Heigh sentence" to be effective cannot rely exclusively on a naked proposition, but must enclose its exposition in "solaas" and perhaps "myrthe" as well. Likewise, a "lusty" effort is never quite devoid of "lore." A literary performance may, by virtue of its kind, tend to one extreme or the other, but, in the successful production, both functions are inevitably and inextricably entwined.

While "lust and lore" may tell us a good deal about Chaucer's sense of the ends and means of literature, another of his familiar antinomies, "experience and auctoritee," serves a more comprehensive purpose. Explicitly or implicitly, it may be said to inform the structure of his imaginative work throughout his career. As with the other pairs, the issues it raises are central to an understanding of the literary experience, though the angle of attack is somewhat different. Rather than form and function, "experience and auctoritee" addresses itself to the problem of the origins or sources of literary creativity, which leads in turn to an inescapable questioning of the viability of the final product as a source of knowledge.

Like the other antinomies, "experience and auctoritee" proffers a familiar set of alternatives that upon examination prove to be both real and apparent. A casual reading of the terms might lead one to think that they comprehend a process: the transcription of the author's observation of life ("experience") into a verbal form ("auctoritee") which, by virtue of a reverence accorded the written word, acquires an authenticity or authoritativeness.[4] Indeed, this process seems to be implied when the speaker in Chaucer's early poems remarks upon his decision to commit his dream experience to written form, or

5

when the experiences of the Wife of Bath are cited as authorities for the edification of January or Bukton. But these experiences themselves are obviously fictive; their value as authority is qualified, if not totally undermined, by the comic irony. Fiction by definition is something made up, a fabrication, and its benefit to mankind has always been a matter for some anxiety. For Plato, poetry ("making") implied feigning, and in the *Republic* he suggests that its charms may be potentially dangerous to the ideal state. The Middle Ages tolerated and often relished its own poets, while, with a variety of rationalizations, they accepted and even revered the *auctores* of the pagan past. Yet the new religion also revived the Platonic suspicions in a new form. What was the value of secular poetry to the City of God? Apologists were as numerous as objectors, ranging from those who found pedagogical value in the verbal manner to those who allegorized away the offending matter. Yet the question must have nagged at many authors[5]—Chaucer among them, as the endings of his two great poems remind us. The attitude of the Parson to the telling of "fables and swich wrecchednesse" clearly does not reflect the poet's feeling throughout his life, but the "Retraction" in many ways represents a logical conclusion to his poetic career.

Chaucer's elusive attitude toward his avocation can be to some extent clarified by taking a close look at the complications and obscurities accruing from his unsystematic use of "experience and auctoritee." The antithetical terms are conjoined by their reference to kinds of knowledge or information. Commonly they denote the intellectual basis of a given utterance, the raw materials upon which the speaker is drawing. Authoritatively, he may cite a proverb or scriptural text, or he may reproduce an entire book—in translation (*Melibeus*), adaptation (*Troilus*), or in summary abstract (the *Somnium* in the *Parliament of Fowls*). But the material comes from the written page and usually from the remote past; it constitutes a vicarious acquaintance with another man's conscious reshaping of his own apprehension of reality, as, for example, when Chauntecleer's men of "auctoritee" are defined as transmitters of what they "han wel founden by experience" (*NPT*, 2978). Written sources are then assumed to be in opposition to what has been acquired through direct observation, what the senses have perceived of the natural or social worlds and what the mind has or has not made of it, by memory, imagination, or reason, or by the less controlled processes of fantasy and dreaming. All of Chaucer's major works depend structurally on this opposition: of what the speaker has read against what he experiences in a dream; of the old books that he scrupulously follows against the experience of the narrator in reproducing them. In the fictive world of the Canterbury pilgrimage, this polarization is exaggerated into the confessional autobiography of the Wife of Bath at one extreme and, at the other, the pathetic failure of Chaucer the pilgrim to come up with anything better than "a rym I lerned longe agoon." Such purely literary associations for "experience and auctoritee" are simple to isolate, not very new or intellectually taxing. Horace, in fact, offers similar alternatives in his advice to poets: "Aut famam sequere aut sibi convenientia finge" (*Ars Poetica*, 119).

Of the two terms, "auctoritee" is probably the more familiar to students of the intellectual history of the Middle Ages, but, largely because of the excesses of the medievals themselves, it has suffered, like rhetoric and allegory, from imperfect understanding and a consequent lack of sympathy. The process by which *auctoritas* came to mean a written document, obscure in English usage, has been usefully clarified by Fr. Chenu's analysis of a semantic history that antecedes the medieval development:

> An *auctor* among the Latins was . . . a person who took the initiative in an act. More properly, an *auctor* in common law was a person who transferred to another person, subject to liability of some sort, a right for which he could vouch. A seller, for instance, was in respect to a buyer an *auctor*. The guarantee itself was called an *auctoritas*. . . .

Whether taken in its juridic meaning or in the wider sense of dignity, *auctoritas* originally signified that quality in virtue of which a man—whether magistrate, writer, witness, or priest—was worthy of credit, of consideration, of credence. By metonymy, the word designated secondly the person himself who possessed this quality. Soon after, by a transposition of meaning from the human subject to his outward act, the word came to designate the writing, the document in which the judgment or the decision of this human subject was expressed. This instrument was invested with authority, or what comes to the same, was considered authentic. This meaning, naturally, applied first of all to official documents. . . . Through a new metonymy, the text itself was directly called an *auctoritas*; no longer was it just qualified as having authority, the text itself which was called to witness was an authority.[6]

The dependence upon received authorities in medieval writing resulted to a great extent from the paucity of books in even the best libraries and from the pedagogical methods, themselves inherited from the past, that were constrained by such practical considerations. Overriding all such external matters, however, was the spiritual justification for all learning, the primacy of theology as the queen of the sciences, and the reverence for scriptural authority, the revelation of the divine Author, which set the model for all intellectual endeavor. Yet, as Chenu persuasively demonstrates for Aquinas, the recourse to standard texts soon became a convention, used as often for "purely dialectical support," or for mere ornament, as for authority. The practice, though much abused, did not prevent the best medieval minds from "developing the processes of thinking and pushing research far beyond the trajectory described by the original text."[7] And so it is that in Chaucer one finds the word "auctoritee" on the lips of Theseus when he is stretching his intellectual resources to their utmost limit, though more typical no doubt is the crowing pedantry of Chauntecleer or the greedy hypocrisy of the Summoner's

8

friar. Whatever the occasion, Chaucer's deployment of the term has well-attested precedent in learned discourse. Its antithesis, "experience," however, is another matter. In Chaucer's usage both terms seem to evoke a second referential model and this complicates their import to literary theory.

This other model, or universe of discourse, may be called philosophical or theological, depending on which side of the watershed of the great scholastic synthesis one chooses to dwell. (In the parlance of modern philosophic inquiry, logic, epistemology, and metaphysics are all pressed into service.) Chaucer's way of defining the materials of fiction implicates, as we have seen, the question of what one knows with that of how such knowledge has come to be. In the medieval world when such philosophical problems were colored by the assumption of an absolute Truth, the comparative validity of alternate ways of knowing inevitably enters into reasoned discourse. "Experience and auctoritee" are more than just intellectual phenomena or mental baggage: as Theseus's famous Boethian speech illustrates, they constitute alternate modes of veridication, competing ways of getting at the truths of the human condition:

Ther nedeth noght noon auctoritee t'allegge
For it is preeved by experience.   (*KtT*, 3000–3001)

Ideally, the proof of a metaphysical proposition can be discovered by either epistemological process, but as the opening of the *Wife of Bath's Prologue* aggressively reminds us, the two may not in every instance be equally available or, even worse, may be found contradictory and irreconcilable.

But if, as so many passages in Chaucer imply, there was a model in theological discourse for the conjunction of experience and authority, where is it to be found? Chaucer's usage suggests that it was a commonplace, and many Chaucerians have proved remarkably credulous. But the antithetical terms one finds running through medieval discourse are "faith" and "reason":[8] the one founded on the revelation in Scripture of the Word of God, the preeminent and uncontested authority

9

in matters of faith; other kinds of knowledge result from the application of human reason, itself a divine endowment, to the Book of Nature, God's other great work. Though Augustine devised ways of entertaining pagan philosophy, especially that of Plato, bringing "rational insight into the contents of Revelation," there was seldom any question of the "primacy of Faith": "Understanding is the reward of faith. Therefore seek not to understand that thou mayst believe, but believe that thou mayst understand."[9] But in spite of Augustine's classic formula, a scholarly methodology with its training in the liberal arts became an essential tool for a proper interpretation of scriptural letter and spirit.[10] When the text was less than Scripture, more than interpretation might be required, and questionable human authority demanded that it be put to the test of human reason. In Augustine's *Soliloquia*, a passage of some importance for aesthetic theory allows Ratio to explain the difference between the falsehoods of deceivers and the untruth of an authority, in this case, a fabulist:

> Farces and comedies and many poems are full of fables whose purpose is to give pleasure rather than to deceive, and almost everyone who tells a joke, tells a fable. But that one is rightly called fallacious or deceiving whose sole aim is to deceive someone. Those, on the contrary, who make something up, but do not do it in order to deceive, no one hesitates to call fabulists, or if not that, tellers of fables (*vel mendaces tantum, vel si ne hoc quidem, mentientes tamen vocari nemo ambigit*).[11]

So, too, in the ninth century John the Scot advised publicizing the findings of reason where authority other than Holy Scripture was concerned:

> For now we must follow reason, which investigates the truth of things and is not overborne by any authority, and is by no means prevented from revealing publicly and proclaiming to all men the things which it both zealously searches out by circuitous reasoning and discovers with such toil.[12]

Though by the twelfth century the neo-Aristotelians, and the "School of Chartres" in particular, had injected their renewed interest in nature into theological discourse, Chaucer would still hear from the mouth of Alain de Lille's plaintive Natura a witty play on Augustine's formula, its fundamental antithesis undisturbed:

> And it is not strange if here theology does not extend me her friendship, since in many matters, we are conscious, not of enmities, but of diversities. I attain faith by reason, she attains reason by faith. I know in order that I may believe, she believes in order that she may know. I assent by perceiving and knowing, she perceives by assenting. I barely see the things that are visible, she comprehends in their reflection things incomprehensible. I by my intellect hardly compass trifles, she in her comprehension compasses immensities. I, almost like a beast, walk the earth, she serves in secret heaven."[13]

In the first half of Chaucer's century such conflicts—between nature and theology, reason and faith, philosophy and theology—acquired even greater significance as the scholastic synthesis, brought to its highest pitch by Aquinas, was seriously challenged and eventually split apart. What Gordon Leff has called the "Age of Scepticism" had begun with Duns Scotus and a "redefinition of what could be known about God":

> The distinction between faith and reason, which St. Thomas had so firmly held, was taken to make each self-contained; the natural and the supernatural were not merely on different planes but without a meetingpoint; since they dealt with different truths they could not inform one another.[14]

Scotus had "set reason loose from the guidance of authority, . . . from matters of faith and restricted it to natural phenomena."[15] In the fourteenth century Ockham further widened the gap by emphasizing the epistemological distinction:

The whole force of Ockham's theory hinges upon the divorce between the thing known and the process of knowing; knowing does not guarantee the truth of that knowledge. Consequently, where Duns Scotus and others had used intuitive and abstractive knowledge to distinguish experience from intellection, Ockham used it to demarcate truth from speculation. For the former, the object and the intellect alone sufficed; . . . reasoning became the property of terms, or signs, not things.[16]

Ockham's isolation of "intuitive knowledge" from matters of faith is crucial to an understanding of theological controversy in Chaucer's time and of the poet's own attitude toward the relationship between knowledge and language:

"Intuitive knowledge of a thing is that knowledge by virtue of which can be known if the thing exists or not. . . . Perfect intuitive knowledge is that of which it should be said that it is experimental knowledge, and this knowledge is the cause of universal propositions, the principle of art and science." Consequently, "nothing can be naturally known in itself, unless it is known intuitively."[17]

The consequences of Ockham's redefinition of reason were not to deny faith or authority, but to make them totally independent: the one resting on "empirical observation and natural causation," the latter on citing its own truths, a positive theology "without the need of intermediaries." Thus "a growing empiricism was giving rise to a growing fideism,"[18] a theological position which Sheila Delany has recently claimed for Chaucer, though we have no evidence for his acquaintance with Ockham.[19]

The Nun's Priest, however, testifies to the poet's familiarity with at least the name of Bradwardine, the great opponent of Ockham and his followers, proctor of Oxford and Archbishop of Canterbury. Bradwardine's great work on free will and predestination, *De Causa Dei*, reasserted an orthodox position but paradoxically merely furthered the dissociation of faith and reason. Bradwardine, refusing "to concede anything to fact or natural evidence . . . saw all truth as revealed truth," theology "a self-contained body of laws and principles which had no call on the resources of natural experience."[20] The tension between two ways of knowing, two kinds of proof, charged the intellectual atmosphere of Chaucer's day, though the standard antinomy continued to be authority (or faith) and reason, as in Wyclif's petition to King Richard, the Duke of Lancaster, and the Parliament, asking them "to here, assent, and mayntene the fewe articlis or poyntis that ben seet withinne this writing, and proved bothe by auctoritee and resoun."[21] What then lies behind Chaucer's preferred coupling of "auctoritee" with "experience," varied only occasionally, as in the *Legend of Good Women* (2394), by the ambiguous "preve"?[22]

"Experience is one of the most enigmatic concepts of philosophy," according to a modern encyclopedist[23] who is, however, worrying more about post-Cartesian developments than the medieval situation. But even Middle English usage is difficult to sort out, and the editors of the *MED* will perhaps forgive me if I rearrange their illustrative citations. One might begin with the common and still current notion of "that which is apprehended by the senses" (*MED* 3), knowledge of worldly or temporal things, as experience of natural phenomena, of love, of marriage, of fools, and especially, experience of time. The citations in this category indicate that the word means, not merely sensory observation, but repeated occasions that breed a familiarity with some matter of practical concern, which has thus become a quasi-abstraction. Hence, this meaning shades off into the next: "Knowledge, information, 'know-how,' or skill acquired through personal experience or practice; expert knowledge; also, good practical sense, understanding, or wisdom (as distinct from natural intelligence)" (*MED* 4). The parenthetical distinction would have raised an outcry among many medieval philosophers, and the definition really combines two ideas. First, the best experience depends on age, "*oold* experience" (*Mel* 2359), as when Plato, in the final citation, uses his experience to advise that the young may be given good counsel "by right grete experience." Or, as Chaucer puts it in the *Knight's Tale*, "Men may the olde atrenne, and noght atrede" (2449).

But the generalized experience of longevity and accumulated memory (see under *MED* 3 the passage from Lydgate's *Pilgrimage*) is quite different from that which culminates in a practical skill or professional knowledge, as in the citations scattered through definitions 2, 3, and 4, which allude to medicine, hawking, "algorismes," astronomy, magic, natural science, moral philosophy, and theology, and to their written formulations, "reedying off bookis" (Lydgate, under 4) or "experience of word outward" (*The Cleansing of Man's Soul*, under 2). This conscious use of the faculties to acquire a skill, craft, or profession leads one to the synonymy of "experience" with "experiment." "Experience" is a testing of, and potentially a discovery from that which is external to the senses (*MED* 2). In the two versions of the Wycliffite Bible at Genesis 42:15, both words are used for the Latin *experimentum*; and Aquinas uses that term to encompass all the meanings discussed so far. "Experiment" is also associated with the Greek "emperic" (*MED* 3), suggesting the Aristotelian origin of this semantic complex. It can refer to the sacred experience of "experimental witnessing" (see *MED*, adj.) or the dubious mysteries of magic and alchemy (*MED* 4), and in the phrase, "bi experiment" (*MED* 5), it seems to mean the mutable condition of this "fals world."

The philosophic sense of "experience" (*MED* 1), however, is regularly opposed to the "doom of resoun" (Pecock), or "science" (*Roman de la Rose*, and Wyclif), or the "sotyle compassement of wytt" (Mandeville). But whereas "Auicen" is cited as holding that "experience ouercometh reson," Lydgate (*Pilgrimage*) refers to their interdependence: "Ffor speculatyff. . . . / Withouten good experience / Avaylith lytle or ellis noght." Pecock, on the other hand, in two citations, gives the orthodox view that both are subject to "credence," or "rehercyng of eny text of feith . . . in the bible."

Middle English lexicography, then, gives a range of meaning that may be some help in understanding Chaucerian usage. We may begin with the absolute subservience of "experience" to "auctoritee," as long as authority means the revealed truth of the Bible. But as soon as authority means something less, the balance is altered. What is written may have apostolic or patristic or ecclesiastical authority, but it is the work of man and, whereas in some instances it may be thought of as divinely inspired or mystically revealed, in others it may be simply the product of better informed or superior reason. It may even represent the unadulterated product of experience itself—if not the common variety, the experience of reading, the gathering of the posies of the wise into an anthology or "florilegium." Once one removes "reason" from the coupling, one has an antinomy with an ambiguous middle: "auctoritee" comes to mean "whatever is written" and therefore presumed reasonable; while "experience" may draw upon the full capacities of the human mind, in which case it ought properly to include "reason."

There can hardly be any question that, for Chaucer's age, experience could not be considered superior to reason (except, of course, in the mystical sense). The faculty psychology of Aristotle's *Posterior Analytics* prevailed among scholastic philosophers and was set apart, but not rejected by the fideists like Ockham. Aristotle's analysis accounts for our popular notion of "animal instinct" as well as our common meaning of "experience":

> Sense impressions persist in certain animals while in others such impressions do not extend beyond the actual perception of things. Man is able to store up the data of exterior sensation in the form of images. . . . He is also capable of systematizing such data, with the result that memory is born. Moreover, out of frequently repeated memories ἐμ-

πειρία or *experience* is begotten, since experience is the fruit of much remembering: αἱ γὰρ πολλαὶ μνῆμαι τῷ ἀριθμῷ ἐμπειρία μία ἐστίν. From experience, in turn, originate the skill of the craftsman and the knowledge of the scholar: ἐκ δ' ἐμπειρίας . . . τέχνης ἀρχὴ καὶ ἐπιστήμης.[24]

The most elaborate and influential development of Aristotle's theories was that of Thomas Aquinas. In his commentaries on the *Analytics* and the *Metaphysics* as well as in his own *Summae*, he offers a complex description of the "interior senses," which are responsible for conducting the data of the senses to the higher intellectual faculties. Briefly, intellectual cognition functions in this way:[25] the *imaginatio* has the power to reproduce the phantasms or images received by the sense after the object is no longer present. *Memoria* "is limited to the formality of pastness to the image, that is, to endowing the image with a peculiar character by which it is recognized as reproduction."[26] It is the function of the *sensus communis* to synthesize these recollected images, bringing together the impressions of the different senses and forming the perception of a unified object while yet attributing to it the various properties apprehended by the five external senses. The last of the "internal senses" is the most difficult. In animals, it is the *vis aestimativa*, the "instinct" that estimates the distinctions between what is dangerous or harmful and what is good or useful. In man, this power is called the *vis cogitativa*, and while in some ways it resembles the "reason," unlike that higher faculty it is still attached to the particulars of sense experience:

> In man, the estimative power works like a particular reason: so that the insensate aspects of objects are appreciated by him either ideationally, or by particular reason operating in conjunction with universal reason. The special discursive activity of particular reason terminates in what Aquinas calls an *experimentum*—the highest type of sensitive experience possible to man.[27]

16

This, then, is the "experience" that underlies the Middle English definitions. It is more than the apprehension of the senses or a collection of remembered objects; it is a unifying activity linking actual perception to what has been apprehended in the past. Thus, to cite Robert Brennan's helpful summary:

> the *experimentum* may be said to have its origin in a kind of discourse, exercised by particular reason working under the guidance and control of intellect. It cannot be called rational discourse, in the strict sense, because it is concerned with particulars. We may, however, dignify it by the name of sensitive discourse, since its function is to draw together and compare all the concrete informations of both the external and internal senses.[28]

The distinction between "experience" and "reason" might be compared to that between the proverb, grounded in graphic particulars, and its reformulation in abstract or universal terms.

The usefulness of such a term to a writer of Chaucer's dramatic range is obvious. It can include the *experimentum* of the Wife of Bath's marriages while it also describes the basis for the knowledge and skill of the craftsmen and professionals, on the one hand, and an aspect of the speculations of the Clerk, the Parson, and perhaps even the Knight, on the other. But strictly speaking, as Aquinas points out in his last lecture on the *Posterior Analytics*, only the Wife's kind of "scole-iyng" may properly be called "experience," for

> reason does not stop at the experience gathered from particulars, but from many particulars in which it has been experienced, it takes one common item which is consolidated in the mind and considers it without considering any of the singulars. This common item reason takes as a principle of art and science. For example, as long as a doctor considered that this herb cured Socrates of fever, and Plato and many other individual men, it is *experience*; but when his considerations arise to the fact that such a

species of herb heals a fever absolutely, this is taken as a *rule of the art of medicine.*[29]

Only in the jesting of the Friar, or perhaps in the fictionalizing impulse of her *Tale*, might the Wife of Bath be said to rise beyond experience to rational knowledge, for as Aquinas summarizes his position in the *Scriptum super Sententias*:

In quantum ex multis sensibus fit una memoria, et ex multis memoriis unum experimentum, et ex multis experimentis unum universale proprium, ex quo alia concludit et sic acquirit scientiam.[30]

But St. Thomas, no more than St. Bernard, "ne saugh nat all, pardee!" There was another tradition that may well have been known (perhaps better known) to Chaucer and that also originated in the recovery of Aristotle in the high Middle Ages.[31] In this case, however, it was the scientific as much as the metaphysical works that proved attractive, and it was Robert Grosseteste, Chancellor of Oxford and Bishop of Lincoln, who established the basis for new research in linguistics, translated the essential scientific writings of the Greek philosopher, and founded a new school of experimental inquiry. By the twelfth century, philosophy had come to terms with "the distinction between experimental knowledge of a particular fact, and 'rational' or 'scientific' knowledge of the cause of the fact."[32] But the methodology for a logic of natural science, which we owe to Grosseteste, could not depend exclusively on deductive argument. To inquire fully into an observed phenomenon, the "fact," one had to discover the "reason for the fact," the efficient as well as the formal and material causes. This required first "induction," the breaking up of the composite phenomenon into its component elements or principles, and then "composition," the theoretical reconstruction of the phenomenon. Scientific truth could then be assayed by comparing the theoretical composite, or "model," with the composite of observation. Experimental verification, however, could only observe the principle of economy: "nature operates in the shortest way possible." Hence, Grosseteste maintained that demonstrations in natural science were "probable rather than strictly scientific."[33] In spite of its acknowledged inferiority to mathematics, practical experience or experimentation, as justified by Grosseteste, became enormously important in the following centuries. Just as the Bishop's theological writings were later to influence Wyclif strongly,[34] so his scientific theories were very much alive in the schools as well as in the alchemical goings-on of Chaucer's century. In particular, Grosseteste may be held responsible for the empirical cast that enlivened philosophic study at Oxford from the beginning.[35]

Grosseteste's most audacious disciple was Roger Bacon (d. 1294), the English Franciscan who insisted on pursuing his own untraditional course of study, preferring the acquisition of positive knowledge to formal logic.[36] He claims in the *Opus tertium* (1267) to have labored for twenty years "in studio sapientiae," spending sums on "experientias varias, et linguas, et instrumenta, et tabulas."[37] His goal was to work out a systematic and scientific treatment of the various branches of knowledge, but he only managed the preambular *Opus Majus* and two works of summary with some additions, most notably one on alchemy, which was responsible for his legendary role in English literature. A large portion of this comprehensive survey was to be devoted to the natural sciences, demonstrating their unity and protesting that the experimental method was the final judge of the assertions and reasonings put forth in these fields. It may, in fact, be to Bacon that we owe the opposition of experience and authority. The first part of the *Opus Majus* is devoted to the four general causes of human ignorance, the first of which is "fragilis et indignae auctoritatis exemplum,"[38] and in the second chapter he cites many authorities to prove his point, while in the third he uses "experientia." Later, he castigates the pretense to knowledge, claiming that the simple often surpass the learned in wisdom. Perfection of human knowledge is impossible; all men err. He enumerates, "by example and experience," the mistakes of the greatest Doctors of the Church, who often corrected one another, rebukes the early Church's neglect of philosophy, of Greek science, of mathematics, and of accurate philology. In short, he attacks the very bases of late medieval scholasticism and anticipates Chaucer's reduction of authority to fallible human experience or knowledge that happens to be set down in writing. There is only one perfect authority: "Una sola est sapientia perfecta, ab uno Deo data uni generi humano propter unum finem, scilicet vitam aeternam, quae in sacris, litteris tota continetur."[39]

All philosophy must be tested by the "intellectus agens" that is God in man.[40] But the human faculties have often been imperfectly or inadequately used:

> For there are two modes of acquiring knowledge, namely, by reasoning and by experience. Reasoning draws a conclusion and makes us grant the conclusion, but does not make the conclusion certain, nor does it remove doubt so that the mind may rest on the intuition of truth, unless the mind discovers it by the method of experience (*via experientiae*); for many have the arguments relating to what can be known, but because they lack experience they neglect the arguments, and neither avoid what is harmful, nor follow what is good. . . . Therefore, reasoning does not suffice, but experience does.[41]

There are, however, two kinds of experience. That which employs the bodily senses, aided by instruments and the evidence of trustworthy witnesses, should be supplemented by the experience of spiritual things, which needs grace. According to Ptolemy, "duplex est via deveniendi ad notitiam rerum, una per experientiam philosophiae, alia per divinam inspirationem."[42] Of the latter there are seven steps, the highest being the mystical state of rapture. This wide range of the meaning of "experience" may well stand behind Chaucer's witty exploitation of the dream-vision form in the *House of Fame* and particularly the *Legend of Good Women*, where the dreamer's experience in the *Prologue* combines the evidence of privileged witnesses with visionary rapture to parody the operation of divine inspiration. But "experience" as sensory apprehension remains the primary meaning for Chaucer; scientific demonstration and visionary rapture are specialized extensions the poet uses to stress dramatically a point of aesthetic theory. Nevertheless, the term in Chaucer's mind seems to mediate the two theological traditions.

The link between the scholastic use of *experimentum* as a faculty and Bacon's formulation of the experimental method is perhaps Aquinas's teacher, Albertus Magnus. Not only did Albert influence the Thomistic definition of faculty psychology but he has also become known as "the first scientist" because of the vast corpus of descriptive works that reveal him as an indefatigable observer of nature.[43] The scientific tradition of neo-Aristotelianism, then, represents not a contradiction to the Thomistic evaluation of *experimentum*, but a shift of emphasis brought about by the new interest in experimental observation of natural phenomena, the particulars toward which the *vis cogitativa* has estimative response.

The most extreme statement of this position that I have found occurs in Bacon's *Compendium Studii*:

> The student's business should lie in chosen and useful topics, because life is short; and these should be set forth with clearness and certitude, which is impossible without *experientia*. Because, although we know through three means, authority, reason, and *experientia*, yet authority is not wise unless its reason be given (*auctoritas non sapit nisi detur ejus ratio*), nor does it give knowledge, but belief. We believe, but do not know, from authority. Nor can reason distinguish sophistry from demonstration unless we know that the conclusion is attested by facts (*experiri per opera*).[44]

For a man like Chaucer, with his evident curiosity about scientific instruments such as the astrolabe, his fascination with astronomy and alchemy, and his wide acquaintance with natural philosophy, there seems to have been available a tradition that allowed "experience" a respectable place on the epistemological ladder.[45] That there was even good authority for preferring "experience" to "auctoritee" in Bacon and Albertus, gives added comic point to Chaucer's identification of himself with the written word when a captive audience to that archetypal experimental scientist, the Eagle of the *House of Fame*, traditionally a figure for divine inspiration.

Whatever the specific philosophic occasion for Chaucer's repeated use of "experience and auctoritee," it is unquestionably more than a catch phrase. In its apparently commonplace terms it captures a fundamental polarity, a binary structure that informs his imaginative thought at every level. But the imaginative forms Chaucer is drawn to—whether generic, narrative, or dramatic—are consistently directed toward the dissolution of the antithesis, toward the exposure of the interrelatedness of these apparent opposites. As the poet grows older, we will sense a steady erosion of their epistemological validity, a bemused, but not unamused skepticism regarding their value, in alternation or in tandem, as ultimately significant ways of knowing.

POETIC FICTIONS:

"CRAFTY IMAGYNACIONYS OFF THINGYS FANTASTYK"

Aucunes genz dient qu'en songes
n'a se fables non et mençonges.

GUILLAUME DE LORRIS

❧

CHAUCER'S early poetry combines precisely those elements one would expect in a writer who was to give his vernacular a new dimension of suppleness and dignity. The English he had learned from popular romances[1] became in his hands a suitable poetic medium for addressing with the requisite urbanity an aristocratic audience on occasions ranging from a casual court entertainment to those of the highest seriousness. Against the diction and metrics of the native tradition, he exerted distinctly foreign pressures, importing from the continent an enriched vocabulary and, eventually, a new verseline. The generic model for his earliest major efforts, however, was entirely of French extraction —not the romance, which had long since been vulgarized into a popular native form, but the elegant artifices of the dream-vision, uncorrupted and by definition unsuited to the common minstrel. To this unlikely amalgam of easy colloquial English and stiff Gallic conventions, he brought that unaccountable touch of genius that made him the "father of English poetry," a native Homer, and the "well of English undefiled" for centuries to come.

For our purposes it is Chaucer's attraction to a fashionable generic structure and the pliancy he found in its conventions that prove most revealing—of an inherent bent to his imagination as well as of the shape of things to come. The rhetorical and narrative *topoi* of the French dream-vision, imported though they often are in large blocks of close translation, are as radically transformed in Chaucer's early works as is the idiom of the English romances. The unmistakable originality so immediately apparent in the supple language, vivid and suave in its tonal variation in spite of occasional prolixity and rhetorical exuberance, is perfectly complemented in the generic sea-change. The modishly elegant but mechanical and inert artifices of Machaut, Deschamps, and Froissart are not merely anglicized; they emerge fresh and revitalized by the new and highly individual poetic voice.

Chaucer's imagination was keenly responsive to the potentialities of form. Again and again in his career, he displays a particular sensitivity to the independent identity of formal conventions—investing new meaning in apparently outworn patterns, dramatically quickening what had been lifeless abstracts of human behavior, and even postulating what may be taken as "realistic" motivation for the rehabilitation of familiar structural or generic models. From the aristocratic French literary tradition of his time he expropriated a form of unbounded potentiality, but which had of late been subject to dulling and arbitrary carelessness. The dream-vision gave him an open field for experiment with many varieties of tone and subject matter, but was in itself a convention inherent with kinds of meaning that had been left dormant in the recent French practice.[2]

The genre by its nature liberates the imagination: imitating the inconsequence of actual dreams,[3] it generates a freedom to conceive without the constraints of empirical causality, the capacity to penetrate realities that, at its most exalted reach, bespeaks the authority of the visionary, at its humblest, the validity of psychic experience. Chaucer exploited the dream-vision energetically; his four exercises in the genre are strewn with extravagant figures and incidents, with hardly any repetition of subject, theme, or even of specific rhetorical conventions. Yet though his dream-visions are unlike one another in style and content, a consistency in the larger structural patterns betrays certain persistent though unstated preoccupations on the part of the poet, which were in turn peculiarly nourished by that genre.

Chaucer was fond of beginning these poems with a statement about the dream experience—its value and authority, or the nature of authority itself—then developing a narrator who responds to the experience of the poem in such a way as to raise questions about its nature and authority. The dreamer-narrator listens in a literal-minded way; he sees and describes without comment, reads and transcribes without engaged response. He may occasionally be moved to pity or terror, but never for long or with sustained seriousness. He resides innocently upon the surface of his experiences, shaping them and containing them by his presence, but rarely interpreting or generalizing the powerful sensations forced upon him. The dreamer's reactions are arrested at the first stage of perception, the Thomist *experimentum*; he stands before a brave new world distinctly not of his making, though nominally his by virtue of the dream fiction.

The famous Chaucerian persona,[4] his strikingly personal version of a medieval commonplace and a device he never abandoned, may be a happy by-product of his apprentice work in the dream-vision form. The French dreamer-poet was more often than not merely a convenience for the introduction of an allegorical *débat* or a tableau commemorating a court celebration. Chaucer makes the poetic "I" very much his own. The ironic self-portrait, a mixture of fact and fiction, of self-deprecation and self-effacement, adds a new dimension to the narrative, a consciousness of the split between the poet's public and private selves and of the creative process through which they negotiate. It is his reliance upon a persona that, as much as

27

anything else, lends that epistemological cast to Chaucer's poetry that it retains, with modifications of the device, throughout his career. The dreamer of the early visions becomes in the *Troilus* the narrator of an old story who cannot prevent himself from becoming caught up in the dramatic unfolding of the events narrated. In the *Canterbury Tales*, the fictive storyteller is further anatomized by his reduplication in a multitude of narrators. But from the beginning Chaucer uses the persona to make us vaguely conscious of the creator who perforce lives outside of the created fictive universe. He appears in the poem as a rough approximation of his true nature, a crude paradigm of the author in action. By such indirections, he directs and controls our awareness of how the poet functions—what he works from and to what end. The posture of the narrator in the dream-visions is calculated to bring to mind the creator of the fiction, the man who actually wrote the poem yet did not, as the persona claims, himself dream the dream. The disengaged attitude of the dreamer throughout his narrative carries an intriguing resemblance to that of the poet when he steps back from his manuscript and suddenly sees his poem, not as a vital experience in which he has been deeply immersed, but as ink on parchment to be copied by a scribe, as a mute quire to which he can say "go, litel bok, go" in a gesture of resigned and detached paternity.

Of course, poets probably do not spend much of their time worrying over the first steps of their verbal offspring unless they need a convenient way to bring a poem to an end. The rhetorical *topos*, if it has any basis in experience, may reflect only incidental moments in the creative process, when, for example, the craftsman is suddenly reminded that his work belongs to a certain tradition or fashion, when he stands sufficiently apart from his own achievements to see them as mere artifacts. But that is precisely how he sees the works of other poets and, as a maker himself, what most interests him about them. Perhaps this kind of response in the experience of Chaucer, the apprentice poet, accounts for one other element he characteristically includes in his dream-visions, namely a self-contained fiction.[5] The dreamer encounters, in some relation to his dream, a literary work spread out before him, but his reaction to the work, though it may include wonder, sympathy, fear, or curiosity, is as shallow, unanalytic, and short-lived as that to the dream proper. The fiction itself, though it may be as rich and intense with human interest as the surrounding matter, intrudes upon the poem as a very different kind of experience—an artifice (a book, mural, or inscription), something composed, shaped and ordered by human agency and not a part of nature. "Auctoritee," here the vicarious experience of fiction, is placed side-by-side with the extraordinary and powerful sensory "experience" of the fictively actual dream.

The persona of the dream-visions, by his inability to engage either "experience" or "auctoritee," by remaining uncommitted to his perceptions as either reader or dreamer, indirectly raises questions about the nature of the fictional experience, its relation to the first-hand experience of life and to truth itself.[6] For, though the dreamer's responses may be limited or even mute, there is no question that the poet Chaucer asks us to see and hear much more, more perhaps than he would have been able to say. With a characteristic amalgam of intellectual curiosity and obliquity, Chaucer in his dream-visions constructs aesthetic models, hypotheses about the nature and uses of fiction for which there was no theoretical formulation available to him.

The three dream-visions examined in this section do not constitute a chronological unit, a "period" in Chaucer's career. The two octosyllabic poems belong to the poet's "youth," while the *Legend of Good Women* came along considerably later, when he had already established a reputation and found the verse-line that was to dominate English poetry until the present century. But these three works, in spite of the great diversity of their ostensible occasions and strategies, share a more or less explicit preoccupation with the poet and his world. Whereas in all of Chaucer's poetry one perceives a consciousness of the fiction-making process that must be taken

29

into thematic account, these three poems have about them more of a self-consciousness. We are aware, for instance, of the poetic persona, the "Geoffrey" of these poems, as standing in closer proximity to the actual Chaucer than the narrators of the major poems. Though the details of the comic pose vary little, the industrious story-tellers of his major works strike one as suave rhetorical devices, easily absorbed into the total artifice, contributing to and pointing us toward its particular kind of "meaning." The narrator of the *Troilus* invites us by his ubiquity to take him as another character in a story whose dimensions he significantly enlarges; and the Chaucer of the *Canterbury Tales* slips almost imperceptibly into the procession as another pilgrim. But the dreamer of the visions, in part because of the fiction that these are his experiences, in part perhaps because they are addressed to specific occasions, carries more of the actuality of his maker, an aura of the man himself, sensitive to his particular audience and conscious of himself making things up before their very eyes and ears.

In the *Book of the Duchess* the resistance of actuality may be noted in the characterization of the dreamer, taken by some critics to be tactful and sophisticated, by others to be obtuse and flat-footed. Perhaps the problem in this case is not entirely with the critics and may indeed have been unavoidable when one considers how many delicate negotiations the poet was conducting within and without his poem. In the *House of Fame* the unexplained tonal residue, a negative attitude in excess of the apparent subject matter, as well as incidental private references deflect our thoughts to the man behind the poem. The *Prologue* to the *Legend of Good Women* reveals a mastery over the public role comparable to the metrical accomplishment it exhibits, but the occasion alone implicates the actual poet and his literary activities in a substantial way. There is no need to exaggerate this comparability; the grouping is, of course, to some extent arbitrary and a matter of critical emphasis. Yet in more ways than one, these poems direct our attention to the process and its occasion as much as to the made object itself, to the self-consciousness of the maker grappling with his own audacity.

Side by side with the pleasure of the creative act, the excitement of exploration and experiment, Chaucer conveys a sense of responsibility, almost of an accountability—to more than his immediate audience—for taking on the perilous role of creator.[7] The reliance on a persona, in all his major works, represents both an evasion and acknowledgment of complicity. The "I" of the poems, the visible (or audible) Chaucer stands before us in all the humility of his bumbling, naïve, portly, well-meaning humanity, asking our indulgence and our complaisance toward the actual poet, who hovers at a distance, sensible of his power and presumption. He is the usurper of Nature, a would-be *vicarius Dei* with no greater claim to the office than the tarnished *imago Dei* within him. The verbal worlds of his manufacture possess no objective reality beyond the applause and patronage of his audience. They may dissolve in an instant before the cold strictures of a St. Paul or his admirer, the Parson, who will have no truck with "fables and swich wrecchednesse" on the irrefutable grounds that they are by definition falsehoods, made-up things. Before the stiff-necked assembly of reason and morality, the responsible poet is severely tried, especially when he sports the garb of courtly maker.

Chaucer does, however, mount a forceful case in these three poems, though like the persona the argument is oblique. The *House of Fame* might have been the closest thing to an open brief for poetry, but the line of thought is smothered in ironic qualifications. The *Prologue* to the *Legend*, on the other hand, transforms a slight and potentially contentious court occasion into an eloquent defense that inverts Fame's seamy view of the poet's complicity in the secular occasions and their probably loose morality. Most indirectly of all, the *Book of the Duchess* posits correspondences between the creative imagination and the restorative powers of the human mind. With astonishing virtuosity, Chaucer extracts from the dream-vision form a wide variety of powerfully suggestive, if tentative, analogies by which one may properly assess the capacity of

31

the imaginative faculties. Recurrent in these explorations is the hypothesis that experience and authority, in their various connotations, are not mutually exclusive; as unduly polarized aspects of a single process, they are equally implicit in the act of the imaginative understanding. In the image-making power of the mind and its manifest activity, the making of fiction, experience and authority prove mutually supportive and together confirm the respectability and worth of poetic fiction as a viable epistemological mode.

Such extravagant and anachronistically phrased claims may seem to set up Chaucer as more of a philosopher than he was, and to heap on more intellectual baggage than these rather fragile poems can bear. The aesthetic implications of the three works will be extended—logically, I hope, though admittedly far beyond the tonal fabric of the verse. Much of what has often been dismissed as courtly convention or irrepressible comedy leads us again and again to the same fundamental issues lying half-articulated beneath an otherwise preoccupied surface. Taken together they force upon us a respect for Chaucer's responsiveness and intellectual responsibility to his chosen art.

CHAPTER I

THE *PROLOGUE* TO THE *LEGEND OF GOOD WOMEN:*

"MAISTRESSE OF MY WIT"

Et quae non sunt praesentia
in locis in quibus sumus,
scimus per alios sapientes
qui ex parti sunt.

ROGER BACON

ONE feature of Chaucer's dream-visions intriguing to scholars of a more historically minded generation is commonly brushed aside or ignored by modern critics. They were almost certainly occasional poems, written to commemorate a public event and designed to accommodate the poet's voice to a public reading of the text. The demands of an occasion as much as the choice of a fashionable genre help to account for the implicit speculation on the nature and validity of the poetic process.

Though the *House of Fame* has had the conclusive evidence lopped off and the *Parliament of Fowls* generalizes its occasion beyond historical recognition, the other dream-visions seem to be sufficiently grounded in a specific event to confirm the pattern. The heraldic pun, the lady's name, and Chaucer's external reference to the poem testify to the occasion of the *Book of the Duchess*, inferred by later editors. The *Legend of Good Women*, however, is something of a special case. It celebrates an event not confined to the great aristocratic world but one that includes the poet

33

as an actor. Consequently, it deserves priority in a search for Chaucer's notions about his art and its relation to an external world of unfictive realities.

There seems little reason to doubt that the *Legend of Good Women* was the result of patronage and that its *Prologue* records in a playfully transmuted form the origin of the poem in a royal commission. Lydgate's testimony that this "legende of martyrs of Cupide" was written "at the Request of the Quene"[1] is corroborated by the lines of the F version:

> And whan this book ys maad, yive it the quene,
> On my byhalf, at Eltham or at Sheene.[2]   (496–97)

And the poet, in spite of his pretense of devoting all his time to poring over old books or worshipping the daisy, is clearly by now a man of some reputation, with at least two large books to his credit—a translation of the *Roman* and his own *Troilus*. His humility and self-deprecation were no doubt familiar to his audience as a witty expropriation of conventional devices to ease the poet's public appearances in his semi-official capacity. Here they accommodate him gracefully to the critical strictures of his social, if not literary, betters. It is hard to believe that any one at the court took with absolute seriousness the idea of Chaucer's "sin" against the code of love, but it is not improbable that the subject for the new work grew out of a discussion of the "morality" of his fictions. The ingenious idea of calling the resultant commission a "penance," however, seems to have proved less amusing in the event. In spite of the modest size of the anthology—nineteen short legends, with presumably that of Alceste to complete the score— the testimony of the manuscripts and the dullness of the performance seem to justify Lydgate's conclusion that no amount of Chaucerian industry "Was importable his wittes to encoumbre / In all this world to Fynde so greet a noumbre."[3]

Though the poem itself turned out to be a colossal blunder[4] and may already have seemed so in the poet's lifetime, the *Prologue* is one of Chaucer's triumphs. It was a great favorite in the last century for its apparent innocence and simplicity and its romantic devotion to that perennial favorite of English poets, the humble daisy. Even the less impressionable and less critically impressionistic twentieth century has admired its easy grace and freshness, though its naturalness and love of nature have been reassessed in the light of literary convention.

Like the *Book of the Duchess*, the *Prologue* is heavily indebted to the French tradition, particularly the "cult of the marguerite." Perhaps the closest of Chaucer's poems to the French dream-visions in structure, it depends on a single tableau, a formal encounter of the poet with figures of authority, and not on a dramatic interplay of character or incident. The "conflict" in the dream is quickly resolved by the Queen's intercession, and the poet's attempted self-defense is perfunctory and speedily dismissed. As a prologue, the piece ought not to assert too obtrusive a dramatic identity; accordingly, it pushes rapidly forward to introduce the matter at hand, while concurrently portraying in suitably flattering terms its "only begetters." Nor does the dreamer linger over a piece of "reading" (Ovid, Virgil, Cicero) as in the other dream-visions—not surprisingly perhaps, since the ostensible purpose is to inaugurate a literary work, not to celebrate an event. The fiction will be simply that this new collection of short narratives has been brought into being by the dream experience interacting with the dreamer's scholarly resources, those "olde appreved stories" (21) to which he had previously been only intermittently devoted.

The *Prologue*, then, is in many ways less complex, less dense than the other dream-visions and is fully taken up by an "occasion" outside of the works of fiction to follow. The event commemorated here apparently concerns less the subject matter of poetry than the impulse for creation, but creation seen less as a problem of the poet's inner world or the imagination than of the social context in which a poet functions, the world of patronage and audience. Yet obviously Chaucer is toying with some of the standard topics raised in any theoretical discussion of the creative act: the poet and his audience; the subject matter and its purpose; the authorial shaping and the inner experience. The royal critics in the vision raise obtuse but difficult questions about the meanings of Chaucer's fictions. He accedes to their interpretations (or perhaps only to their superior power), but in doing so turns the imposition of their will into a graceful tribute to their apparent inspiration. The exercise as a whole transcends the banal event; the commission becomes an occasion to explore, with well-disguised intensity, the intricate relationship between authority and experience. Paradoxically, it is this relatively flat and inauspicious occurrence—a royal command—that prompted Chaucer to his most aesthetically suggestive reworking of the dream-vision convention.

The theoretical implications of the *Prologue*, as well as its poetic merit in general, have been overlooked in most recent studies. The *Prologue* has either been pulled down by *Legends* to the critical basement or been scuttled by its historical entanglements and the frivolousness of its ostensible topic. The major exception to this criticism is Robert O. Payne, who uses the text as a cornerstone for his study of Chaucer's poetics, *The Key of Remembrance*.[5] Though we differ on many points, I wish to reinforce Payne's analysis here. The primary reason for our common interest is that in the *Prologue* Chaucer dramatizes with uncommon vividness the split between what I have called "experience and auctoritee." By first adducing a written authority that depends upon an extraterrestrial experience, then setting it at odds with an observation of nature that rises to impassioned devotion for a single flower, Chaucer pushes the dichotomy to extremes bordering on burlesque. But what may put off some critics by its fancifulness intensifies the theoretical issues and should insure their consideration. In the G version, Chaucer softens the antithesis by making the daisy-worship a part of the dream. For my purposes, unlike Payne, I prefer the F text, which is generally conceded priority and stresses the uncontestable divorce between the waking worlds of bookish authority and natural experience.[6]

36

The first clue to Chaucer's strategy lies in the *Prologue*'s opening lines, which wallow in sententiousness yet seem to have no relevance to what follows beyond a justification of the speaker's slavish respect for old books:

A thousand tymes have I herd men telle
That ther ys joy in hevene and peyne in helle,
And I acorde wel that it ys so;
But, natheles, yet wot I wel also
That ther nis noon dwellyng in this contree,
That eyther hath in hevene or helle ybe,
Ne may of hit noon other weyes witen,
But as he hath herd seyd, or founde it writen;
For by assay ther may no man it preve.
But God forbede but men shulde leve
Wel more thing then men han seen with ye!
Men shal not wenen every thing a lye
But yf himself yt seeth, or elles dooth;
For, God wot, thing is never the lasse sooth,
Thogh every wight ne may it nat ysee.
Bernard the monk ne saugh nat all, pardee!   (1–16)

The written word gives access to kinds of knowledge otherwise unavailable to common experience; books are the collective memory of mankind—"of remembraunce the keye" (26). But, this said, the impulse of the impressive introduction is allowed to falter; the passage, cut off from the body of the poem, seems to have been merely a "correct" rhetorical tactic, entered for local effect only. The description of the poet's devotion to scholarly pursuits through most of the year serves as a foil to brighten the enthusiastic exception, the competing worship of the daisy "whanne comen is the May" (45).

Of course, there is more here than at first meets the eye. Chaucer has unobtrusively set up a frame of reference, a complex of terms and ideas, that he will exploit heavily in the ensuing dream. The opening lines insinuate the language of religious experience into the innocent discussion of reading; the exalted diction is then imperceptibly extended to the "adoration of the daisy": "to the doctrine of these olde wyse, Yeve credence" (19–20), "honouren and beleve" (27), "feyth and ful credence" (31), "reverence" (32), "devocioun" (39). The real issue in the opening lines is the need for faith, a faith without which much knowledge would be impossible, and the proposition is made in terms that a medieval audience would have considered self-evident.[7] The knowledge of heaven and hell can only have proceeded from divinely inspired authority—if not Scripture itself, something nearly as venerable. Yet the narrator's concern is not, as it turns out, the documents of theology but "olde appreved stories," histories of a human past where the subject matter may be "of holynesse," but equally "of regnes, of victories, / Of love, of hate, of other sondry thynges" (22–23). This mindless drifting from analogy to analogy culminates in the revelation that the true object of the speaker's passion is not old books at all but the daisy, and not only in May but for the larger part of his poem. The enthusiastic pedantry of the narrator's apologia allows Chaucer to extend the reach of devotional discourse, first to secular writing where the ambiguous concept of "authority" provides an easy, unconsidered transition, and then into the worship of the daisy, where the charming nonsense of the poet's behavior assures us that more is meant than meets the ear.

Such an ingenious strategy would not have been required if Chaucer had in mind only the conventional and commonplace expropriation of the language of Christian belief for secular, amorous purposes. But the subject of this poem, unlike that of the other dream-visions, is not love, and its "lady," whether Anne or not, was certainly not the object of Chaucer's extra-poetical passion. Nothing of this has prevented Chaucer, however, from using the most extravagant terms of devotion, the language of the ecstatic visionary. What makes this tour de force possible is not only the exquisite handling of the tone but the thoroughness with which Chaucer prepared and worked out the religious analogy. The kind of experience alluded to in the opening lines implies more than common piety; it involves that divine condescension to human inadequacy, known as inspiration, by which knowledge of things beyond this world is communicated to mortal beings. Privileged recipients of such vision range from prophets of old to the monastic contemplatives, for whom Bernard of Clairvaux was apparently proverbial. St. Bernard became known for his veneration of the Blessed Virgin and for the heightened language of his devotional exercises, to which the diction of this *Prologue* has a special debt.[8] Equally celebrated as the great visionary, his sermons being a classic source for the definition of the mystical experience, he is almost certainly the subject of the colloquial tag, slipped in with deceptive casualness, "Bernard the monk ne saugh nat all, pardee!" (16). With such incidental strokes as these, Chaucer prepares the way not merely for the language of devotion but for a thoroughgoing transformation of the conventional dream-vision into a secular parody of the greatest reward a contemplative may receive, the gracious animation of the object of his veneration into the divine reality itself—the mystical vision.

Chaucer manages to make his exercise in daisy worship so convincingly engaging because the posture is totally realized in rich detail. Our disbelief is not suspended by mere historical knowledge of the conventionality underlying such absurdities. The dreamer develops and extends the analogy with ingenuity and compelling logic. The devotion to the daisy, though seasonal, has the uncommon absoluteness of a true vocation. The canonical hours, though only two, are observed with zeal, first at dawn "To seen this flour ayein the sonne sprede" (48), then again,

> whan that hit ys eve, I renne blyve,
> As sone as evere the sonne gynneth weste,
> To seen this flour, how it wol go to reste.   (60–62)

And the object of contemplation, though called a "relyke" (321) later in the poem, is obviously instinct with life for the worshipper, hence the shift to a feminine pronoun. Moreover, the daisy has an established spiritual valence as well as physical beauty: "Fulfilled of al vertu and honour" (54). This

39

vitalization intensifies to such an extent that it is soon impossible to think of the object of veneration as merely a flower. The transformation reaches a climax in a rhapsodic passage of praise: the inspiring force of the daisy assumes analogously the power of grace customarily reserved for the Blessed Virgin:

> She is the clernesse and the verray lyght
> That in this derke world me wynt and ledeth.
> The hert in-with my sorwfull brest yow dredeth
> And loveth so sore that ye ben verrayly
> The maistresse of my wit, and nothing I.
> My word, my werk ys knyt so in youre bond
> That, as an harpe obeieth to the hond
> And maketh it soune after his fyngerynge,
> Ryght so mowe ye oute of myn herte bringe
> Swich vois, ryght as yow lyst, to laughe or pleyne.
> Be ye my gide and lady sovereyne!
> As to myn erthly god to yow I calle,
> Bothe in this werk and in my sorwes alle.   (84–96)

The secular reference is carefully maintained—she is an "erthly god" and her governance is over the wit not the soul of the worshipper—but the rhetorical posture can hardly fail to recall such hymns to the Virgin as Dante assigns to St. Bernard, a text Chaucer knew well.[9] The secular plea for inspiration incorporates the Christian's petition for prevenient grace, that grace which "goes before" and in fact prompts the desire for, as well as the words of prayer. On another and more straightforward occasion Chaucer appropriates Dante's formulation of that doctrine; in their Canterbury prologues, the Second Nun and the Prioress ask for Mary's help in a literary endeavor that, like the dreamer's here, is both a public performance and an act of personal devotion.

At this point Chaucer reminds us of his initial statement about the need for faith in old books (97ff.), but his "besy gost" (103) hurries back to the scene of his devotion where we are given an extended picture of the spring setting in which the poet "knelying alwey" (117) contemplates "the resureccioun of this flour" (110–11) till nightfall. The birds in their amorous pursuits provide a choral background, and the poet is even prompted to imitate the hagiographers by providing an etymology for his "saint's name" (184).[10] Chaucer has given adequate intimation that the ensuing dream, though it may seem merely, in the French manner, to introduce a debate among allegorical characters, is in fact an elegantly parodic account of what Macrobius termed an *oraculum*.[11] The dream comes as a reward for devotion, but confers a grace far in excess of possible merit. The dreamer is in a state of sin, the nature of which he will come to know shortly.

The graciousness of this divine condescension to visionary appearance seems all the more remarkable when we discover that the dreamer does not recognize his deity. He can name the God of Love, but significantly his apprehension does not extend to the true identity of the queen. Her costume tells him that she is his daisy, here seen in that spiritual reality of which the earthly flower was but a token. In this knowledge, he hymns her praises in a *balade* that defines her essence as the epitome of all the virtues embodied separately by the nineteen heroines of antiquity. We can see in retrospect that the dreamer has an intuitive sense of who she is, but at this stage she is simply "My Lady."

The main "plot" of the dream follows the spiritual progress of the poet—the discovery of his sin, the wrath of the God, the intercession of the Queen, and his penance. But his enlightenment is correlated with another kind of action—the sequence of revelations during which the dreamer acquires a complete awareness of the identity of his divinity. Both processes are vital to the poem: the first is what brings us to the legends; the second gives the *Prologue* a coherence and integrity of its own. When the dreamer knows his lady in all of her manifestations, he becomes capable of integrating fruitfully those seemingly disparate impulses in his waking life— the conflicting devotions to old books on the one hand and to the daisy on the other.

The kind of spiritual illumination that Chaucer dramatizes parodically here is a familiar component of religious allegories, especially those in which a debating format proclaims a distant kinship to Boethius's *Consolation*. The Middle English *Pearl* comes immediately to mind. There, too, the dreamer's progressive understanding of his own spiritual state is figured symbolically in a corresponding enlargement of the meanings found in the "pearl."[12] The figural technique in the two poems is remarkably similar. The literal gem (like the daisy) most probably had a historical reference outside the poem to the dreamer's lost child (Chaucer's Queen Anne). In both dreams the symbol assumes the scarcely recognizable form of an appropriately costumed, courtly lady. In the ensuing debate, the pearl acquires many abstract connotations, but its final metamorphosis—as one of the virgins in the Procession of the Lamb—brings together the emblem and the reality of spiritual salvation. So, too, Chaucer's daisy appears first in floral masquerade, but her royal station alludes to a "historical" level of meaning (Chaucer's patron and Richard's queen) and anticipates the further allegorical development. Only when the dreamer has experienced her virtues in action is her true identification as Alceste, bride of the God of Love and archetype of wifely devotion, revealed. As daisy, Lady (Anne), Queen of Love, and Alceste, she moves on many planes of symbolic being, whose identity emerges dramatically from and correlates with the increasing spiritual enlightenment of the dreamer.

The interrelation among the various levels is so complex that it may be helpful to review them in terms of Dante's fourfold allegory of the poets.[13] The literal level, the daisy, penetrates the three allegorical realms. The "Lady" wears a robe and crown that associate her with the flower; and Chaucer concludes with the provision of an Ovidian metamorphosis for Alceste, which strongly suggests the anagogical dimension. Her stellification sets the final symbolic seal on her exemplary nature, "kalender" to all women, lovers, and wives (542–45).

Her story, presumably, would have set the capstone to all the "other small" legends of good women (549–50). The historical level admittedly involves some conjecture. What Queen Anne may have had to do with the daisy is lost forever among the other mysteries of fourteenth-century English court life. But the game of the flower and the leaf was perhaps not as irrelevant to the *Prologue* as Chaucer's disclaimer of partisanship suggests. That Anne was the "inspiration," or at least patroness of the poem at hand, is more evidently implied by the text. Her historical activities as intercessor and peace-maker[14] won her for centuries to come the popular epithet, "good Queen Anne," and it is possible that Alceste's speech to the God of Love (Richard) on the responsibilities of royalty dramatizes in epitome the historical basis for that reputation. Finally, and unquestionably, praise as the pattern of ideal wifelihood, asserted in the identification with Alceste and confirmed by the doting protectiveness of the God of Love,[15] would have rounded out, in a cycle of appropriate associations, the elegant compliment to the poet's royal patroness.

For Chaucer the dreamer, the pulling tight of all the symbolic threads has profoundly imagined implications. The dream has provided (as the trip to the House of Fame was presumably meant to) the hapless author with matter for his poetry. The experience of the vision has led him back to the books and study, abandoned for the daisy. But in the process, that faith in "olde appreved stories," proposed as an incidental component of the poem's introduction, receives a new justification, infused now with presumedly supernal authority. At the outset it had seemed as if the two kinds of existence were totally unrelated, if not incompatible. The world of books on the one hand and that other world associated with nature and love, each demanding intense and absorbing dedication, seemed quite distinct from each other in their laws and governance, threatening the dreamer with devotional schizophrenia. In the visionary realm, they are discovered to be interpenetrating and inseparable. The false dichotomies of the waking world disappear with the revelation of an essential reality, where the mysterious forces inspiring the creative act can be seen face to face.

But the visionary apprehension of Chaucer's dream is, of course, only a secular parody. Its deities walk firmly on the ground, in spite of the political theories that hedge the Christian king with divinity and in spite of the historical Richard's profligate attempts to realize those theories in ostentatious display. Furthermore, by turning an onerous commission into a graceful compliment, Chaucer is by no means conceding any substantial creative authority to his temporal master and mistress. The protective device of the persona shields him from such an heretical abdication of his rights as creator, as it does from the accusations of literary sin. Yet with all these qualifications, all these sober reminders of the *Prologue*'s obvious playfulness, it remains true that Chaucer could conceive an analogy, even if parodically, between the secular creative impulse and divine inspiration. Deeply embedded in the artifices of court charade and the multileveled audacities of comic ingenuity, lies an intuitive sense of the constructive powers inherent in the poetic imagination.

CHAPTER II

THE *HOUSE OF FAME:*

"EXPERIENCE THOUGH NOON AUCTORITEE"

Poetry—a thing sweet and varied, and that would be thought to have in it something divine; a character which dreams likewise affect. But now it is time for me to awake, and rising above the earth to wing my way through the clear air of Philosophy and the Sciences.

FRANCIS BACON

ACON'S notion of a lofty flight may not have been precisely what Chaucer had in mind in his first large-scale allegorical quest, but a shift in direction from the French tradition seems marked. The *House of Fame* is not, however, a poem one can speak of with confidence. Its incompleteness, of course, is a major stumbling block,[1] but not the only one. There is reason to doubt Chaucer's own satisfaction with what he was about. While Book II has moments that anticipate Chaucer's most delightful comic spirit, the surrounding books contain some of the flattest stretches he ever wrote. Imaginative sympathy with his subject is wanting, and the manner falters correspondingly. It appears that he deliberately set out to produce a "big work," to imitate, either in earnest or in game, the reach of Dante. But once the sizable plan was laid out, he found himself filling in the pieces mechanically, plodding through the story of the *Aeneid* and working out almost mathematically the petitioners to Fame and their rewards. One senses that something was imposed uncongenially on the poet

45

—whether the form or the subject matter or both, it is futile to surmise—and, as in the case of the *Legend of Good Women,* the effort was finally abandoned.

In spite of its unfinished state, the poem has not lacked interpreters. Their wildly varying readings need not be catalogued here. Recent full-dress treatments have ranged from the patristic allegorical illogicalities of B. G. Koonce[2] to the sober historical documentation of J.A.W. Bennett,[3] whose exhaustive annotations provide only minimal support for his aesthetic interpretation. A persuasive study by Sheila Delany subtitled "The Poetics of Skeptical Fideism" supports at many points the tenor of my discussion in this chapter, systematically uncovering the skepticism, if not the fideism, that pervades the poem. Delany differs from her predecessors in locating the "meaning" of the poem, not in a "unity . . . of subject matter and plot development" or "explicit content," but in the method of "structural repetition."[4] With remarkably little distortion of the text through critical ingenuity, she demonstrates that the *House of Fame* is characterized throughout by a skeptical examination of recurrent instances of conflicting opinion and perspective. Unresolved dilemmas produce a continuum of dissatisfaction toward all modes of human judgment, which in turn yields logically to fideism. While I find that Delany has defined with uncanny accuracy the temper of Chaucer's mind in this poem and perhaps in his work as a whole, I tend to believe that Chaucer at this juncture is less fideistic than skeptical and that the explicit content of the *House of Fame,* though it may never divulge an unassailably demonstrable unity, merits further inspection of its development, with full acknowledgment and respect to its inconsistencies, irresolutions, and attendant puzzles.

The problem is not merely the missing evidence; there is also an equally troublesome abundance of material—too many tantalizing motifs that recur, but do not add up. Chaucer seems to have been unable to keep his creative mind on the matter at hand. The poem gives the appearance of rambling "gothic" parataxis, and one could not predict from its example that Chaucer would eventually produce such sophisticated organic structures as the *Parliament* or the *Knight's Tale*. Some hypotheses may, however, be put forward tentatively concerning its shaping forces: the poem is probably occasional; the subject involves love and fame; and the writer is simultaneously attendant to his poetic activity and conscious of himself as maker.[5] In all these concerns and important to their interrelations is the unsteady tone of the poem, perhaps the most serious obstacle to our understanding.

In spite of its moments of geniality, a faintly unpleasant tone lingers about the *House of Fame*—throughout, but especially at beginning and end. The dream itself is an anti-vision with deliberate inversions of the conventional season and landscape,[6] and the dreamer suffers anxieties unknown to his counterparts in Chaucer's other dream poems. In fact, the poem takes on the quality of an *insomnium*, a nightmare governed by uncertainties and the deep fear that comes from dislocation in a sterile or unstable atmosphere. The "Proem" warns us of the parodic character of what is to follow. We learn nothing of the dreamer's personal life, of his sleeplessness or his devotion to books. Instead an exhaustive catalogue of the kinds and causes of dreams, shot through with reminders of the speaker's ignorance—"nought wot I"—is framed by the helpless exhortation, "God turne us every drem to goode!" (1 and again 58). The effect of this, when set against the affirmative *sententiae* that introduce Chaucer's other dream visions, is enigmatic. Rather than point the thematic direction of what follows, it suggests a lack of direction, a deep-seated uncertainty. We are given no assurance that this December dream is invested, like the Macrobian *oraculum*, with authoritative truth. And the "Invocation" to an Ovidian Morpheus and a Dantesque eternal "Mover" adds little to our confidence. The poet asks the first to help him "telle aryght" his dream and the second to reward those who interpret it correctly, but the weight falls on the concluding imprecation and the "pseudo-sinister reference" to Croesus. If this is meant to be "pleasantry," a *jeu d'esprit* as Bennett suggests,[7] the tone

is not entirely convincing, and the inference is inescapable that
this dream is peculiarly susceptible to misjudgment.

The question of judgment is central to this book of Fame,
and the first part of the dream, the visit to the Temple of
Venus, exemplifies the problem the last book will allegorize.
The romantic retelling of the *Aeneid* dwells upon the unreli-
ability of popular reputation. Dido yields to love, is betrayed
and commits suicide rather than face the world's judgment of
promiscuity:

> 'Loo, ryght as she hath don, now she
> Wol doo eft-sones, hardely.'   (358–59)

Yet the faithless Aeneas—and the digression on false lovers
insists on this characterization—escapes, apparently unstained,
to found Rome and be immortalized by Virgil. The structural
emphasis of the *Aeneid* is reshaped by the inclusion of the
Ovidian version in equal measure, highlighting both Dido's
experience and the role of the temple's presiding deity. Venus
energetically protects Aeneas from the wrath and storms of
Juno, Jupiter's wife, and provides him sanctuary in the arms of
Dido, where he is allowed to do "al that weddynge longeth
too" (244). This "achievement" of the hero's adventure is
Venus's triumph (461–65), justly celebrated on the walls of
her temple, yet the picture of love it presents is almost bitter-
ly ironic. It is not merely that the relationship is extramarital,
immoral in the public view, but that Aeneas breaks the pri-
vate bonds of trust between lovers and destroys faith in such
experience:

> Allas! what harm doth apparence,
> Whan hit is fals in existence!   (265–66)

The Venus whose spirit informs this temple is a far cry from
the passive deity who in the *Parliament of Fowls* luxuriates
within an overheated allegorical establishment where love is
conceived as an end in itself. Here she is a "naked fletynge"
(133) agency whose particular force and influence in the af-

fairs of men and gods alike manipulate them to other purposes—security, power, empire, fame.

It is probably impossible to recover the historical situation for the *House of Fame*. Yet most of these dream visions, Chaucer's and others', seem to be occasional, and the Eagle and the cage of Rumor seem to promise the poet not just "tydinges of Loves folk" (644-45) but material from his immediate world of experience, perhaps even as close as from his "verray neyghebores, that duellen almost at thy dores" (649-50). What precisely these tidings were, the manuscripts choose not to say, but the structure of the poem seems to prepare us for an occasion that involves love and reputation and perhaps the great world of politics and power. If so, and if the implications of Book I are intended, the poem's final reticence hardly needs explanation. But whatever the historical magnitude of the event, we are given no cause to expect anything very pleasant. The tidings the Eagle promises in such abundance will include "both sothe sawes and lesinges" (676), and though his catalogue of examples gives roughly equal time to the good and the bad, the specified variety in the false kinds —"discordes," "jelousies," "murmures," "novelries," "dissymulacions," "feyned reparacions," "berdys," and finally even "eschaunges"—leaves a far from sanguine impression. Nothing in the Palace of Fame with its capricious judgments or in the confused House of Rumor with its emanations of "fals and soth compouned" (2108) leads us to expect anything but an occasion where at best the truth of the matter is well nigh impossible to ascertain and at worst the behavior of the participants has been distinctly unattractive. Such an hypothesis seems consistent, at least, with the concept of Love and Fame in Book I and the inversions of the dream-visionary conventions as well.

When the dreamer emerges from the temple he finds himself, not surprisingly, in a desert. The landscape is utterly devoid of human habitation and all that is natural. The scene reaffirms the pattern of the *insomnium* in which the expecta-

tions of true dream poems—scenically a luxuriant springtime—
are ironically inverted. The prospect is not merely unpleasant
in nature; it is un-natural, of a different order of experience:

> Ne no maner creature
> That ys yformed be Nature
> Ne sawgh I, me to rede or wisse. (489–91)

Dante dreamt himself into a dark wood, but this is a realm
of pure nightmare, of "fantome and illusion" (493). The
Italian found Virgil, an (allegorically) reasonable interpreter
through the infernal regions, though at a later time he chose
more elevated authority for his loftier flights. Chaucer's dream-
er, too, recognizes the need for superior assistance to escape
from his unnatural surroundings, and his prayer for a guide is
promptly answered.

But Chaucer pursues a relentless course of ironic parody:
the guide is only partly formed by Nature, and the other-
worldly goal will be only partly concerned with truth. There
is a consistency in the *House of Fame*, at least in mode: noth-
ing is quite what it seems, either in the form or the content of
the poem; everything is subjected to ironic valuation. Unlike
the *Parliament of Fowls*, where the dreamer emerges from the
Temple of Venus into a startlingly different atmosphere and
the symbolic value alters accordingly, here the desert landscape
seems of a piece with what has gone before. This temple has
not been very alluring in its delineation of the moral conduct
of the world; nor, on the other hand, has it been especially
appealing as an aesthetic experience.

The temple episode in *Fame* corresponds loosely with the
passages in the *Book of the Duchess* and *Parliament of Fowls*
that proffer some reading matter from old books. Indeed, the
temple as an artifact is curiously realized; it seems more an
excuse to retell the *Aeneid* than an architectural entity. The
first lines of Virgil are closely translated on a "table of bras"
(142), but thereafter it is hard to tell if what is graven on the
walls is plastic image or mere words. Though the structural
pretense is flimsily maintained, the vagueness permits the

story to be told efficiently. Great chunks of the *Aeneid* are disposed of summarily—the last six books in ten lines—but the Dido episode is inflated rhetorically: surrounded by the *sententiae* and the *exempla* on treacherous lovers, a spoken complaint in the Ovidian mode gives the narrative a central moment that verges on dramatic realization. As a representation of the experience of an "old book," the whole episode stands midway between the vivid and empathic rendering of the story of Alcyone in the *Book of the Duchess* and the tonally dry, schematic abstract of the *Somnium Scipionis* in the *Parliament of Fowls*. There is a moment when the observer's or the reader's emotions may be said to be engaged, but the dominant impression is flat and denatured, as unflattering as the Venusian ideal being celebrated. The desert into which the dreamer emerges seems to be correlative with both the symbolic value and the experiential character of the temple.

The Eagle, of course, brings escape from all that the desert symbolizes of moral and aesthetic sterility. By an imaginative act of dream-like compression, the symbols of Book I seem also to stand for the dreamer's past life, when the days in the Customs House were followed by nights during which, in the Eagle's words,

> also domb as any stoon,
> Thou sittest at another book
> Tyl fully daswed ys thy look
> And lyvest thus as an heremyte,
> Although thyn abstynence ys lyte.   (656-60)

The bookishness of the temple achieves a clearer focus retrospectively as the Eagle defines what had been lacking. In fact, throughout the remainder of the poem, the ostensible subject matter—tidings of Love's folk—finds a larger perspective. What the tidings were—the presumed occasion of the poem—takes second place to the questions of the nature and origin of tidings in general.

The revelation of the "man of gret auctorite" (2158) might have brought these thematic issues in balance and order once

51

again, but, as we have it, the poem is all process, and we can only speculate on the ultimate goal that would—Chaucer's other visions lead us to expect—have hauled in the Venusian strands of Book I. Even the literal narrative with its absorption in the fact of journeying—unparalleled in these dream poems—points to a preoccupation with the way things are known, which Chaucer here allowed to become the primary matter.[8]

What makes the Book II so engaging is not alone the characterization of the Eagle, but Chaucer's willingness to indulge his dramatic propensities and create a situation in which two comic, because single-minded, characters confront one another as embodiments of two apparently incompatible ways of knowing. The Proem gives us a hint of what is to come: after a parody of popular minstrelsy[9] and a perfunctory invocation of Venus and the Muses, the poet translates a line spoken by the pilgrim Dante on the brink of his infernal journey and about to come to terms with his "reasonable" guide:

O Thought, that wrot al that I mette . . .   (523)

[O mente, che scrivesti ciò ch'io vidi, *Inf.*, ii, 8]

The rendering of "mente" by "thought" may have been due to an imperfect grasp of the Italian, but may also be intended to circumvent the limiting associations that "memory," like imagination, had acquired in faculty psychology. The less precise word, "thought," though it makes the remainder of the passage difficult to follow, suggests a more daring claim than Dante's. The pilgrim to Hell is merely insisting that the experience he is about to relate already exists in his memory, "la mente che non erra," and the Muses will help him show it forth. Dante's statement is part of the fiction of the pilgrim narrator. In Chaucer's version, "thought" not only experiences the dream and shuts it up "in the tresorye . . . of my brayn" (523–24), it is also the instrument of reproduction: "Now kythe thyn engyn and myght!" (528). Dante's "ingegno," in apposition to the Muses, becomes "engyn" and must refer to the engineering ingenuities of the human mind.[10] Whether or not Chaucer is making a conscious appeal to something like the creative imagination, the passage is a clear warning of what follows, for the theme of Book II is unmistakably the processes of mind that transmute experience into fiction.

The method of the new book continues in the parodic vein of the first, and the tone, though admittedly lighter, is consistently ironic. The plump, timorous book-worm of a dreamer parodies, of course, aspects of Chaucer's own nature, but the Eagle's character alludes to a large and complex tradition. Explicitly he is Jove's bird and comes on an errand of something like inspiration (if the word can be applied to this performance). Like St. John's emblem and Dante's several references to the symbol, this bird obviously represents a kind of "thought"—and not by any means the least exalted reaches of the mind. Chaucer himself implies this interpretation of the Eagle and his journey when he cites Boethius

That writ, "A thought may flee so hye,
Wyth fetheres of Philosophye,
To passen everych element." (973-75)

The Eagle parodies human guides as well—Africanus in the *Dream of Scipio*, who engineers a similar high flight; Dante's Virgil, who represents the highest reaches of human reason unaided by revelation; and especially Boethius's personification of Lady Philosophy, who could literally, when she chose, heave up her head so that "sche percede the selve hevene so that the sighte of men lokynge was in ydel" (I, Pr. 1, 20). There are, in fact, several things about the Eagle's long disquisition on the position of Fame's dwelling that recall Boethius: the reasoning by analogy, the use of alternate explanations to justify a phenomenon difficult for the human imagination to comprehend, and the delight in suiting the terms of discourse to the condition of the audience:

"A ha!" quod he, "lo, so I can
Lewedly to a lewed man

53

Speke, and shewe hym swyche skiles
That he may shake hem be the biles,
So palpable they shulden be."   (865–69)

The element of parody is immediately apparent in the self-important, zealous, and patronizing tone of the Eagle. Supporting this is the ironic inversion of the conventional function of the guide in allegorical dream-visions, particularly the philosophic ones. Though he flies high, the Eagle's flight is merely physical, and his goal is exalted in only a literal sense. The would-be allegory collapses when one compares the purpose of Lady Philosophy in the *Consolation*, leading her charge to his true country, to a true knowledge of himself and his place in the universe. Though the Eagle may be called philosophic, he is only a natural philosopher. He expounds a kind of *lex naturae*, and his analogies depend upon observable phenomena.[11] He makes the air his experimental laboratory—and his lecture room as well—when he condescendingly vulgarizes his science. His goal—Fame—is of a very low order of abstraction to begin with, but in his realm of experience it assumes a concrete though high floating actuality—a house. The ultimate comedy of the Eagle depends upon the combination of our expectations and the philosophical mode persuading us that something significant is going on, even if the tone is light. But we are finally forced to recognize that nothing is as it seems, and the Eagle's excursion is just as devoid of reliable substance as Fame herself. The celestial journey proves to be allegorically earth-bound.

The dramatic climax of the book comes just after the dreamer has been thinking of literary precedents for his heavenly journey—in Martianus Capella and Alain de Lille. The mindreading Eagle dismisses his "fantasy" and proposes another lecture, this time on the stars. But the dreamer now has the confidence to refuse—"for y am now to old" (995). The Eagle tries to tempt him with a prospectus but is rebuffed, then insists again, with the literary argument that such first-

hand experience of the constellations will help in the reading
of astro-mythological poetry:

> "For though thou have hem ofte on honde,
> Yet nostow not wher that they stonde."
> "No fors," quod y, "hyt is no nede.
> I leve as wel, so God me spede,
> Hem that write of this matere,
> As though I knew her places here;
> And eke they shynen here so bryghte,
> Hyt shulde shenden al my syghte,
> To loke on hem." "That may well be,"
> Quod he.   (1009–18)

The dialogue perfectly catches the "two cultures" energeti-
cally and determinedly failing to communicate. For the Eagle,
a true disciple of Roger Bacon, scientific observation is the
exclusive, inescapable mode of experience. For poor Geoffrey,
books are sufficient to his belief: too much experimental reality
is more than his human eyes can bear. Experience and au-
thority, what one sees and what the poets say, what one's
neighbors are doing and what Virgil wrote, two modes of
knowledge implicitly contrasted in the narrative of the first
two books, here dramatically confront one another in their
purest incarnation. Yet the comedy includes unawares a para-
doxical insight: the authorities of the dreamer produce in
him a kind of experience, eliciting an emotional response
while conveying knowledge of human behavior and the hu-
man condition; the dreamer himself becomes an "authority"
in turn, writing his experience of the dream; and he is, at a
further remove, the fictional experience of his maker, Chau-
cer. So, too, the Eagle, for all his eager faith in the evidence
of the senses and the logic of physical analogies, expends his
energies identifying poetic metamorphoses in the sky and,
best of all, prides himself on his ability to demonstrate by "ex-
perience" the reasonableness of that flimsiest of Ovidian po-
etic fictions, the House of Fame. Once more, nothing in this

poem is what it seems. Even the authoritative status of the poet's art is deprived of its familiar security. But this undermining of traditional categories is itself provocative, neither the first nor the last time Chaucer will intimate that the opposition of experience and authority is an illusion, a false dichotomy of the philosophers; that they are perhaps merely aspects of a single process, different facets of a unified way of knowing through the imagination; and above all that their unmistakable interdependence somehow lends validity to the process as a whole. The parodic dissolution of the epistemological antithesis verges on yet another indirect apology for the poetic imagination.

Indeed, Book III opens with a reference to the "art poetical" (1095), and this has led many critics to take the poem as some kind of aesthetic manifesto. But the *House of Fame* is far too slippery; like its subject, it is built on ice. I share wholeheartedly Bennett's remark on this third invocation that Chaucer "is the first Englishman to share Dante's sense of the worth of poetry and of the act of poetic creation."[12] Yet Chaucer's prayer to Apollo or "devyne vertu" (1101) follows Dante only in the choice of deity and the reference to the laurel tree. Whereas Dante in the *Paradiso* is approaching the True Light, Chaucer's Apollo, as a pagan "god of science and of lyght" (1091), serves only as the object of burlesque veneration. Where Dante offers to seek out the laurel in order to crown himself, Chaucer in mock humility promises to "kysse yt, for hyt is thy (Apollo's) tree" (1108). If Dante has "made of the pagan god a heavenly muse," as Bennett (p. 101) reminds us, Chaucer fixes his deity in a luminous but firmly secular context. The "art poetical" he speaks of is merely technical; the humble author disclaims, as he will again in the *Canterbury Tales*, the "diligence to shewe craft" (1099–1100), to get the rhyme and meter right. The arch rhetoric of the invocation may be aesthetically suggestive, but an *ars poetica* is not at all the stated matter, the "o sentence" (1100) of this final book.

This is not to suggest that the third book does not have as much to say about the nature and the function of poetry as the preceding two; but like theirs, its statements are qualified by a persistently ironic mode of presentation. The obvious, if not overstressed, theme of the Palace of Fame and its wicker-work appendage concerns the nature of worldly reputation. The goddess, her house and her attributes, all reiterate the capricious and arbitrary relation between intrinsic worth and its communication to an earthly audience. Rumor's domain increases geometrically the proportionate unreliability of the final report, for the petitions to Fame come first through that house where any veracity is systematically confused or confounded. In this context, poetry has an important place, but it would be hard to maintain that its ultimate worth does not share the dubiousness of all worldly reporting. The Palace of Fame is ornamented externally with images of all sorts of entertainers—musicians of small and large noises, minstrels, jugglers, and magicians, while the great poets of antiquity within have pride of place, holding up the pillars to the nave of this flamboyant shrine. Clearly they are superior to the anonymous rabble without; the fame they confer has a grandeur and a temporal reach far beyond that of the casual performer. But their incorporation into a single building dedicated to the production of empty sound—copious verbiage but uncertain truth—makes them equally complicit in the capriciousness of Fame and as undependable as the street singer or the village gossip. The inclusion of the great pagan poets in the Palace confirms the general case, of which the performance of Virgil, spelled out in Book I, was the specific example; and Dido's reproach of Fame finds an echo in the goddess's hall itself. The contention between the Eagle and dreamer is here symbolically reconsidered, too, but again inconclusively. The great books of old may prove questionable in authority—witness the lies told about the Trojan War—yet in experience as in the architecture of the Palace, they loom large and rich, with an impressiveness to be esteemed, though cautiously, by the poet's audience. Whatever the ironic qualifications, the *House of Fame* still manages to suggest that poetry is a fitting and imposing support to earthly fame.

After his sight of the ministrations of Fame, the dreamer is asked if he has come to seek personal fame. He replies that it is enough for him if no one drags his name into law suits; his personal experience suffices in and for itself:

"I wot myself best how y stonde;
For what I drye, or what I thynke,
I wil myselven al hyt drynke,
Certeyn, for the more part,
As fer forth as I kan myn art."   (1878–82)

He comes only for the famous tidings, subject matter on which he can presumably exercise his public art. Again the statement looks as if it were addressed to a particular event. Whether or not the *House of Fame* is an occasional poem is not central to my thesis, but if it is, the narrative apparatus seems to be making some such claim as this: the devotion to Love and her scriptures, elevated by Thought but grounded in the wisdom of experience, produces a comprehensive vision of the operations of Fame and the offices of Poetry to confer renown upon earthly events. Read ironically, the poem makes the same point but withholds any unqualified assertion of value: neither written authority nor observed experience has any claim to truth, but combined in the efforts of the poet they provide the best available access to earthly fame. Poetry has the enduring power to celebrate an event, no matter how disagreeable its actuality; it may even immortalize a lover, however dubious his distinction. Perhaps Chaucer's final irony is to suggest that the poet, by acknowledging the ambivalence of his task, may remain untarnished by the questionable gilding of the laurels he receives. Moreover, by the same logic he may still profess a substantial claim to well-deserved and eminently justified patronage.

CHAPTER III

THE *BOOK*
OF THE
DUCHESS:

THE KINDLY
IMAGINATION

"I was saying, what is
the reality
Of experience between
two unreal people?
If I can only hold to the
memory
I can bear any future.
But I must find out
The truth about the past,
for the sake of a
memory."

T. S. ELIOT

HAUCER'S EARLIEST dream-vision, the *Book of the Duchess*, appears in retrospect to have tackled the problem of the value of fiction head-on. It differs from the later dream-visions in that we find the dreamer literally "using" a work of fiction. The story of Seys and Alcyone, directly or indirectly taken from Ovid's *Metamorphoses*, serves therapeutically to divert the narrator from an insomnia induced by an imprecisely defined melancholy. He responds, however, to the reading matter in two distinct ways that are tonally differentiated with great care. This complex reaction prepares in turn for the unconventional "consolation" the elegy will propose.

The story records the loss of a much-loved husband and king, and the dreamer evinces great sympathy for the suffering queen, reminding us that he is both reader and himself a "maker," with (perhaps) similar sorrows of his own:

> Such sorowe this lady to her tok
> That trewly I, which made this book,
> Had such pittee and such rowthe
> To rede hir sorwe, that, by my trowthe,
> I ferde the worse al the morwe
> Aftir, to thenken on hir sorwe.   (95–100)

Chaucer has, in fact, adapted the Ovidian story so that it proceeds quickly to the sorrowful and sorrow-inducing image of the wife: Ovid's extended description of the fateful sea voyage is severely compressed, and the grief of Alcyone is made to follow hard upon it. Ovid's heroine is allowed to revel in premonitory distress before her husband departs, yet her prayer to Juno is primarily intent on keeping her husband faithful. The fiction Chaucer's dreamer happens upon has been tailored to his need for an emotional involvement with something other than his own self-pity as well as to the poem's actual subject, the bereaved lover.

The dreamer's second response, tonally different, is directly expressed only after the reading is completed. Although he initially describes the tale as "a wonder thing" (61), its wondrousness seems ultimately to rest not in such everyday matters as grief and sleeplessness, but in the mythological superstructure that animated that now unfamiliar time "while men loved the lawe of kinde" (56). Reverting to what he calls his "first matere" (218; also 43), the dreamer quite forgets the emotionally compelling fate of Seys and Alcyone, and Chaucer obligingly suppresses their reunion through Ovidian metamorphosis. Juno and the "goddes of slepying" (230) turn out to be the real news:

> Me thoghte wonder yf hit were so;
> For I had never herd speke, or tho,
> Of noo goddes that koude make
> Men to slepe, ne for to wake;
> For I ne knew never god but oon.
> And in my game I sayde anoon—
> And yet me lyst ryght evel to pleye . . .   (233–39)

And in this playful tone, which he acknowledges to be at odds with the tale just read and his own mood as well, the dreamer proceeds to ape Machaut's lover in *La Fonteinne amoureuse* by pledging a wittily appropriate sacrifice to the newly discovered Morpheus—a featherbed and a sleeping chamber accoutered in black and gold.

The fanciful manner with which the grievous episode seems to be dismissed is not, however, without point. On the one hand the gesture seems to be effective; the dreamer is launched into his dream. Though it too contains a narrative of loss and sorrow, this "real dream" is set in a natural landscape that conveys something of the lighthearted exuberance of the dreamer's petition, while its "kindliness" contributes significantly to the final statement of the poem. On the other hand, even the telling of Alcyone's sad tale, though it begins and ends with solemn and uncompromising declarations of loss, is not unrelieved by this sense of "game." The very supernatural portions that induce the dreamer's playful paganism unfold in such a way that no other "reading" would be appropriate. Chaucer lingers over the cave of Morpheus and the absurd postures of the sleeping gods, then substitutes for Ovid's radiant-bowed Iris an urgent messenger whose horn-blowing and repeated cries of "awake" shatter their sleep and their mythological dignity as well. Thus "sorwe" and "game" contend tonally in the recounting of "Seys and Alcyone" as much as in the energetic responses of the dreamer.

Again and again in his poetic career Chaucer will reveal this penchant for looking at a fictional event simultaneously in more ways than one. In the *Book of the Duchess* a dual perspective, realized tonally, is both inherent in the narrative and reflected in the superficial reactions of its immediate audience. The two tones distinguish two aspects of the fiction itself and two points of view, or modes of apprehending, the same story. These in turn are related in intricately significant ways to the dream that follows. Explicitly, the playful excursion into the supernatural provides the technical means—a mock, sleep-inducing ritual—by which the dream is arrived at, but the burlesque begs to be forgotten once its comic point is made. The "first matere" of the dreamer, a frivolous narrative device, does not encourage us to attach much significance to his remedies for sleeplessness, nor does the professed ignorance of pre-Christian mythology ("I ne knew never god but oon," 237) persuade us to anticipate a "revelation" truly momentous.

Placed against so much playful irrelevance stands the obvious structural importance of the sorrow of Alcyone, forgotten by the dreamer, but clearly mediating between his own wakeful unhappiness and the grief of the Black Knight, which will dominate his dream. But the two tones and the two related perspectives on the tale serve useful functions in determining the meaning of the poem as a whole. The grief of Alcyone and the "comforting" speech of Seys delineate the quality of the loss as well as the nature and limits of the consolation experienced by the Black Knight. The comic apparatus of pagan gods, with their ability to induce sleep and consequent dreams, projects a hypothetical mythic analogue for the processes of the human mind and tells us something about those faculties that produce both grief and consolation—perhaps love and poetry as well.

Seys and Alcyone are the human actors of their story and, not surprisingly, are most easily related to what follows in the *Book of the Duchess*. Initially, the "hertely sorowful lif" (85) of the queen establishes a new emotional dimension in the poem. The cause of the dreamer's melancholy is designedly left imprecise, perhaps meant to suggest a convention of the love-complaint, but unspecified and hence unrealized. All that we are given are its consequences for the dreamer. It is for Alcyone to introduce into the poem the concept of a love between husband and wife that is deep and passionate, all-consuming, reaching beyond life itself. The quality of her love provides a needed link, dramatically and thematically, to the situation of the Black Knight. The difference of sex, rather than an obstacle to understanding, belongs to a deliberate pattern of indirect or unstated similitudes in the poem; Alcyone is noble (literally, royal) and wedded like John of Gaunt, but

not precisely like the Black Knight, whose estate on both ac-
counts is ambiguous.[1] More subtly, her experience of love an-
ticipates that ecstatic mutuality with which the Black Knight
concludes his vision of the past (1287–97), the poet's finest
compliment to his lost Duchess.

Still more important to the poem as a whole are the basic
differences in the situation. Alcyone does not know for cer-
tain of her husband's death, though she is gloomier in her
suspicions than Ovid's heroine. She petitions Juno:

Send me grace to slepe, and mete
In my slep som certeyn sweven
Wherthourgh that I may knowen even
Whether my lord be quyk or ded.   (118–21)

She requires knowledge of a simple, ineluctable fact, life or
death, and this is precisely what Juno grants in Seys's blunt
"I nam but ded" (204). The divine message, though softened
by tender reminders of affection and gentle sadness, is clear
and uncompromising:

And farewel, swete, my worldes blysse!
I praye God youre sorwe lysse.
To lytel while oure blysse lasteth!   (209–11)

We are told no more of the story but that the dream has
brought release from sleeplessness and uncertainty, and that
her ensuing death has set an end to the queen's grief. If we
press the analogy to the Black Knight's case, there seems little
occasion for hope or likelihood of consolation. Again, the lines
of similitude are oblique and subtle. The Black Knight is not
to be consoled by death, neither in a romantic ecstasy nor by
riding off to the New Jerusalem.[2] This would be an absurd
breach of decorum by a poet with a very lively, albeit grieving,
patron to consider. The point of contact between these two
parts of the poem lies in the fact of knowledge. Alcyone, dis-
covering that Seys is dead, escapes the grievous ignorance
that made her life sleepless and without meaning, a living
death of suspense from which death and the clear knowledge

of death offer a release needing no Ovidian metamorphosis to sentimentalize its stark and absolute purity.

The Black Knight grieves too, but not in ignorance. Whatever the dreamer does or does not hear, the song of the Knight, "My lady bryght . . . is fro me ded and ys agoon" (475–86), reveals that he possesses the fact of death. But the physical state of the Knight reminds one of Alcyone before her dream, and this analogy in turn raises the possibility that he too may be wanting in knowledge. The Black Knight may know that his lady is gone, but his inability to relate the full meaning of such words to his present reality proves to be as injurious as the ignorance of Alcyone. He will require a long process of re-education, of coming to know his true self, before he can adopt Seys's simple assertiveness and say, without the mask of songster: "She ys ded" (1309).

The *Book of the Duchess* is in essence a poem about the processes of body and mind in which the greater battles between life and death, Nature and Fortune, are microcosmically reflected. In the opening lines, the state of the dreamer's mind is given greater consequence than would seem warranted by his subsequent role in the poem. He is not, after all, the lover himself as in so many French dream-visions, and the identification of the Black Knight with John of Gaunt makes it unlikely that he is also a surrogate for the narrator.[3] Nevertheless, the dreamer's mental condition commands attention in and for itself and is described at some length. The combination of sorrow and resultant insomnia affect body as well as spirit, destroying appetite, sensation, and the ability to distinguish what is good:

> For I have felynge in nothyng,
> But, as yt were, a mased thyng,
> Alway in poynt to falle a-doun. (11–13)

His condition is *contra naturam*, "agaynes kynde" (16), destroying the life-giving forces, slaying the "spirit of quyknesse" (26). The reading matter chosen to divert the dreamer from this unnatural state contains fables that descend significantly from a time, "while men loved the lawe of kinde" (56).[4] The queen Alcyone suffers as does the dreamer, from sorrow, but not only is the cause specified, the physical release of frequent swooning and the spiritual recourse of prayer to the goddess of marriage is available to her as a woman and a wife. The divinely inspired vision, accorded her in such a sleep as was denied the dreamer, marks an end, albeit tragic, to her suffering. The "lawe of kinde" moves mysteriously, but with ultimate beneficence.

The state of the Black Knight when he enters the narrator's dream brings to mind both sorrowers, but especially the dreamer's carefully anatomized suffering. The Knight's black form turns away from a green and blossoming natural landscape, instinct with life, where the poverty and suffering of winter is past, cold mornings and sorrows are all forgotten (410–13). But, his back against an oak, the Knight's posture of self-absorbed suffering repudiates the message of awakened nature. A motto for the emblem he composes might well be "agaynes kynde," as the comment of the narrator suggests:

Hit was gret wonder that Nature
Myght suffre any creature
To have such sorwe, and be not ded.   (467–69)

As in the prologue, the bodily consequences of emotional distress are dwelt upon in great detail, this time in precise physiological terms. The heart faints and the vital spirits decline. Observable pallor indicates that the blood has rushed to the heart to discover the cause of sorrow "by kynde" (494), for the heart is "membre principal of the body" (495–96). The extreme bodily suffering puts the Knight in danger of losing his mind; he appears to be beyond the mediation of even Pan himself, the "god of kynde" (512).

These three extended depictions of a common physical and mental condition—in the dreamer, Alcyone, the Black Knight —do much to unify the poem, of course, and they lend substance and seriousness to what in the opening lines might have been taken as familiar and idle convention. With the diagnosis of the body's sympathetic vital spirits, a concrete physicality supplements the sense of unnaturalness in the emotional realm, where sorrow and sleep have been the antagonists of an invisible battle. But the mind's contribution to this unhealthy experience had been singled out in the dreamer's initial statement: "For sorwful ymagynacioun / Ys alway hooly in my mynde" (14–15). Chaucer suggests that the life-denying condition of sorrow, which seems to absorb everything into itself, can be understood in terms of medieval faculty psychology, where the imagination is the mediating power between the senses and the reason. The imagination of the three sufferers has become a dead end, or an end in itself. It has failed in its natural role as transmitter of recorded and collected sensory experience to a higher faculty; short-circuited, it merely reproduces the same sensation again and again, the contact broken between the directive faculties of human nature and the external world. The consequence is that paralysis of mind and body observed in all three figures: "Suche fantasies ben in myn hede, / So I not what is best to doo" (28–29).

There is no evidence that Chaucer knew or was interested in the intricate and often contradictory systems of the medieval descriptive psychologists.[5] He need have known no more than the passage in the *Consolation* in which Boethius alludes to the simple formulation of the early Christian Neoplatonists—*sensus, imaginatio, ratio,* and *intellectus*:

> A man himself is comprehended in different ways by the senses, imagination, reason and intelligence. The senses grasp the figure of a thing as it is constituted in matter; the imagination, however, grasps the figure alone without the matter. Reason, on the other hand, goes beyond this and investigates by universal consideration the species itself which is in particular things. The vision of intelligence is higher yet, and it goes beyond the bounds of the universe and sees with the clear eye of the mind the pure form itself.[6]

There is, however, evidence that Chaucer knew the moral consequences of the diseased imagination or fantasy. The last books of the *Troilus* dramatize various unhappy attempts to project images of the future or resurrect those of the past. And the Merchant's tale of the senile and lecherous January, subject to "heigh fantasye and curious bisynesse" (*CT*, IV, 1577) as he revels in the process of selecting a wife, provides a precise figure of the diseased mind—a mirror set up in a marketplace receiving and thoughtlessly collecting the fair shapes and features of luscious young girls. The unhealthiness of this kind of imagining first coyly attributed to the blindness of love, is then sardonically reduced to literal blindness.[7]

The defect of the sufferers in the *Book of the Duchess*, however, is not dramatized as a moral one; there is nothing of the wilful imposition of unreasonable choice by which January is condemned. The fault is an excess of feeling or sensibility to which the imagination contributes, and the danger is to the life of the body not the soul. The cure, like the disease, lies in the imagination, but the imagination considered as a force more significantly constructive than the faculty of the descriptive psychologists. This alternative concept of the imagination, which may owe something to Plato's notion of divine inspiration, survives in Christian mysticism, but is not generally associated with the term itself in the Middle Ages, when it carried, as it still does popularly, the implications of moral or intellectual unreliability. Whereas the imagination in the facultative scheme must be subordinated to and directed by the reason, the notion of an inspired fury in the madman, the prophet, or the poet circumvents the objections of the psychologists by the attribution of the act of imaginative creation to God not man.[8] In the Christian era the prophetic visions of the Old Testament, the parables of the Gospels, and the revelation of St. John provide authoritative substance for such a view, while the dream theories of Macrobius[9] and others lend philosophic support. The power of symbolic images to convey truths may be postulated, if divine inspiration is understood to replace and supersede human reason in the creative act. The visionary is always unreasonable, but madness and even idiocy may be touched with higher wisdom; and if the lunatic may, so analogously (on occasion) the lover and poet, too, may "reason with a later reason." In theological terms, apprehension through the material symbols of created Nature shares with natural reason validity as means of approaching the ultimately unknowable mystery of divine truth.[10]

Nevertheless, for the medieval, the products of the human mind were always somewhat suspect. The act of creation could take on vicarious authority as an imitation of divine activity,[11] but the fallibility of human agency was always there to undermine complete assurance.[12] Christian imagining is necessarily a compound of pride and humility. Dante brought off his great work by hiding the arrogant poet in the fearful pilgrim, and tangling the images of his own fancy in systems of received theology. Chaucer's creativity was of a different order, and his view of the secular works of the imagination was undoubtedly equivocal. At the end of his career he would retract all of his works that could not be justified by explicit pious or prudential concern. But in the beginning, his talents were engaged by forms and images of a predominantly secular orientation, and indeed his genius was always attracted more by the actual processes of human behavior than by moral philosophy. Submerged in his earliest work is an exploration of the mechanics, power, and value of the creative imagination.

The *Book of the Duchess* opens with a view of the imagination as a diseased faculty of the mind, but as the poem moves into the realms of fable and dream, a new conception of the image-making power as a source of restorative value gradually unfolds. The first stage, the tale of Alcyone, operates within the metaphysical limitations of the "lawe of kynde," limitations reinforced by the comic tone of the supernatural episodes and the dreamer's professed ignorance of other gods "but oon." The tonal attitude toward the supernatural here is a key to the kind of significance it will support.

The playful treatment of Juno's messenger and the gods of sleep concedes their fictive nature. This is not God; these are creatures of the imagination. But they belong to an order of human experience that, though pre-Christian, had access to a type of knowledge—the wisdom of the workings of nature, the law of kind—that is valid still. The pagan gods survive as ways of understanding the mechanics of the human temperaments and the processes of causality on earth and beyond. They are fictions, they stand for something that could perhaps be stated in abstract formulae, but they have nonetheless an enduring vitality. Their survival bespeaks a capacity to hypothesize realities with greater economy than the most refined abstract proposition and without a loss of the wonder and awe evoked by their ultimate mysteriousness.

What the pagan supernatural does in the Alcyone episode is quite simple. It gives us a paradigm, a schematic representation of how the image-making power of the mind functions. Juno answers the queen's prayer by having Morpheus awakened; vitality is introduced into sleep itself. He then takes on the form of the dead Seys.[13] What appears to Alcyone is the body of her dead husband animated by an otherworldly power able to speak to her not only of the fact of death but of their former love as well. The dream is a form of knowledge that has the unmistakable authority of supernatural agency but is transmitted in an image that combines past memory and present reality. The experience has all the force of a prophetic vision because of the supernal complicity. But because the divine agents are acknowledged as mere fictions who behave at times undignifiedly, and because the knowledge provided is not of the future but of a past and present, empirically verifiable but not fully available to the dreamer, the vision equally suggests facultative powers that are analogous to supernatural forces, but actual in the human mind itself. In short, the tale of Seys and Alcyone is both a parable of grief and resolution and a paradigmatic fiction of the image-making power of the mind.

In the dream of the Black Knight, the paradigm is realized

in purely human terms: the perceptive powers of the imagination in intimate cooperation with memory bring about a release from the paralysis of sorrow—all within an exclusively natural context. In fact the thrust of the elegy as a whole is toward Nature, specifically human nature, and away from a familiar revealed metaphysic. If the Christian God appears in the action of this poem, it is only in the general sense that the Creator is immanent in all human history, and perhaps in the particular sense that His image, the special endowment of man's creation, is revealed in the activities of the human imagination.

The imagination of the Black Knight is, however, unblushingly literary; his heart proves to be a rag-and-bone shop of well-worn motifs from the French tradition of dream-visions and romance. What is nevertheless remarkable in Chaucer's performance is that even at a novicial stage he betrays an instinctive feeling for the psychological implications of rhetorical conventions. Although nothing the Black Knight says is particularly original, the elements of his speech have been set in a pattern of such uncanny dramatic accuracy that C. S. Lewis found not only the Knight, but his lady as well, more convincing than any of their great elegiac rivals in English.[14]

Every device of the Black Knight's rhetorical repertoire is a viable means of communicating the emotions of grief and love, but individually they are commonplace and derivative. In the sequence of the dream, however, they form a pattern that moves away from an emphasis on separation and sorrow toward an assertion of the unifying force of love. Simultaneously the devices themselves become progressively less artificial and give us an increased sense of vivid actual experience. The Knight is first overheard in a short and rather banal complaint against death. Its chief function is to dramatize the singer's self-absorption and isolation from nature and human commerce. When the dreamer intrudes upon his presence, the awakened instinct for proper social amenities effects a notable transformation:

Loo! how goodly spak thys knyght,
As hit had be another wyght.   (529–30)

When the dreamer then offers to ease the sorrow of his heart
by providing a willing audience "yif that yee / Wolde ought
discure me youre woo" (548–49), the Knight replies at great
length, but with the most self-conscious diction. An emblem
of suffering to be contemplated by all who know pity (574–
76), he thinks of himself as having traded a particular human
identity for an allegorical label: "For y am sorwe, and sorwe
ys y" (597). He luxuriates self-indulgently in the easy pro-
liferation of oxymora to characterize his unnatural condition:

My wyt ys foly, my day ys nyght,
My love ys hate, my slep wakynge, etc.   (610ff.)

As the cause of this living death, an allegorical agent, For-
tune, is conjured up, equipped with a correspondingly dupli-
citious nature:

She ys th'envyouse charite
That ys ay fals, and semeth wel.   (642–43)

And even the allegorical action that follows—a game of chess
in which Fortune wins his "fers"—is bemoaned with helpless
detachment, for understandably she only "took the beste"
(684).

To all this self-pitying allegorical obfuscation the dreamer's
reply is sympathetic but obtuse and literal minded:[15] he never
heard of anyone getting so upset about the loss of a chess
piece. This blunt refusal to accept the conventions of allegory
forces the Black Knight into direct reminiscence. His auto-
biographical account of a youth of idleness, informed from
the start by a "kyndely understondyng" and homage to love,
culminates in the discovery of one lady among a fair com-
pany, whose look pierces his eye and heart and binds him to
her service. The entire passage (759–847) reads like a sum-
mary of de Lorris's *Roman de la Rose*, from the awakening

71

of the lover until his capture by the God of Love, after he has spied his favored bud among the roses on the bush. This, however, is not the allegorical narrative but the actual sequence of events and emotions that de Lorris's poem has transmuted.[16] The Black Knight still speaks in conventional generalities, but he has moved an important step toward a direct confrontation of experience.

The full-scale portrait of the Lady, which follows, is also a convention of courtly poetry, but here it is quickened by a dramatic sense of the portrayer's involvement. Piece by piece he conjures up the image in his mind, and in the process she stands before him as a living being:

Me thynketh I se hir ever moo.   (913)

She who was herself so full of life that "dulnesse was of hir adrad" (879) confers a new vitality upon him through her image. After a catalogue of those inner virtues that match her outward beauty, he can declare:

For certes she was, that swete wif,
My suffisaunce, my lust, my lyf,
Myn hap, myn hele, and al my blesse,
My worldes welfare, and my goddesse,
And I hooly hires and everydel.   (1037-41)

The image resurrected in his mind has brought with it a memory of love, the deep response to something outside himself needed to loose the bonds of self-pitying grief.

The superlatives of the Knight simply bring out the realist in the dreamer. Almost gratuitously he suggests that the Lady's ideality lay only in the eye of the beholder:[17]

I leve yow wel, that trewely
Yow thoghte that she was the beste,
And to beholde the alderfayreste,
Whoso had loked hir with your eyen.   (1048-51)

The Knight, of course, insists on the objective reality of his vision and is provoked into further reflection on the ability of sight to banish sorrow:

That, whan I saugh hir first a-morwe,
I was warished of al my sorwe
Of al day after, til hyt were eve.   (1103-1105)

Her image has now fully reestablished itself in his heart
(1108) and only one further question from the dreamer is
needed to extend and animate his memory with the full story
of his courtship, from the first song and the first refusal to
the final acceptance. Throughout the narrative he emphasizes
her power: from the beginning, "she was lady of the body"
(1152-53), until at the last:

In al my yowthe, in al chaunce,
She took me in her governaunce.   (1285-86)

The final experience is a resurrection "fro deth to lyve"
(1278), and the long tale concludes with the ecstatic union of
their two hearts:

Oure hertes wern so evene a payre,
That never nas that oon contrayre
To that other, for no woo.
For sothe, ylyche they suffred thoo
Oo blysse, and eke oo sorwe bothe;
Ylyche they were bothe glad and wrothe;
Al was us oon, withoute were.
And thus we lyved ful many a yere
So wel, I kan nat telle how.   (1289-97)

What was once achieved in life can now only be relived in
the recollections of the imagination, but the experience has
been fully realized. The fact of death can now be unflinch-
ingly stated and understood. The Black Knight's "she is ded"
recalls Seys's equally laconic announcement, but it, too, comes
quick with the memory of love and with a clarity of knowl-
edge that implies a release from sorrow even in the face of
loss. The ending of the *Book of the Duchess*—the abrupt ex-
change of words, the end of the hunt, the heraldic landscape,
and the awakening—operates dramatically. We apprehend not
logically but psychologically.[18] Whatever consolation there is,

is certainly not theological. The poem consoles like an act of nature, spring after winter and after suffering, sleep and dreams. The poem ends with a dramatic affirmation of life that outsounds the words of death, and that affirmation has been arrived at, in the dream, by a combination of memory and the creative imagination.

The experience of the Black Knight implies a great deal about the meaningful power of the imagination to apprehend reality. Recreating the image of his lady and their past love, dredged up from beneath a layer of smothering false emotion, he provides a model of the mind's image-making faculty in an act of restoration harmonious with the vital processes of nature. What the Knight acts out in the dreamer's vision is the psychic actuality for which the dream of Alcyone describes a fictive paradigm. That dream in turn is contained within a fiction that is responsible for inducing the restorative sleep required by the insomniac narrator of the poem. By such indirections as these, the young poet of the *Book of the Duchess* smuggles into his remarkable elegy a subversive claim for the creative imagination and the constructive use of fiction reaching far beyond his contemporaries' demand for moral application. Like many another poet of his stature before and since, Chaucer at this early stage reveals a sensitivity to problems inherent in the creative act, more basic and vexing than questions of technique and form. The proper value of the imagination and the place of fiction on the scale of human endeavor are matters that admit no simple or abiding definition. Chaucer tangled with them throughout his life: in fact, it can be said that they expose a significant contour of his poetic achievement. But, though he will return again and again to an exploration of the process of imagining and raise the questions about the uses of fiction, never again will it be with the easy confidence and exuberant enthusiasm of the *Book of the Duchess*.

PHILO-SOPHIC FICTIONS:

"PLAINS DE PHILOSOPHIE, GRANT TRANSLATEUR"

The mere understanding, however useful and indispensable, is the meanest faculty in the human mind and the most to be distrusted; and yet the great majority of people trust to nothing else; which may do for ordinary life, but not for philosophic purposes.

DE QUINCEY

Scribendi recte sapere est
et principium et fons.
rem tibi Socraticae poterunt
ostendere chartae,
verbaque provisam rem
non invita sequentur.

HORACE

THOUGH the three poems considered in the previous section fall roughly into the first half of Chaucer's poetic career, they cannot be said to define a tidy period in his development. He was, apparently, still tinkering with the *Prologue* to the *Legend of Good Women* in the 1390s and gives no indication of downgrading even the octosyllabic poems when compiling his poetic catalogue for the "Retraction." Yet it is not unwarranted, I believe, to view these poems as a group and to consider their thematic propositions as a preliminary groundwork for future exploration of the possibilities and limitations of fictive art.

The dream-visions provided Chaucer with a flexible and liberating form, a fashionable one as well, which could be fitted to any courtly occasion. Public performance, however, obliged him to seek a means of accommodating his private and creative self to its exigencies. In response, he found it useful to create a persona and to re-create the genre, that he might satisfy public demands upon his talents, make his reputation, yet retain his privacy and

77

artistic integrity. These external pressures and a non-professional's indulgence in technical experimentation combined to produce works that found a ready audience and gave the language a new poetic voice. Chaucer's genius, moreover, turned these literary opportunities into occasions for probing the elusive nature of his art, a chance to ask the whys and wherefores of the creative process in the very act of creation itself.

Though the terminology belongs to a later era, one finds intimations in these dream-visions of a concept of imagination and a grasp of its theoretical implications, astonishing in their scope and profound seriousness. By the playful disposition of "mythic allegories"—the vision of Alceste, the journey to Fame, and the resurrection of Seys—Chaucer proposes a kind of poetic metaphysics; the narratives "analyze" the imaginative process, from its external stimuli to the working of its internal mechanism. Again and again Chaucer implicitly defines the imagination as a mediating force between the outer and inner worlds: on the one hand, the public world of patron and audience and the verbal and formal structures by which it can be intelligibly addressed; on the other, the private domain of contending thoughts, acquired knowledge and personal feelings, spurred by a not wholly accountable impulse to exteriorization. The conflict between these opposing forces, between the finished product of "auctoritee" and the searching process of "experience," becomes for Chaucer that tension of poetic consciousness, which may be called the "intellectual imagination."

These notions are, of course, merely implicit in Chaucer's early work. They can be discovered by attending to the recurrent fictive patterns and following the indirection by which he confers upon certain terms, such as "experience and auctoritee," a philosophic resonance. Chaucer, no more than Shakespeare, was a conscious theoretician. The suggestion that he dabbled in aesthetic theory would have bewildered his audience and surprised or amused the poet. But Chaucer's just claim to some of his earliest accolades—"noble philosophical poete," "Who was hier in philosophie / To Aristotle, in our tonge, but thow?"[1]—has of late recovered some of its original force. The relationship between the more familiar brands of philosophic speculation recognized by his contemporaries and the wrestling with problems of imaginative fiction, latent in the dream-visions, will, I trust, justify the seemingly "romantic" biases of the preceding section. But the specifically limited aesthetic concerns can only be fully appreciated when they take their place in the larger perspective of Chaucer's development as a maker of philosophic fictions.

By "philosophic fiction" I mean a work in which the narrative has been pressed into the service of a philosophic idea or speculation. Whatever modern bias one may hold on the matter,[2] a respectable tradition of poetic philosophizing was available to Chaucer, its form distinguished by Macrobius as the *narratio fabulosa*.[3] Beginning in the *Republics* of Plato and Cicero, the tradition was continued in late antiquity by Martianus and Boethius, emerged again with the twelfth-century Platonists, especially Bernardus Silvestris and Alain de Lille, then spread into the vernacular. At least one of Chaucer's works, the *Parliament of Fowls*, stands squarely in this eminent company,[4] though of course with numerous Chaucerian modifications. But the *House of Fame* with its celestial journey and visit to an allegorical potentate comes even closer to the formal archetype employed by Martianus, Bernardus, and Alain. I have separated the *Parliament* from the other dream-visions because it seems to me much less explicitly concerned with the activity of making poetry than the others, the qualifying adjective in "poetic" or "philosophic fictions" referring more to the thematic content than the form.

The organization as well as the designation of these groups of poems has been chosen to underscore a kind of logical shape or progression, somewhat though not rigidly chronological, to Chaucer's poetic career. The self-consciousness and underlying seriousness of the "poetic fictions" lead predictably to the awareness of a potential purpose for fiction other than the fanciful incarnation of a particular occasion or the meditation upon the process by which such metamorphoses are effected. In fact, the sensitivity to their aesthetic implications that Chaucer exhibits in this first collection of poems presages

79

a new direction in both formal and thematic ways. If it is agreed that Chaucer, even in his earliest works, raises questions about the theoretical assumptions underlying poetic activity, it is equally likely that he was alert to the possible use of fiction to explore philosophical ideas other than the aesthetic. The interdependence of such "discoveries" is as obvious and inevitable as the identity of form and content.

Not all, if indeed any, of the "philosophic" poems in this group entirely satisfy Macrobius's concept of the *narratio fabulosa*.[5] Even those "presented beneath a modest veil of allegory" admit events and characters either less respectable or less divine than that sober commentator requires. One might argue that these poems are not entirely innocent of "a decent and dignified conception of holy truths," but their literal, often quite unallegorical, fictions are too firmly anchored in secular experience and its literary counterparts to appease some medieval and more recent demands for "high seriousness." Chaucer's metaphysics is unorganized and not central to his thinking; he was not interested in competing with the Chartrian Platonists on their own terms, though he did not hesitate to appropriate some of their ideas and images.[6] He owes a far greater intellectual debt to Boethius, to a philosophy concerned more with the human predicament than metaphysical speculation.[7] The very form of his most famous work reveals Boethius's affinity with Chaucer's kind of poetic imagination, its fondness for the dramatic situation and psychological observation.[8] So, too, Chaucer's philosophic muse descends into a recognizable earthly setting, whether it be a prison or a garden.

The works that illustrate Chaucer at his most philosophical share familiar themes—Nature, Love, Fortune—and they have been arranged here in a sequence that may represent the order of their composition. The sequence suggests a progression of thought, what might be taken as identifiable stages of intellectual development, if the chronology were more certain and if one believed such spiritual biographies can be extracted from this kind of poetic canon. I do not pretend to any such conviction. The arrangement is a matter of convenience; the job of suggesting thematic definitions is facilitated, and I hope the discriminations are made finer, by such juxtapositions. Of greater import to the critic is the literary activity itself, the fact that Chaucer directed so much of his creative energy to the fashioning of such narratives, and the process by which the materials of fiction come to acquire such philosophic consequence as they do.

One further characteristic of this group of poems may be noted. From one point of view, they are among Chaucer's least original works; the fictions here deployed are unashamedly second-hand. The *Parliament of Fowls* is a special case, a fascinating arrangement of bits and pieces, but the remaining tales—those of Troilus, of Palamon and Arcite, and of patient Griselda—closely follow the originals of Boccaccio and Petrarch. In fact, this "philosophic" grouping may appear to some as a resurrection of what was once called Chaucer's "Italian period." The presence of Boethius as an important secondary source may, however, justify my choice of terms.

More significant to my thesis is the phenomenon that these works have never been seriously thought of as unoriginal. Chaucer has so comprehensively reworked his borrowed narratives that they seem to most readers entirely new, remarkably different works, and—*pace* the Italianists—decidedly superior. C. S. Lewis has even claimed for Chaucer the astonishing feat of propelling the Troilus story out of the Renaissance back to the Middle Ages.[9] What distinguishes these poems—and what will occupy most of our attention—is not so much the fiction itself, but the shaping of it. That Chaucer should have expended so much creative energy in refashioning ready-made narratives supports my depiction of the poet as arriving at a sufficiently theoretical sense of the uses of fiction that he might test it on the fictions of others. And when the narrative receives predominant attention, as it necessarily does when a writer is reworking an established story, there is a predictable thematic emphasis as well. Looking at Chaucer's philosophical fictions, then, requires particular attentiveness to the formal procedures by which the old matter is recast into new shape and new meaning.[10] The critic must imitate the artist's sensitivity to the actual process of using a fiction. Only then, perhaps, may one infer with accuracy its particular "philosophy" and what it means to create a "philosophical fiction."

The philosophic fictions to be analyzed share their dependence on a source, a text with an integrity and autonomy of its own, and their use of a narrator whose independence from the original telling tends to heighten our awareness of that autonomy. Though the activities of the narrator are less conspicuous in the *Knight's Tale*, in each of these works the narrative has been reshaped—expanded, abridged, interpolated—in such a way that, not merely the form, but the thematic implications are notably affected. The narrator both contributes to and alerts us to these transformations, but the range of possibilities for narrative involvement is extensive: in the *Parliament* the dreamer is passively acquiescent to a series of "experiences" or "fictions" whose consequence is left for the audience to interpret, while the *Knight's Tale*, as adapted to the Canterbury pilgrimage, relies upon our acceptance of its concerns and ethos as appropriate to the teller. The narrators of the *Troilus* and the *Clerk's Tale* respond energetically to their fictions; as an intermediary audience, they more or less deny complicity in the actions they describe, but are cunningly used by Chaucer to negotiate his audience's emotional involvement and thereby complicate its philosophical evaluation of the performance as a whole. Whatever the narrative method, these works all testify to a strong sense on Chaucer's part of the unavoidable implication of the teller in the thematic import of his fiction. The idea that a story could have a meaning independent of and unaffected by the formulations of its narrator is a naïve assumption that Chaucer thought better left to the fictional story-tellers themselves and perhaps a few in his own audience. That it still holds a claim on some modern readers provides a final justification for this review of Chaucer's authority as a "philosophic poet."

CHAPTER IV

THE PARLIAMENT OF FOWLS:

"EVENE NOUMBRES OF ACORD"

EDWARDS: *'You are a philosopher, Dr. Johnson. I have tried too in my time to be a philosopher; but I don't know how, cheerfulness was always breaking in.'*

BOSWELL

THE *Parliament of Fowls* bursts into the Chaucerian canon with a dazzling show of exuberant, self-confident mastery. The octosyllabic poems seem in retrospect poor things indeed or, in their technical aspect at least, limited and jejune. In the *Parliament* Chaucer rolls out decasyllabic lines of effortless metrical and tonal variation, assembles them into rime-royale stanzas of equally varied flexibility, and shapes his dream-vision with an assurance of formal control that enables its cohesive but mercurial surface to enclose a complex structure of philosophically provocative images. Everywhere one looks at the *Parliament*, one is struck by the deceptive artlessness of its artistry. Ostensibly another courtly occasional piece—if not for some aristocratic coupling, at least for St. Valentine—it invites, and has received,[1] comparison with the weighty "fabulous narratives" of Bernardus Silvestris and Alain de Lille, whose figure of Natura it appropriates and acknowledges. In the disarmingly ingenuous voice of a narrator merely reporting everyday experience, it manages to bring together within a few hundred lines the immortal longings of a Cicero and the quacking of an articulate duck.

The sophistication of tonal complexity in the *Parliament* appears in the first stanza.[2] The opening line englishes a familiar Latin tag[3] of medical origins, with a simplicity of diction, regularity of accent, and rhetorical balance that positively invites the lapidary chisel: "The lyf so short, the craft so long to lerne." But what "craft" is meant by this sober, resonant announcement of a new art? Perhaps, knowing the poet, the *ars poetica* that was for some reason abandoned in the back regions of the *House of Fame*; perhaps, given his portentous tone, an *ars moriendi*; in any case, something worth devoting one's life to. The next two lines are so close to the first rhythmically that one scarcely notices the modification of subject:

Th' assay so hard, so sharp the conquerynge,
The dredful joye, alwey that slit so yerne . . .   (2–3)

The chiasmus, yoking two nearly synonymous adjectives of suffering at the center of the second line, distracts from the military image and the qualifying notion that this "craft" is something that can after all be "conquered." The third line concentrates the antithesis before the caesura, emphasizing again, in the near oxymoron, the emotional character of the issue, while the clause imitates its ephemeral nature by lightening the rhythm. But if this last phrase constitutes an echo of the "short" life in line one, something has gone wrong with the system of contrasts; logically one would expect that the "craft" was being subjected to further definition. If, as Brewer says,[4] the first three lines are "an example of *interpretatio*, or different ways of saying the same thing," the "thing" has become intricately paradoxical: "craft," when opposed to "life," suggests the unnatural, but turns out to be more a matter of the emotion than artifice; and its pleasures, though long in the learning, are short-lived. If we have read carefully, perhaps more carefully than the firm rhetoric invites us to do, we are prepared for the explanation of what has become al-

most a riddle: "Al this mene I by Love." But it is still possible
to ask, is this an art of love or an art of loving? A treatise of
philosophical objectivity or a practical handbook? Both possi-
bilities seem to inform the opening lines.

A kind of answer is offered by the remainder of the stanza.
At issue is something called "felynge," the emotional experi-
ence presumably responsible for the bewildering contrasts and
paradoxes of the first lines. The rhythm and rhetoric make
this clear by a deliberate stylistic contrast: the verses now
avoid the imposing caesura; they hurry along, lighter in move-
ment; syntactic continuity (or hypotaxis) encourages enjamb-
ment, and the diction is less calculated, almost colloquial:

Al this mene I by Love, that my felynge
Astonyeth with his wonderful werkynge
So sore, iwis, that whan I on hym thynke,
Nat wot I wel wher that I flete or synke.   (4-7)

These lines, like the final image, convey the sense of having
been caught up in a powerful experience that confuses the
laws of gravity. The stanza as a whole pivots magnificently
on the word "Love," balancing grave, poised rhetoric against
light-headed confession. The rhetorical contrast seems all in
all to be pitting authoritative *sententiae* against the unself-
conscious spilling-out of experience.[5]

Even this apparent antithesis is not quite so tidy as it at first
seems. The speaker's feeling may be in question, but he in-
forms us that his experience has been provoked by an intellec-
tual act: "whan I on hym thynke" (6). This hint becomes the
subject of the next stanza where the dizzying experience of
love proves to be vicarious and literary. Love's power is no less
real, however; in fact, his divinity, also hinted at in the first
stanza ("his wonderful werkyng," 5), is now conceded mirac-
ulous as well as wrathful capabilities, and exacts a laconic
obeisance from the speaker:

I dar nat seyn, his strokes been so sore,
But "God save swich a lord!"—I can na moore.   (13-14)

85

This closure allows for a shift of subject in the next stanza. Ostensibly we are getting down to the real subject—namely, reading (17). But stanza four further delays the true "purpos" with another *sententia*:

> For out of olde feldes, as men seyth,
> Cometh al this newe corn from yer to yere,
> And out of olde bokes, in good feyth,
> Cometh al this newe science that men lere.   (22-25)

Among all the deviations and apparent red herrings of these four stanzas is scattered an impressive number of related antinomies. After those explicitly connected with love come these concerning books. Reading is for "lust" or for "lore" (15), "olde bokys" produce "new science" by analogy to a natural process; authority becomes the experience of a reader, who in turn becomes an author that he may transmit the new knowledge he has harvested. The interpenetration of experience and authority is a central fact of the speaker's existence and is obviously not unrelated to the attitudes toward love expressed in the second stanza and implied by rhetorical strategies of the first. The ramblings of the narrator permit Chaucer to suggest without stating explicitly that the poem will be concerned with the inseparability of the authoritative and experiential approaches to love: love can only be understood after acknowledging that experience needs to be subjected to the generalizing perspective of authority, while authority in turn must also be constantly renewed in the localized dynamics of experience. If the poet can claim any philosophic advantage over the philosopher, it lies in just such a capacity for authoritative abstraction or generalization without losing the touch of experience upon empirical reality.

In spite of the narrator's diverting equivocations, the first stanza of the *Parliament* does state Chaucer's theme. The poem is about that well-known phenomenon of human behavior called love, of whose emotional confusions and contradictions the narrator reminds us while disclaiming firsthand knowledge. But it is also about love as an idea, a concept of wider-reaching physical, social, political, and even metaphysical ramifications. To be expert in the true craft of such a love takes longer than does the access to my lady's chamber. Since a theoretical view of this order would come more logically from literature than life, the narrator's bookish inclinations now appear an advantage. At any rate Chaucer seizes the opportunity to maneuver us through a rather dry epitome of the *Somnium Scipionis*, but only to have his dreamer exasperatingly confess that his labors have made him sleepy.

> For bothe I hadde thyng which that I nolde,
> And ek I nadde that thyng that I wolde.   (90-91)

The *Somnium* contains the kind of information true philosophers purvey, but in spite of Cicero's efforts at a "mythic" vitalization of his ideas, their stiff abstract by the narrator here merely suggests an epistemological inadequacy. The dissatisfaction expressed by the dreamer may also reflect the limited relevance of their pagan formulation to his Christian mode of experience. Cicero's cosmic images and notion of "common profit" are important contributions to the *Parliament* theme, but the dreamer, unable to "know feelingly" by means of such dry stuff, is, paradoxically, rewarded only by sleep and dreams —though he does salvage a guide for his dream.

While the dreamer allows himself to drift without comment through the dream landscape, refreshed but apparently unenlightened, the Ciceronian passage has offered in one of its images—the celestial music of the spheres (59-63)—a version of the *Parliament*'s informing principle, a motif that determines both its thematic coherence and its structural integrity. Like its erotic and societal analogue in the roundel near the poem's end, the essential point about this heavenly harmony is its concordant unity proceeding from diverse and disparate sources. Just as Nature will mate the individual birds into a social contract that produces a song of seasonal celebration, so the *primum mobile*, moving in one direction, sets the spheres moving in another, but at differing speeds, and the friction of their unequal motions produces separate tones resolved into a single harmony. Governing all such natural concords, cosmic and sublunar alike, is the divine principle of creation, love, bringing harmony out of dissonance, unity out of multiplicity. Like the allegories of the Chartrian Platonists,[6] the *Parliament* does not emphasize the God of redemptive history and the sacraments, whose love is *caritas* and of the spirit; it subscribes instead to the God of Nature, the Creator who is immanent in every aspect of his work, present in the smallest atom as well as the distant stars. He is even apparent in physical coupling of his animal creatures, the act by which Nature perpetuates his creation, and which is in some instances also called love. But on the First Cause itself, the poem is reticent; like Boethius's great work (to which this concept of love is indebted), the *Parliament*, while not incompatible with Christian doctrine, is by no means obtrusively Christian in its metaphysical assumptions.

The *Consolatio Philosophiae*, in spite of its remoteness from Chaucer's poem in tone and genre as well as time, glosses the *Parliament* with useful economy and accuracy. In the last meter of Book II, Philosophy, discoursing on friendship, describes that force by which the world with stable faith varies its changing yet concordant process; by which an everlasting law contains the warring seeds of things; by which day and night, sea and earth are held in bounds:

Hanc rerum seriem ligat
Terras ac pelagus regens
Et caelo imperitans amor.[7]

(Al this accordaunce of thynges is bounde with love, that governeth erthe and see, and hath also comandement to the hevene.)

This same power binds people together by its holy bonds, and sacred marriages by its chaste loves, faithful friends by its laws. Later after a long disquisition on Divine Providence, Lady Philosophy returns to the theme of that love that holds the stars and planets to their assigned places: "Sic aeternos reficit cursus Alternus amor" (IV, m. vi). The passage deserves full quotation, even in Chaucer's translation:

And thus maketh Love entrechaungeable the perdurable courses; and thus is discordable bataile yput out of the contre of the sterres. This accordaunce atempryth by evenelyke maneres the elementz, that the moiste thingis, stryvynge with the drye thingis, yeven place by stoundes; and that the colde thingis joynen hem by feyth to the hote thingis; and that the lyghte fyr ariseth into heighte, and the hevy erthes avalen by her weyghtes. By thise same causes the floury yer yeldeth swote smelles in the first somer sesoun warmynge; and the hote somer dryeth the cornes; and autumpne comith ayein hevy of apples; and the fletyng reyn bydeweth the wynter. This atempraunce norysscheth and bryngeth forth alle thinges that brethith lif in this world; and thilke same attempraunce, ravysschynge, hideth and bynymeth, and drencheth undir the laste deth, alle thinges iborn. (p. 371)

Above this world of process sits the Creator, judging and regulating all motions, all directions:

Hic est cunctis communis amor
Repetuntque boni fine teneri,
Quia non aliter durare queant,
Nisi conuerso rursus amore
Refluant causae quae dedit esse.[8]

(This is the comune love to alle thingis, and alle thinges axen to ben holden by the fyn of good. For elles ne myghten they nat lasten yif thei ne comen nat eftsones ayein, by love retorned, to the cause that hath yeven hem beinge.)

These meters of Boethius constitute the "inner source" of the *Parliament*. The principle of a divine force that binds discordant and contentious elements informs every aspect of the poem and regulates its structure. We have seen how the conflicting attractions of love and books operate in the "Prologue," shaped by the speaker's indirection into a complex statement of theme. In the climactic scene of the poem, the figure of Nature allegorically represents the principle we have been discussing. She is the *vicaria Amoris*, the binding force even at the most elemental level:

> Nature, the vicaire of the almyghty Lord,
> That hot, cold, hevy, lyght, moyst, and dreye
> Hath knyt by evene noumbres of acord. (379-81)

And of course her right to govern the parliament stems from her being the *lex* as well as the legislator. She knits together those eternal opposites, male and female, in a harmony of joyous mating, executing the divine plan as surely here as in the constitution of basic matter, perpetuating created life by procreation.[9]

Nature brings together not only the sexes but also all types and classes. The four orders of fowls allude without precise equation to the ranks of society, and the catalogue of birds (337-64), like that of trees earlier, defines a range of character types or "temperaments," social conditions, and functions. The union of these multifarious contrarieties under Nature's aegis implies a political theory in which the social or governmental contract expresses a need or desire as natural as the sexual urge—and as often disrupted or perverted by the selfish assertion of individual will.

But in the *Parliament* taken as a whole, the societal and even the cosmic implications of love recede before the dominant image of human sexuality.[10] It colors Cicero's notion of "commune profit" to the extent that the wrongdoers punished after death include both "brekers of the lawe" and "likerous folk" (78-79). The class warfare that disrupts the orderliness of the parliament itself stems from the differences among the avian orders as to how the sexual urge is to be incorporated into civilized social intercourse. The aristocratic birds of prey perform those "spiritualizing" rituals that take up the time of the idle rich with psychological refinements and exclusive, self-generating rhetoric. The rationale of this elitist behavior is impenetrable to the impatient, practical-minded water and worm fowl, who want simply to get on about their business.

But the ceremonious debating of the tercelets is absurdly profit-less only to those who are obviously less interested in the wel-fare of the community than in "looking after number one." Nature's resolution of the conflict acknowledges the justice on both sides. The natural promptings of society must not be in-definitely suspended while the nobles debate, yet their right to set a more deliberate pace and more elaborate rites for themselves is conceded, though kept within bounds. The only satire of *fin amor* one finds in these exchanges is both indul-gent and double-edged.[11]

Serious reservations about aristocratic love are expressed not in the parliament scene but in the structure of the poem as a whole. The juxtaposition of the Temple of Venus with the "launde" and flowery hill of Nature engages a far more search-ing analysis of erotic behavior than the squabbling fowl can provide. The contrasts in setting, in atmosphere, in sound and movement reinforce the basic distinctions between the two goddesses, which Bennett and others have thoroughly docu-mented. Equally significant is the dramatic mode in which human behavior is depicted. In the parliament, a densely populated, hyperdynamic scene, the independent wills of the feathered spokesmen contend in spontaneous though reason-ably governed freedom; in the lifelessness of the temple, the human lovers are dwarfed by the murky shrine, their experi-ence figured only by the broken bows and painted images of disastrous affairs at the conclusion of the episode, while the allegorical sequence of static abstractions that prefaces the scene systematically uncovers the dark ambiguities of courtly "likerousnesse." The formal balance of the two scenes urges upon us a dialectically qualified appreciation of the erotic phenomenon they hold in common.

The whole fabric of the *Parliament*, tenuously held together by the uncritical receptivity of the narrator, is densely pat-terned with figurations, small and large, of the principle of love binding the discordant into harmony, the contentious into unity. The figures are as multifarious as the ambivalences of the concept. Some examples, like the black and gold inscriptions on the gate to the park (127-40), define the conflict in terms of the human response to love's overpowering but unprovoked visitations. The brief invocation to Cytherea may be intended as a reminder of the celestial manifestation of the goddess, a heavenly Venus, theologically less at variance with divine Nature than the one we actually observe in the poem. But the larger units necessarily carry the weight of meaning. The dream of Scipio not only provides a cosmic overtone to the harmonics of the narrator's dream, it confers upon the dreamer's experiences a political and moral serious-ness that survives the irreverent treatment of the borrowed guide, Affrican. The two dreams are knit together by such superficial formalities, but at the same time the texture of the dreams is conveyed in such a way that they come to embody two very different orders of experience—the orderly, reasoned, but aridly abstract world of books against the vivid, fluid, teeming, uncontrollable sensations of dreaming. An alertness to the interpenetration of these distinctive forms of knowledge emerges as an inescapable precondition to any serious appre-hension of the complex and mysterious idea of love.

Chaucer has fashioned his "philosophical plot" in a sequence of three seemingly independent fictions: the first, admittedly borrowed from Cicero, is teleological and moral but remote from common experience by virtue of its unrealized historical figures as well as its eternal perspective. The second, unac-knowledged from Boccaccio, is rich in sensuous description of the natural scene and the human figure, but lifelessly alle-gorical and static. The concluding fiction completes a process of increasing involvement in the dynamics of human per-sonality, while a balance is preserved between the uniqueness of the individual and the generalizing philosophic vision by the happy choice of the representative human institution and the avian participants who speak with distinctive yet typical voices. Each fiction refines and expands our perceptions with-out requiring us to abandon the insights acquired on the way. A true philosophical poem, the *Parliament* is an epistemologi-cal process.[12] By unfolding a progress that makes us conscious of how we know, it implies more than one might expect about what we can know.

The indispensability of the Chaucerian persona to such strategies is self-evident. He functions as a kind of suspension medium in which a multiplicity of poetic events may be floated without the poet's having to prescribe their values or relationships. Such events may be more deeply imagined than those constrained by logical discourse or restricted by allegorical coherence alone. Moreover, a kind of tension is set up between the persona and the poet, analogous to the epistemological process embedded dramatically within the fiction. In such works as Boethius's *Consolation* and its Middle English descendant, the *Pearl*, the audience merely follows the guided enlightenment of the dreamer within the poem. Chaucer's method is characteristically more oblique, his objective less limited and less predictable. It may be better understood, though not explained, by exploring a point of sympathetic resemblance between the poet and his persona—their bookishness. Whereas the narrator simply tells us of his literary habits, summarizes one book, and then goes on to experiences of an entirely different order, behind him stands the poet who has put all of this poetic entity together from innumerable bits and pieces of books.

The sources of the *Parliament of Fowls* are surely more diverse than those of any other Chaucerian work. Beside the general debt to the French dream-visions and the *Roman*, and major set pieces from Cicero and Boccaccio, there are many minor borrowings as well: to make the transition to the dream, Chaucer models one stanza on Dante, another on Claudian. The park gates are inscribed with Dantesque echoes and its trees are Ovidian. Only the final scene of the parliament appears to be less derivative—except for Nature herself who is introduced by her credentials from the "Pleynt of Kynde." What is remarkable about this "unoriginality" is how unapparent it all is. Only the annotation of a century of scholarship alerts us to the presence of so many old Romans and recent Italians lurking beneath the seamless texture of the verse. Not

93

only has Chaucer achieved the technical mastery of an authentic voice, he has so thoroughly made the works of his great predecessors his own that they have become an integral part of his poetic experience, part of the raw material on which he can draw when he wishes to set the stamp of his authority on the "new science" of his imagination. In the making of the *Parliament* Chaucer must have felt an amused and ironic sympathy for his bookish dreamer whose varied experiences he pieced together out of his own encounter with books. The genesis of the poem represents yet one further analogue to its informing theme—the creative power of love, once again making out of multiplicity a new whole, out of the discordant babel of poetic tradition assembling a new harmony.

CHAPTER V

PALAMON
AND ARCITE:

"MYRAKLES AND
CREWEL YRE"

*But though I cannot
admit that machinery is
necessary or essential to
the epic plan, neither can
I agree with some late
critics of considerable
name, who are for ex-
cluding it totally, as in-
consistent with that
probability and impression
of reality, which they
think should reign in this
kind of writing. Mankind
do not consider poetical
writings with so philo-
sophical an eye.*

HUGH BLAIR

THE *Parliament of Fowls*
joyously celebrates a world
of avowed unreality, a uni-
verse of dreams and talking birds,
a fabric of studied artifice em-
broidered with courtly conven-
tions. But it evokes a higher re-
ality, the ghostly paradigm on
which the appearances of our
mundane reality play, the sub-
stance underlying our workaday
accidents. The *Parliament* offers
an essential vision of Nature, re-
moved by a dream from the con-
tingencies of actual experience.
The natural landscape, the con-
tentious birds, even the sensuous
allegorical figures may seduce us
by the vitality of their dramatic
cohesion into crediting their fic-
tive substantiality, but neverthe-
less they are not the thing itself
as we know it. We may accept the
"humanity" of the avian orders,
but in spite of all their recogniz-
able inflections of attitude and in-
dividuality, they represent a dis-
tinct and limited selection from
the totality of human experience.
To put it one way, these feathered
couples mate, and even undertake
courtship, but do they marry?
Chaucer's Nature, presiding over
a gathering of birds, is much less

95

literally *pronuba*[1] than even the ambiguous Hymen in the works of Martianus and Alain, where at least the allegorical couples have recognizable human form. But the sacrament of marriage, with all of its ethical and theological implications, was an inescapable fact of human society as Chaucer knew it, defining even in its absence the courtly liaisons of *fin amor*.

To observe love in its universal aspect Chaucer, by the ingenious device of animating the birds on Natura's robe, managed in the *Parliament* to distract attention from the many problems love raises in other guises. Following the example of the Chartrian Platonists, Chaucer created a fiction or "mythos" in which human love finds its place in a hierarchy of analogues ranging from the elemental to the ethereal, correlated by the principle of the union of opposites. The harmonious coupling of male and female defines Nature's beneficent governance: the Temple of Venus opposes natural human love with something not explicitly immoral, but simply dispirited, factitious, and abortive, an unhappy progress toward death. The natural bond of love delineated in the *Parliament* has a philosophic viability, perhaps even a (natural) theological one. But the poem arrives at its particular kind of statement by declining to enter into the process of human experience and all of its contingencies. Love, life, and death in this dream-vision are abstracted from all but the idea of flux. Even the fiction itself is conducted as an argument in imaginative logic, linking together a series of independent units whose thematic coherence must be sought far beneath the surface appearance of random inconsequence. Sequential events, related to one another as cause and effect, determined by human motives and choices, lend themselves to philosophical speculation of a different kind. Ethical considerations become more insistent, metaphysical implications more problematic as they are subjected to existential testing. The sustained narrative settles ineluctably into the kind of historical flux dream-visions rise so confidently above. It is arguable that Chaucer turned to such storied fictions as much for the philosophical challenge they offered as for their more obvious and immediate attractions.

Sometime in the middle of his poetic career, when his involvement with Boethius's *Consolation* was still fresh, Chaucer seems to have acquired the texts of two large works by Boccaccio. The extensive treatment of love in the *Teseida* and *Filostrato* came to him embodied in congenial fictions of a density and amplitude beyond, apparently, his power or inclination to invent. They presented him with the raw material needed to pursue some of the philosophic issues, implicated but left unexplored in the *Parliament*. Transmuting the lush but often facile verses of Boccaccio into poetry of deeply felt thoughtfulness, Chaucer created in the *Knight's Tale* and in the *Troilus* two romances on a grand scale that remain philosophically provocative to this day.

Both of Boccaccio's poems contain autobiographical elements. The passion of a great love, achieved then lost, is anatomized with lyric tenderness and at great length. The two works differ generically, however: the *Teseida*, an epic, Virgilian (or Statian) in its structural appurtenances but Renaissance in its combination of the martial exploits of its titular hero with the love triangle of the secondary characters; and the *Filostrato*, looser in structure, freely indulging its idealizing lyricism, yet often cynically psychological and more transparently allusive. Chaucer's adaptations retain some of these distinctions: an aura of epic grandeur still hovers over the story of Palamon and Arcite, and the *Troilus* retains much of the intimacy of its original. Yet both Chaucer's works are more remote, the narratives more "distant": the *Knight's Tale*, often characterized as a kind of "poetic pageant,"[2] depends heavily on set speeches and descriptions and is organized into great tableaux where the choice of setting, the entrances and placement of its actors figure as symbolically as the actions; while the story of Troilus is held at arm's length by its sympathetic but self-consciously "different" narrator.

Chaucer, in fact, makes capital of the idea that these are

97

adaptations, though of course he never mentions their true source. He reshapes the narrative material with a will. While there remain great stretches of close translation, there is also ruthless condensation—particularly in the *Knight's Tale*—as well as expansion and interpolation from other sources, most notably from Boethius. One incident, the celestial journey of Arcita's soul, is omitted from the *Teseida* adaptation, but transferred to the other story, as part of the "Epilogue" to *Troilus*. Clearly, these new narratives are anything but slavish imitations. Chaucer has approached Boccaccio's firmly modeled originals as if the clay were still wet, pulling and tugging at their components until a recognizable but essentially new form emerges. The classical twelve books of the *Teseida* have been reduced to four carefully balanced narrative units, stripped of the rhetoric of epic formality; while the nine irregular cantos of the *Filostrato* are remodeled into a five-act design with tragic associations, classical as well as medieval,[3] and punctuated with invocations in the high style. The generic implications of this new structure play intriguingly against those of the original, while the reorganization as a whole points to Chaucer's confident sense of the potentialities of narrative fiction as a vehicle of meaning, a mode, far more rich and complex than the moral exemplum or even the dream-vision, of philosophical imagining.

Another feature of these two Boccaccian poems that no doubt contributed significantly to Chaucer's reshaping is that evident love of antiquity once thought peculiar to the Renaissance. But although the legendary, titular hero of the *Teseida* lends authenticity to the genre, camouflaging the less classical behavior of the young lovers, the poet's autobiographical surrogates, the invention of Troilus's love story, based on hints in the Trojan romance-histories, is on Boccaccio's part admittedly no more than "a cloak for the secret grief of my love."[4] In Chaucer's hands, however, these stories of antiquity take on some of the qualities of romance, begging to be consigned by the literary historian to "The Matter of Greece and Rome." Chaucer was nevertheless genuinely intrigued by the paganism of this material. Its heroes, like Seys and Alcyone, lived "while men loved the lawe of kinde" (*BD*, 56), the order of Nature, supervised and executed by a pantheon of energetic deities, anathema to the theologian but heaven-sent to the poet-philosopher. While the philosophers of antiquity—Plato, Cicero, and others—had entertained monotheism as a serious cosmological proposition, their anticipation of revealed Christianity had only limited reference. The pagan world, therefore, as Shakespeare was later to see, provided an ideal setting in which to explore the mind's grasp of fundamental metaphysical issues, suspending for the nonce some of the central tenets of Christian faith and its sacramental view of life. While the *Parliament* viewed earthly love as a harmonious part of the great scheme of Nature, but as only one particular manifestation of the larger principle of regeneration, these narratives depict a uniquely human response to love—less universally perhaps, but in a historical and representative context, where its characters and consequences cannot be blithely equated with the mating of birds.

Something of the supernatural orientation of the *Parliament* survives in these pagan fictions, but significant generic barriers re-form once vision is replaced by quasi-realistic narrative. The narrator is obliged to observe, with greater precision and amplitude, the limitations of human psychology as well as the limits of human knowledge. Chaucer uses these Boccaccian stories of antiquity to imagine, with all the historical restrictions of time and space, the mind attempting to come to terms with its situation—social and political as well as metaphysical —while simultaneously forced to acknowledge and cope with its own inadequacies. The antique setting encourages the analysis of human behavior functioning without the resources of Christian faith; the "uninstructed" mind is left to its own devices, obliged to read the book of nature by the power and intuitions of its unaided reason, to seek not the comfort of Christ but the consolation of philosophy. And it is, of course, because Boethius attempted to do much the same thing that he intrudes so frequently and decisively upon these narratives.

In the dialogue of the *Consolatio Philosophiae* Chaucer found an analogue of epistemological progression, from which moments of partial and tentative insight could be spliced with dramatic propriety into his reshaped Boccaccian narratives of a pre-Christian condition.

In spite of its sustained narrative, the story of Palamon and Arcite[5] is in some of its formal aspects reminiscent of the *Parliament.* Its story is shaped into large, symbolically organized scenes, depicting, for the most part, structured public confrontations—parliaments, in fact, at the climax of Parts III and IV. The dramatis personae include planetary deities of awesome power, and the human actors are correspondingly limited and not substantially realized as characters. They are closer to the representative abstracts of human behavior found among the parliamentary birds than a Troilus or Criseyde. The radiant and flower-like Emelye, as many have noted, has nothing of her Italian counterpart's worldly womanliness, those flashes of Boccaccio's difficult but captivating muse. Emelye is merely the ideal object of desire necessary to produce in her suitors the whole catalogue of Ovidian symptoms that constitute the lover's disease.

Palamon and Arcite, in spite of numerous attempts to distinguish them, remain as alike as two peas or two tercelets.[6] Even Boccaccio's heroes, though scarcely well-rounded characters, at least do not look alike; "Palemone was strong-limbed, somewhat dark, clever in speech, subtle, solemn in movement and bold. Arcita was rather slender, blond, open in speech, active and agile."[7] Chaucer's lovers worship at different shrines, but their goal is the same, and every care is taken to preserve the symmetry of their actions.[8] Palamon's priority of vision and worship of Venus may make the ending appropriate, but Arcite's equal love is never questioned and his equal worth is confirmed by his behavior in the impressive death-bed scene and the public recognition of the funeral. In their parallel complaints of Part I, the burden is the same, though Palamon addresses the eternal gods and Arcite, mis-

guided man. To speak of a contemplative or theological Pala-
mon and an active or mundane Arcite[9] is to distort petty dif-
ferences inescapable for the plot and to misjudge the mode
and meaning of the tale. The two characterless. young men
are mere counters in a philosophic inquiry. They illustrate in
a generalized way the various forces that manipulate man's
life; they make no significant choices for themselves; and they
certainly do not "learn" or "develop" as characters. Moreover,
their equality in passion, nobility, and worth is essential to
the structural patterns of the story and to the questions about
earthly justice they insistently raise.

Theseus, more than any other figure in the poem, has at-
tracted critics by the apparent fullness of his characterization.
While the others are merely acted upon, he is the chief actor;
they are playthings of the gods, he the god-like ruler; they
are the moving pieces of a philosophic problem, he is the
philosopher. In his attempt to stand above the vicissitudes of
Fortune, Theseus alone exerts his will, commanding, building,
organizing, always engaged in making choices. Consequently,
he also engages our attention and empathy. His vitality differs
qualitatively from that of the young men: they do the loving,
fighting, dying, and marrying; after the conquest of Thebes,
he merely presides. But his dynamic, which intrigues us be-
cause of its play of mind and will so unlike the helpless
floundering of the lovers, resides nonetheless in the narrative
rather than his character, in the sequence of decisive arbitra-
tions rather than in the complex entanglements of psycho-
logical motivation, such as one finds in a Criseyde, for ex-
ample. Theseus as much as the others is a paradigmatic figure,
embodying a schema abstracted from the contingencies of ac-
tual human experience. He inhabits a philosophic parable
within which an individualized personality would constitute
a serious breach of decorum.

When the interest of characterization is restricted in this
way by schematic simplification, a greater burden necessarily
falls upon the action. In romances of the melodramatic sort,
narrative amplitude is provided by an extended sequence of

episodes, often with bare-faced reduplication. The tale of the
Man of Law is a characteristic example. But when the narra-
tive strives for greater generic and thematic insight, the action
becomes more evidently structured. The unity of the *Knight's
Tale*, as Muscatine has said, "is based on an unusually regular
ordering of elements."[10] The symmetry of character is echoed
by a symmetry in the plot that takes two distinct forms. There
is the pattern of "erratic reversals" or "ups and downs," as
Underwood has called them.[11] The situations of the young
lovers at the end of the first book are cunningly balanced in
equal misfortune: Palamon may still gaze on his beloved, but
is confined in prison, while the liberated Arcite is exiled from
the consolation of his eyes:

> Yow loveres axe I now this questioun:
> Who hath the worse, Arcite or Palamoun?   (1347–48)

By closing the section on this *demande d'amour* Chaucer
forces attention to the structural integrity of its events, which
in turn raises the question of earthly justice or, in this case,
the injustice ingeniously doubled by the symmetrical inver-
sion of the lovers' fortunes. Part II reverses the conclusion of
the first through the agency of Theseus, who removes the
sentence hanging over both knights, offering each an equal
opportunity "be batayle" (*PF*, 539). Their response is as eager
as the "egle tercels' ":

> Who looketh lightly now but Palamoun?
> Who spryngeth up for joye but Arcite?   (1870–71)

The symmetry here is in the formal structure: the two men,
at first equally though differently discomposed, are now equal-
ly ecstatic. The obstacles, unwittingly imposed by Theseus, first
harshly for political purposes, then benevolently as a favor to
his friend, have been removed, and the lovers have the illusion
that they can be masters of their amorous fates.

The translunar perspective of Part III constitutes Chaucer's
most subtly imaginative reshaping of his Boccaccian material.
Theseus, in building the impressive "lystes" to give due public

solemnity to the contest,[12] ironically also provides the setting for religious observances, and the two warriors with their expected prize, Emelye, seize the opportunity to place themselves in the hands of higher powers. The circular amphitheatre with its three oratories becomes an architectural anàlogue for the symmetrical reduplication of the earthly triangle in the planetary deities, Venus, Mars, and Diana. The automatic recourse to supernal aid by the human actors and the equally unquestioning divine acceptance of the responsibility suggest an accord between the two realms of being for which we have been inconspicuously prepared. The fortunes of men depend as much upon forces within themselves as without—it has been the aggressions, martial and venusian, which brought about the miseries of Part I. Love as much as war brings with it discord and violence, turning the chivalrous bond of fellowship into the bloody duel in the grove. And love, like war, often comes uninvited, but once arrived proves to be a power over which its subjects have no control. The planetary deities of Part III return us to the misfortunate world of Part I; they stand for the "ruling passions" of their worshippers, writ large in the heavens.[13] And though Venus and Mars are traditionally "fortuna" and "infortuna minor,"[14] long before they begin their squabble for celestial power, Venus and even Diana have been portrayed at their altars in form and influence[15] almost as sinister and terrifying as Mars. In this unpleasant pantheon Chaucer has introduced a rather subtle anatomy of the concept of Fortune that hangs so heavily over Part I. Those forces lumped together so conveniently but ambiguously under the name of Fortune reside not in the stars alone; they penetrate and intermingle in what we would now call the human psyche. What man sees as a temporal good or evil may indeed be imposed on him from without, but may equally come from within himself. Arcite's complaint can be taken one step further; man's own desires may themselves be his misfortune.

The willingness of Saturn, *infortuna major*, to take on the role of arbiter "agayn his kynde" (2451)[16] brings down the curtain on the celestial scene with an ironic finality that completes the structural parallel to Part I. Part IV presents the "grete effect" promised by its predecessor. Like Part II it depicts a contest between the two knights and works to remove the misfortunate temper of its predecessor. Theseus begins the action with his proclamation of a bloodless combat and after the catastrophe brings the poem to a close by once again striving to mitigate the personal misfortunes of the young men, enlarging the context into a public ceremony. The tournament, funeral, parliament, and marriage are all of his making, all attempts to provide an occasion in which the collective will of a human society can assert—even in the face of all that Fortune may dispose, even death—the dignity and worth of human life. Theseus replaces, in action as in his discourse, the Saturn of Part III with the Jupiter, *fortuna major*, who becomes "the kynge,"

> That is prince and cause of alle thyng,
> Convertynge al unto his propre welle
> From which it is dirryved. (3036–38)

By omitting Jupiter from the celestial parliament and introducing him here as, in Theseus's mind at least, the equivalent of the "First Moevere," Chaucer confers upon his sagacious duke a philosophic insight comparable to that which informs the *Parliament of Fowls*. Like Nature, Jupiter gives spatial boundaries to the elements, temporal ones to the day and night, duration to all things in the mutable sublunary world. The Boethian "fair cheyne of love," which lies behind both of these poetic figures, is predicated upon an eternal principle of creation, itself stable and orderly like the translunar world, but apparent in this world of generation only by a leap of imaginative vision. Confined to the temporal plane, most men, like Egeus, see only the linear progress from birth to death. Theseus, through his belief in Jupiter, understands the divine ordinance by which things corruptible in nature shall "enduren by successiouns" (3014) and thereby achieve something of the stability and order implied in the bond of love. By a submissive, stoical response to this mortal necessity, a virtue may be made of a hero's death. Extending the application of such reasoning, Theseus, as Jupiter's theologian, presides, like Nature in the *Parliament*, over the union of the surviving lovers, to perpetuate that succession which the death of Arcite threatened to break.

That the *Knight's Tale* begins and ends with a marriage is perhaps the most telling aspect of its symbolic structure.[17] The action of the poem imitates the concepts Theseus propounds in his great speech.[18] The symmetries of action and response, the formal parallels of ironically opposed content, all recreate in the fictive world through which Theseus moves, the pattern of order and stability generated by the permutations of time and fortune, the flux and apparent disorder of the sublunary condition.[19] The form of the poem confirms Theseus's insight; from within the natural world of his experience, he draws conclusions that penetrate to the essential principles of creation itself. His observation is circumscribed by the resources of his pagan world, limited to natural philosophy, but the formal construct of his fictional universe authenticates his wisdom.

The limitations of Theseus's speech are serious, however, and more damaging than some admirers of the *Tale* allow. Some of the best readers of Chaucer have been troubled,[20] and one critic has even found ironic comedy in Theseus's inability to do more than assert that the only certainty is death.[21] Theseus's recognition of the order and coherence of natural things may, however, be taken as the theoretical basis for many of his actions in the poem. On the model of nature as he understands it, he attempts to fashion social and political constructs intended to bring a sense of communion and stability to the various multitudes who make up his ordered unities. The organized combat, the ceremonies of state, and the rituals of death are organized to discharge the sense of personal misfortune into the larger field of communal experience. Theseus's articulation of his functions as ruler "anticipates" medieval political theory in its dependence on hierarchical analogies; but though he can rationalize a formal pattern for human conduct, he does not quite answer the philosophic question as posed. He places the problem of death in the larger perspective of natural succession, but he does not explain *Arcite's* death. The question raised in Part I generalizes the problem of justice in human misfortunes; Arcite's totally fortuitous disaster in the midst of triumph, like the classic test-case of the death of an innocent child, revives the issue in unequivocal terms. Saturn spins the conquering hero off Fortune's wheel with grimly ironic speed, and the narrator permits no suspicion of human complicity. Theseus may find order and stability in forces that shape the world, but is there also justice? The identification of the "fair cheyne" with "love" seems to imply more than is in fact corroborated by Theseus's examples and conclusions. In his scheme, human life is indistinguishable from that in the mineral world of hard stones or the vegetable kingdom of long-lived oaks—perhaps even the avian parliament presided over by Nature. The pagan vision does not extend beyond the image of a universal machine in which man is simply a self-important cog that consoles itself by imagining greater cogs.

Such analogies, while not precisely unfair to the actual words of Theseus's speech, certainly do not do justice to their impact in the context of the narrative whole. To better understand the limitations of thought among these poetic pagans, it is useful to set their philosophizing in the perspective of the dramatic argument in Boethius's *Consolation*. The complaints of the young Thebans in Part I belong in spirit to the first half of Boethius's work,[22] which is devoted to a discussion of Fortune. Palamon's address to the cruel gods is adapted from the complaint voiced by "Boethius" himself in similar incarcerated circumstances (Book I, Metrum 5):

> O thou governour, governynge alle thynges by certein ende, whi refusestow oonly to governe the werkes of men by duwe manere? Why suffrestow that slydynge Fortune turneth so grete enterchaungynges of thynges; so that anoyous peyne, that scholde duweliche punysche felons, punyssheth innocentz? (pp. 326–27)

Arcite's speech, on the other hand, incorporates some of the wisdom of Lady Philosophy (Book III, esp. prose 2) on the false felicities of this world in which foolish man thinks to find his true happiness. But Arcite remains as blind as his sworn brother, still believing Emelye to be his supreme good and mistakenly wishing for the wrong thing, release from prison. He will, of course, repeat his error in praying to Mars for victory. Both men err in the same way, as Philosophy would see it: they find in the promptings of Venus (or Natura Pronuba) their greatest desire, and lack that reason which is the *"summum bonum* of human nature,"[23] the key to their true blessedness. Right reason makes clear the folly of desiring any temporal good, which would, necessarily, fall under the sway of Fortune. But what higher good is available to heroes of a secular romance, especially one whose secularity is reinforced by the pagan setting?

The fair chain of love, which forms the basis of Theseus's final argument, derives from those metra used earlier as a gloss on the *Parliament.* What is missing in his speech is the ethical and metaphysical position Philosophy builds upon this magnificent cosmological image in the latter half of the *Consolation.* In Book III, prose 10, for example, she teaches that "blisfulnesse and God ben the sovereyn good; for which it mote nedes be that sovereyn blisfulnesse is sovereyn devynite" (p. 351). But this God, which is both the highest good and highest happiness, is not available to the pagan lovers as a reasonable substitution for their radiant Emelye. Nor is Theseus able to contribute this ethical dimension to his First Mover. Later in the *Consolation* (IV, pr. 6), Philosophy juxtaposes Fortune against Divine Providence, while Theseus has merely compared the linear perspective of the individual life to the enduring and stable cycles of nature. Only by moving outside of time and nature can one perceive the providential plan by which "God hymself, makere of alle natures, ordeineth and dresseth alle thingis to gode" (p. 371). Theseus can only approach such a concept negatively; one is not to grieve, he concludes, that Arcite has departed "out of this foule pris-

oun of this lyf" (3061). Theseus's grasp of the ethical implica-
tion of the fair chain is greater than that of the other mourn-
ers, especially the grieving women who equate "gold ynough
and Emelye" (2836). But though he raises his sights above
the realm of mutable Fortune, beneficent Providence eludes
his natural philosophy. Perhaps on this account Chaucer in-
troduces his appearance in Part II with the long and appar-
ently gratuitous reference to

> destinee, ministre general,
> That executeth in the world over al
> The purveiaunce that God hath seyn biforn.   (1663-65)

In the Boethian scheme, destiny mediates between eternal
Providence and the earthly Fortune visible to men. Theseus
from his first entrance in the poem is seen as somehow im-
mune to the vicissitudes of Fortune, and in the splendid image
that opens Part IV he sits "arrayed right as he were a god in
trone" (2529) imposing his beneficent will on the tournament
through the intermediary of a herald.

Indeed, it is such symbolic moments throughout the poem
that make Theseus's final speech more profoundly resonant
than a literal analysis allows. There is, moreover, another
pattern of scenes, not previously mentioned, which contributes
decisively to the philosophic content of the poem. The first
episode, for which Chaucer added to Boccaccio's version de-
tails from Statius (along with the epigraph), carefully sets
the mode as well as much of the meaning of what is to follow.
Theseus, resplendent as the returning conqueror, meets at the
temple of Clemency the lamenting Theban widows. The vivid
tableau of starkly contrasting colors might be taken as an em-
blem of Fortune, the Duke with his martial banners above,
the black-clothed noblewomen cast down in wretchedness be-
low. The sole gesture of the scene also speaks symbolically:

> This gentil duc doun from his courser sterte
> With herte pitous, whan he herde hem speke.
> Hym thoughte that his herte wolde breke,

Whan he saugh hem so pitous and so maat,
That whilom weren of so greet estaat.   (952–56)

Theseus's pity reveals his gentle heart, and he immediately takes up their cause, abandoning his nuptial festivities. The consequent brutality of the sack of Thebes has pained many admirers of the Duke.[24] It is difficult to know whether our modern sensibility intrudes, whether Chaucer miscalculated in carrying over too much material from his sources once he had omitted the rationale given by the previous Athenian-Theban conflicts, or whether we are indeed to see Theseus here imperfectly assuming the responsibilities of justice.

If some kind of development was intended, Part II supplies the necessary corrective. The episode in the grove—the only one undefined by a symbolic architectural setting—formally recapitulates the opening scene. Theseus's initial response to the confession of the young warriors is one of outraged justice. The gentle pity comes first from the Queen and her sister, who in their plea move Theseus, as Alceste does her lord, to a finer concept of royal justice:

> "Fy
> Upon a lord that wol have no mercy,
> But been a leon, bothe in word and dede,
> To hem that been in repentaunce and drede,
> As wel as to a proud despitous man
> That wol mayntene that he first bigan."   (1773–78)

In pardoning the lovers and setting the stage for a more dignified and conclusive contest, Theseus atones (if atonement is required) for their initial confinement, so apparently arbitrary in this version of the story. These two parallel scenes portray a powerful ruler moved from stern outrage to tender compassion, stirred by the helpless entreaties of kneeling women. Both scenes present emblematically that commonplace of medieval thought, the tempering of justice by pity and mercy.[25] That Theseus requires prompting need not be taken as a sign of his inadequacy; it confirms in symbolic action the accord between the male and the female principles in an ethical realm, implying a deeper significance to such natural conjunction than is ironically conferred upon martial and venusian associations elsewhere in the poem.

In the last two books Theseus works out his destinal role on a grand scale, creating the lists, mercifully prohibiting bloodshed, then arranging for the obsequies, the parliament, and the marriage. Though his ministrations cannot prevent the death of Arcite, even that event provides the occasion for a reassertion of nobler sentiments. Arcite's death-bed speech contains not only the moving statement of the poem's theme, "What is this world? What asketh men to have?"; it concludes with the reconciliation of the sworn brothers and a generous definition of Palamon's nobility and worthiness as husband to Emelye. When, in the final moments of the poem, Theseus returns to Arcite's suggestion that she now take Palamon, his argument to the lady is based upon those significant themes that shaped the earlier scenes. He asks her to manifest her "wommanly pitee," to consider Palamon's great merit, his service and adversity in love, "for gentil mercy oghte to passen right" (2089). In the context of the passage, "mercy" seems to include the gentle feelings exhibited by Palamon as well as the grace requested of Emelye. In any case, by invoking mercy over right in this final scene, Theseus adds immeasurably to the limited Boethian observations of his previous speech. Although he seems to lack the knowledge that will permit him to articulate such ethical concepts into his statement of philosophical beliefs, they are nevertheless a part of his experience as a believer in the operations of the fair chain of love within the natural world. He can translate the idea of mercy from his political world to the private one of matrimony. The dramatic situation lends great weight to the gesture. A wedding may be expected of the conclusion in this romance genre and is required of the comic perspective which implicitly posits a universe of ultimate benignity.[26] Theseus, by bringing the Christian concept of mercy into the most naturally significant of human relationships, imposes an ethical dimension on his pagan world, by his gestures if not by his philosophizing. As the first mover of his dukedom, he imparts by action and example the bond of creative love to his subjects. The bleak condition of pre-Christian antiquity incorporates in Theseus's presence—by what one might call a secular typology—hints and guesses of the benevolent Providence its natural wisdom cannot comprehend.

CHAPTER VI

TROILUS AND CRISEYDE:

"LOVE IN DEDE"

*Vivat amor in ydea,
ne divulgetur opere.*

"Dum rutilans Pegasei"[1]

*"My dear Sir, never
accustom your mind to
mingle virtue and vice.
The woman's a whore,
and there's an end on't."*

SAMUEL JOHNSON

THE story of Palamon and Arcite moves us a considerable distance from the idealized vision of the *Parliament* into a realm of recognizable historical realities. It does not, however, entirely lose the *Parliament*'s range of inquiry, which relates individual human experience to social and political concerns, and human experience in general to cosmological forces. Nor, in spite of its greater mimesis, is the comic perspective entirely abandoned. The price exacted in sympathetic human involvement, however, becomes very apparent once one turns to the *Troilus*. The characters of the *Knight's Tale* are defined by their experiences; they are the functions of a philosophic inquiry that of necessity avoids certain kinds of particularity. Hence, we do not grieve for Arcite, though we may be moved by the image of universal condition he voices. His experience and his words are subsumed within that larger scheme of things that is the poem's narrative as well as its meaning.

The story of Troilus might be said to take up matters from Arcite's point of view. In the Trojan

War the furies of Saturn have a ready-made symbol of *infortuna major*, and Troilus, better than the Theban prince, knows what it is to be one moment with his love, the next "allone, withouten any compaignye." But, in spite of the celestial laughter at the end (granted to this hero at Arcite's expense), Chaucer's retelling of the *Filostrato* is by the poet's own deposition a tragedy, its subject matter a "double sorwe."[2] To sustain a true tragic vision, the poet must convince us that something of value has been lost. Arcite satisfies only the most limited requirements for a tragic hero. As Fortune's fool, he has the necessary "high estate" from which to fall; but his nobility is a "given" in the poem, demonstrated perfunctorily by his chivalric progress and his susceptibility to a certain kind of refined love. We are asked to accept him as a type of recognized value, but we are not allowed the intimacy of particularity. We know him only from the outside, and as outsiders we feel only a general empathy for his condition.[3]

The characters of the *Troilus* also come with established external values; we move in the highest Trojan society. But here gentle birth is no guarantee of *gentillesse*. Each character is called upon again and again to prove his value; and the demonstration has little to do with physical prowess or material wealth. Measured primarily in terms of moral values, they are required repeatedly to make demanding decisions, and their motives are inspected at very close quarters, from the intimacy of the tête-à-tête to the privacy of their inner thoughts. Though a comparison of the *Troilus* to the psychological novel may raise false expectations and misjudgments of its methods,[4] there is unquestionably something almost Jamesian about many of its scenes. Even where we withhold our approval, we have a sympathetic knowledge of its characters unmatched in our literature before Shakespeare.

The emphasis on character is apparent in every aspect of the work. *Troilus and Criseyde* is presided over by a narrator who attempts to guide our sympathies in a sequence of events over which he claims no control. The narrative itself is shaped—or reshaped from Boccaccio—with an eye for the dramatic definition of mental and emotional states. Rather than pose abstract questions about the human condition as does the *Knight's Tale*, the *Troilus* narrative is organized to focus upon the ethical implications of human conduct. The settings, while no less symbolically resonant, are here for the most part interiors, domestic, private. The significant spaces in the poem, close chambers, bedrooms, are loci of meditation and intimate communion; the public occasions represent disastrous intrusions upon the integrity and freedom of the individual.

Time in the *Troilus*, like space, is governed by the dictates of the human psyche rather than the romance conventions of chivalric behavior. Palamon and Arcite spend at least ten recorded years wasting away and fighting over Emelye before they attain more than a distant glimpse of her. The only comparable leap of time in the *Troilus* (at the opening of Book V) startles us, not because of its unrealistic conventionality, but because the consummate experience of Book III—echoing through night after night of perfect bliss, rounded by the mutual aubades—seemed to have nothing to do with such temporal designations as:

> The gold-ytressed Phebus heighe on-lofte
> Thries hadde alle with his bemes clene
> The snowes molte, and Zepherus as ofte
> Ibrought ayeyn the tendre leves grene,
> Syn that the sone of Ecuba the queene
> Bigan to love hire first for whom his sorwe
> Was al . . .   (V, 8–14)

Calendar time belongs to the public world; it marks the separation of the lovers and counts the days of Troilus's anticipation.

Love exists outside of time, or at least gives the illusion of doing so. Its consummation stretches over the years in the seclusion of night. Its coming is sudden, altering time without itself becoming process. Troilus falls in love "with a look":

And upon cas bifel that thorugh a route
His eye percede; and so depe it wente,
Til on Criseyde it smot, and there it stente.   (I, 271–73)

Criseyde experiences a similar moment, when she

gan al his chere aspien,
And leet it so softe in hire herte synke,
That to hireself she seyde, "Who yaf me drynke?"
(II, 649–51)

Her dream that night confirms the change in her affections, even if she cannot fully admit it to herself. Yet the process is entirely different for Criseyde, precisely because it is minutely described for us. The long and devious preparation of Pandarus and the coy pretenses, the self-deceiving rationalizations of Criseyde make her transformation qualitatively distinct from Troilus's. The experience has been subjected to time and all the dangers and duplicities associated with temporal flux. Yet by the world's standard this has been a rapid alteration, a matter of one day,[5] and the narrator takes pains to reassure us that Troilus got her love "in no sodeyn wyse" (II, 679), implying that there would be something wrong if he had. The irony of this miscalculated attempt to save the heroine's honor is double-edged. It is obvious that Criseyde has gone beyond the stage of "inclining to like" the Prince, and the narrator is misrepresenting the facts as much as she herself does. On the other hand, he is trying to make her actions conform to a standard of morality that is clearly not that of the poem; it would have been better for her to fall in love in an instant, as did Troilus, than to require the day of accommodation. The time it takes Criseyde to love reflects the ambiguous character of all she does: like Troilus in some respects, she gives the illusion of ideality; but more profoundly tied to time and space than he, she betrays him through her inability to slip those bonds.

Distinctions among the three major characters can be measured by their responsiveness to time and place. Troilus's instinct, once he has been "converted" to love, is to close himself off from the world of events outside. He finds reality only in the solitary, agonized meditation within his bedchamber, just as later he achieves his only happiness in Criseyde's. His ability to function in the great world is entirely dependent upon his love; otherwise, the world has no intrinsic value or pleasure for him. Pandarus is his perfect opposite. More than a go-between or a voyeur, Pandarus is the manipulator *par excellence*, who finds satisfaction in the activity of arranging time and place, no matter what the end. In one sense only he wins the victory over Fortune. By playing at mutability himself, he is immune to her capriciousness. His energy and good will in Troilus's service are boundless, but thoroughly arbitrary in their goal; if one mistress proves untrue, why then "this town is ful of ladys al about . . . we shall recovere an other" (IV, 401, 406). Like some amoral physical principle, he requires only matter to make evident his capacities. When the rain prevents Criseyde's leaving his house on the fateful night, it is Fortune which is invoked (III, 617ff.) but Pandarus who is responsible for its effect upon human lives.

On the other hand, Pandarus is entirely dependent upon the material world of time and space for his pleasures and values. More than anything else in the poem he exposes the absurdity of writing off Troilus as merely another seeker after the false felicities of this world. The ending of Book I superbly estimates the difference between the two men: Troilus, ennobled by his love, finds each of his former flaws changed "for a vertu"; he moves into a realm of unqualified superlatives:

> For he bicom the frendlieste wight,
> The gentilest, and ek the mooste fre,
> The thriftiest and oon the beste knyght,
> That in his tyme was or myghte be.   (I, 1079–82)

Pandarus on the contrary has contracted to do a job and sets about busily to make the most of the materials at hand:

> For everi wight that hath an hous to founde
> Ne renneth naught the werk for to bygynne
> With rakel hond, but he wol bide a stounde,
> And sende his hertes line out fro withinne
> Aldirfirst his purpos for to wynne.   (I, 1065–69)

That these lines are an adaptation of Geoffrey of Vinsauf's opening advice on poetic invention is one of Chaucer's closet ironies. Pandarus's poem will be an ephemeral thing of time and occasions. Like the *Parliament*'s Nature, he provides for a mating, but if any high purpose is to be served, it is for Troilus to define it.

Much of the poem's definition is sharpened by the Boethian passages Chaucer has scattered through the text. Many of these appear to be later revisions that serve, as Root has said, to "enhance appreciably the serious philosophic tone."[6] One can evaluate the *Troilus* characters, like those of the *Knight's Tale*, by the distance they have traveled with Boethius in his enlightenment at the hands of Lady Philosophy. Here, too, one is made conscious of the limitations imposed by the pagan context. None is able to go all the way to the consolation of Philosophy. Troilus founders on the perennial theological conundrum of God's foreknowledge and man's free will (IV, 957ff.), but he has at least reached the final stage of Boethius's exposition (V, pr. 2, 3). His argument is learned and precise, conducted in some of Chaucer's least elegant verses, but observant of the niceties of Aristotelian logic. This passage, together with the other late addition (from the *Teseida*) of Troilus's celestial journey, claim a great deal for the scope and penetration of the hero's powers.

The Boethian passages in the *Troilus*, unlike those in the *Knight's Tale*, support other character values. In a romance of this kind we expect to be faced with Troilus's superiority in love, but cannot help being unprepared for his formidable intelligence. Pandarus, like the water fowl of the *Parliament*, is no true servant of love; nor is reason one of his strong points. Not that he lacks the ability to persuade; his method,

however, is to bombard his audience with proverbs and ex-
empla until the din wears down his opponent. By the standard
of the schools, he ranks low in reasoning powers; his devices
—proverbs and exempla—form the bottom rung on the ab-
straction ladder, clinging still to the concrete. They consort
better with the village gossip than the schooled rhetorician.
Pandarus's wisdom has more sound than substance. Proverbs
and exempla invite the misapplication and irrelevance of
specious logic. He devotes, for example, several stanzas to the
proposition that "By his contrarie is every thyng declared"
(I, 637) in the hope of proving that a fool's advice will profit
a wise man. And one of the earliest indications of Troilus's
intellectual acumen comes in the reply Pandarus forces out of
him by crying, "Awake":

> He gan to syken wonder soore,
> And seyde, "Frend, though that I stylle lye,
> I am nat deef. Now pees, and crye namore,
> For I have herd thi wordes and thi lore;
> But suffre me my meschief to bywaille,
> For thi proverbes may me naught availle.
>
> . . . .
>
> What knowe I of the queene Nyobe?
> Lat be thyne olde ensaumples, I the preye."
> (I, 751-56, 759-60)

Though finally powerless against Pandarus's insistence, Troi-
lus shows that he knows exactly what his arguments are worth.
Pandarus's bag of platitudes contains, not surprisingly, bits and
pieces of "Boethian" lore, mostly on the changeableness of
Fortune. If Fortune is Troilus's foe, why complain?; she al-
ways changes. If Fortune smiles, be prepared; it will not last.
The mighty argument of the *Consolation* is reduced to an
old wive's tale.

But the truly surprising use of Boethius proper comes in
Criseyde's speech, on the night of the consummation. De-
ceived into believing Troilus jealous, she launches into a dis-

course on the "condicioun of veyn prosperitee" (III, 817) that
almost matches in clerkly method Troilus's later meditation.
It is a piece of very cogent reasoning, rounded off with a tech-
nical flourish:

> "Wherfore I wol diffyne in this matere,
> That trewely, for aught I kan espie,
> Ther is no verray weele in this world heere."   (III, 834–36)

The sentiments are appropriated from the second book of the
Consolation, but are striking in the mouth of the timid woman
who seems in too many ways her uncle's niece. Most of the
evidence to this point has focused on her quick wit and her
ability to penetrate and equal Pandarus's deviousness. Yet
here we have testimony to a different kind of intelligence.
Though its provocation is false and its conclusions quickly
ignored, the speech helps establish dramatically the reasonable-
ness of Troilus's love. Just as Criseyde shows something of
his suddenness in love and will shortly match his facility in
composing aubades, here she demonstrates an intellectual ca-
pacity that partly matches his, phrased in the language of the
schools and supported by the authority of Lady Philosophy
herself. In these astonishingly bookish additions to a courtly
romance, Chaucer pays fitting tribute to the dramatic vitality
of Boethius' great work.

The philosophic burden of the poem rests of course on
Troilus's shoulders. If his career is to be taken as more than
just pathetic, a spectacular because aristocratic example of the
machinations of Fortune, he must convince us of a nobility
more impressive than his princely station, more profound
than his impeccable amorous rhetoric. His great soliloquy in
Book IV does more than establish his intellectual credentials;
it confers a kind of respectability on his conduct, which many
in Chaucer's original audience would have found reassuring.
What prevents him from resolving the contradiction between
God's foreknowledge and man's free will is, at least as Lady
Philosophy would see it, his conception of time. He makes

the mistake of imagining divine knowledge in human terms, existing in time with a past, present, and future. Troilus's paganism is defined, for Chaucer's Christian audience, by an imperfect sense of divine eternality, just as Theseus's was by an inadequate grasp of divine love. What makes both of these cases so poignantly noble is that these metaphysical blind-spots are more theoretical than actual. These pagans lack the concepts to articulate what they act on more or less intuitively. Theseus imitates the benevolence of divine justice, and Troilus loves with an absoluteness that clearly implies the transcend-ence of time. Both heroes of antiquity would have no diffi-culty commanding the respect of a medieval audience, if not, like Trajan, the hope of salvation. By their obedience and conformity to the highest law they know, they both merit celestial seats among the just ancients of fiction.[7] Troilus, of course, has already begun his journey before the poem ends.

The reason Troilus's nobility fails to impress some critics is that his highest law is love and its object a creature of this world. He invites the simplistic critical view that dismisses him as one of the misguided hankerers after temporal riches Lady Philosophy disposes of in the early books of the *Conso-lation*. But if he can truly be so easily accounted for, why did Chaucer deliberately portray him as raising the knotty prob-lems of Boethius's fifth book? The question is not as frivolous as it sounds. One need not require that a character recapitu-late all the steps of Boethius's progress to consolation, to sug-gest that arriving at the final stage of the argument implies having in some sense got beyond its initial problems. Troilus's investment of his love in a temporal good is a consequence of his paganism. The meditation on free will reveals the particu-lar boundaries set to his spiritual reach. Theseus's philosophi-cal limitations do not prevent him from acting in such a way as to improve the human estate; the *Knight's Tale* can, there-fore, offer a qualified comic perspective. Troilus's world, how-ever, admits no transcendent object for his love, and he com-mits the tragic mistake of accepting the earthly object. But, intriguing and attractive as Criseyde is as a character, it is not the object but the quality of Troilus's love that ultimately matters.

The formal structure plays a large part in the proper evaluation of Troilus's experience. Boccaccio's *Filostrato* is an irregularly organized mélange of lyrical outbursts and sinuous narrative. Chaucer, by insisting on the boundaries of each of his five books, creates a structure that emphasizes units of significant action rather than emotional impetus. The first three books—the "rising action"—define the quality of Troilus's love dialectically.

Book I reads like a commentary on Guillaume de Lorris's *Roman de la Rose*, following the stages of Troilus's love from his cynical and prideful disbelief to his virtuous transformation. The experience is for him of such magnitude that it seems to have little to do with the external world. He loves a living woman, but, unaided, it never occurs to him that his emotion need be anything but private, a source of elevating, if painful meditation. His every impulse resists the efforts of Pandarus to translate the ideality of his experience into mundane action. Though he yields at last to the persistence of his friend's seemingly harmless persuasion, he remains inactive, not out of adolescent ineptitude, but because his instincts work against any practical consequence to his love.

Chaucer leaves it to others to suggest the true analogue for Troilus's experience. The narrator opens the book with an invocation that shortly resolves itself into a "bidding prayer"; he speaks as one "that god of Loves servantz serve" (I, 15), elevating to the role of sympathetic intercessors those lovers that "bathen in gladnesse" (22). Pandarus, having by the end of the book extracted Troilus's confession, playfully indulges in "a good conceyte" that rounds out the religious analogy:

"I thenke, sith that Love, of his goodnesse,
Hath the converted out of wikkednesse,
That thow shalt ben the beste post, I leve,
Of al his lay, and moost his foos to greve."   (I, 998–1001)

In this case Pandarus speaks truer than he knows. Troilus has indeed undergone a spiritual revolution that will alter his life and being. The religion of love may have passed for idle rhetoric in much medieval literature, but in this closed pagan world where the alternative is the festival of the Palladium, it assumes significant proportions. Troilus's devotion to love from the very first anticipates and justifies the apotheosis Chaucer was later to provide.

Book II is almost entirely given over to Criseyde and the duel between Bialacoil and Daunger under the supervision of Freend, Pandarus. Troilus is not inactive; he fights the Greeks, rides through the streets, writes passionate letters, and works his way into Deiphoebus's guest room. But the dramatic action centers in the mind and heart of his lady. Criseyde's progress toward love contributes indirectly to a better understanding of Troilus. Her world is a familiar one; her house has an architectural presence that Troilus's palace does not; it is peopled, active with the inconsequential doings of everyday life. Time, as we have said, marks Criseyde's experience as worldly and unlike Troilus's. The contrast is not as yet antithetical; Criseyde moves between opposing modes of being, defined by Troilus and Pandarus. Though she is not fully conscious of the direction her emotions—both love and fear— are taking her, she nevertheless exerts a good deal of rational control over the situation. She knows Pandarus for what he is and plays his games with equal skill. Unlike Troilus, however, she shows herself, in the process, capable of saying one thing while thinking another. Her attitude toward any kind of change in status is cautious, tentative. Troilus's love is for her something that may be reckoned, even debated at length. In the process rationalizations creep in along with extrinsic considerations. Though she may in fact love rather suddenly and powerfully, Criseyde shares with Pandarus a tendency toward worldliness and calculation in matters that Troilus conceives of as absolute and spiritual. Self-deception and even duplicity, urbane and ingratiating as they may seem in this comic action that moves toward the union of the lovers, distinguish Criseyde's love as vulnerable to the mutations of time and place. Book II prepares convincingly for the tragic dé-nouement at the same time it captivates with the possibilities of earthly love that will be realized in Book III.

In the "Prohemium" to Book II, after an invocation to Clio, Chaucer makes capital of his historical milieu to set Troilus's amorous behavior apart from the contemporary world whose conduct will animate the scenes to follow (II, 22ff.).[8] One must not inspect too closely the logic of this justification of the hero's antique ways, when his lady behaves so much like a well-bred member of fourteenth-century society. The point is not that everyone else is anachronistic, but that Troilus's extraordinary capacities would strain credulity in any age, most especially perhaps in a time when his amorous style was such a familiar convention that it was easily satirized or paro-died. The task of substantiating Troilus's claim to more than commonplace hyperbole falls to Book III.

The interruption of the action at the end of Book II, when Criseyde approaches Troilus's side, is more than a coy Ariostan seeking after suspense. The first meeting of the lovers is re-served for the book that massively celebrates unions. While Book II breaks off inconclusively, with Criseyde's hesitant footsteps and tentative love, Book III mirrors structurally the integrity and comprehensiveness of Troilus's feeling. The nar-rative works its way through the comic awkwardness of meet-ings contrived by Pandarus, until there is nothing further for him to contrive and the tone modulates to the lyricism of high romance.[9] The two bedroom scenes wittily reverse the posi-tions of the lovers, but the comedy in each instance results from the intensity of Troilus's passion under the pressure of complicity in Pandarus's machinations. The pretense of ill-ness as well as real agonies of love all but deprive him of prepared speeches at their first meeting, while the fainting spell that gives Pandarus the opportunity to pop him into Criseyde's bed is occasioned by Troilus's inability to cope with Pandarus's ruse of her suspected infidelity:

"God woot that of this game,
Whan al is wist, than am I nought to blame." (1084-85)

The farcical elements of these scenes profess Troilus's inno-
cence at the same time they allow him to benefit from Pan-
darus's fictions.

That such comic invention can yield to the passionate lyri-
cism of the consummation is one of the great feats of English
literature. While the twin aubades testify to the mutuality of
their love, it is Troilus who sets the tone of the scene and of
the book as a whole. He consecrates the union with a hymn
to Love, or "Charite," and to Venus and Hymen. That Cupid
may be addressed in such loaded terms is hardly anachronistic
blasphemy as some critics have alleged. Troilus merely con-
fers on these, the only deities he knows, the most potent re-
ligious associations in Chaucer's vocabulary:

"Benigne Love, thow holy bond of thynges . . .
Here may men seen that mercy passeth right;
Th' experience of that is felt in me,
That am unworthi to so swete a wight." (1261, 1282-84)

To confirm these implications Chaucer replaced Troilo's
speech at the conclusion of the episode in *Filostrato* with the
Boethian song to that creative power that orders the discord-
ant elements of the world into the stable bonds of love:

"So wolde God, that auctour is of kynde,
That with his bond Love of his vertu liste
To cerclen hertes alle, and faste bynde,
That from his bond no wight the wey out wiste." (1765-68)

Troilo's invocation to Venus, now the "Prohemium" to the
Book, in spite of its greater reliance on classical mythology,
has much the same theme:

God loveth, and to love wol nought werne;
And in this world no lyves creature
Withouten love is worth, or may endure. (12-14)

125

The celestial Venus sets the law to all things in the universe, the invisible bond that unites the most unlikely opposites; she knows "al thilke covered qualitiee of thynges" (31–32). By shifting about these great speeches, Chaucer not only disembarrasses Troilus of Boccaccio's heavy classicism and graces him with the authority of Boethius, he also validates, within the poem but outside the temporal limits of its fictive world, the high concept of love Troilus espouses. Structurally the three hymns provide a center and a secure frame to enclose the love which is already secluded from the world in the curtained room, by the darkness of night, and above all, by the finality with which the narrator brings the action to a satisfying close.[10]

That this rounded conclusiveness will prove ephemeral is insinuated by several allusions to Fortune, the most chilling being:

> And thus Fortune a tyme ledde in joie
> Criseyde, and ek this kynges sone of Troie.   (1714–15)

But the impermanence of the object need not invalidate Troilus's attempt to realize in his loving of Criseyde the highest law available to him, an expression of the natural longing, as Aristotle defined *eros*, "of the essentially imperfect for its own perfection."[11] That he should choose Criseyde instead of God is not Augustinian cupidity, but the inevitable consequence of living under the law of Nature, whose most sacred expression was the loving union of opposites, the holy bond of things. That human experience should on occasion, in such blissful consummations of human love as this, seem to be offering a stability and permanence inconsonant with mortal nature prepares for a tragedy far more universal in its resonance than would seem possible to the fragile rhetoric of medieval romance.

Book IV, divided centrally by Troilus's meditation on free will, is constructed as a sad parody of the first books. Once again Pandarus negotiates separately with the two lovers to bring them together, and in the final scene they are reunited in the bedroom, but this time to confer upon and accept their separation. Pandarus is still the energetic go-between, but he can no longer exercise the control he once had. He finds a Troilus who counters his glib opportunism with firm and decisive reasoning. His recourse is to work through the more pliant Criseyde: "Women ben wise in short avysement" (936). Criseyde, urged more by her fear than love, proves equal to the task, managing to rationalize a handful of ways by which she alone will effect a return to Troy. But Troilus's predicament provides the dominant theme of the book. Faced with new and bewildering circumstances he struggles to extricate himself with a vigorous application of reason. Though he can hold his own with Pandarus, his very cogency proves self-defeating when he tackles free will and divine foreknowledge with imperfect premises. Thus demoralized, he understandably capitulates to Criseyde. He listens to her sophistry with both heart and ears, and though "his herte mysforyaf hym evere mo" (1426), he has no alternative but to concede her the freedom of choice he believes to be denied mankind absolutely. The conflict between the mind and the heart is resolved in favor of specious reasoning. Troilus cannot argue against the apparent good sense she boasts. His heart perceives the lack of faith that Criseyde already betrays by protesting too much, but matters of faith are not discerned by the reason as his wrestling with the problem of divine foreknowledge had previously made clear. His reason works against his better interests because he lacks the basic terms. He can no more define his love in the language of Criseyde's sliding worldliness than express Providence in terms of divine eternality. Book IV, then, while it systematically sets about to destroy all that Troilus has found to value, manages at the same time to increase our appreciation for those intellectual and spiritual capabilities he brings to bear upon his dilemma.

Book V portrays Troilus haunting a time and space devoid of animating purpose without Criseyde. Paradoxically the parameters of earthly existence only acquire a presence for him negatively. In the absence of the saint, her palace takes on the aspect of a shrine. Each moment of the ten days is measured against the terminus that proves so elusive in the event. For Criseyde, become a true creature of this world, one day slips into the next imperceptibly. Troilus, on the other hand, determined to invest this earthly frame with spiritual reality, refigures "hire shap, hir wommanhede / Withinne his herte" (473–74) so insistently that when the fatal night comes he can impose her image on "fare-carte." As her absence continues, he withdraws again into a condition of inner suffering, brought on by his inability to temper his image of reality to the external world. His symbolic dream reveals the true state of his earthly affairs while it confirms his access to spiritual truths. Our two final glimpses of Troilus are equally important to the poem's meaning. From the perspective of the eighth sphere he knows the world in all its petty vanity and transitory "blynde lust."[12] But just as memorable is his last dramatized moment in the story, standing on the Trojan walls with Pandarus, who can now only find words to express his hatred of Criseyde. Yet Troilus, befuddled by his undeserved treatment, speaks out a final helpless message to Criseyde:

> "I se that clene out of youre mynde
> Ye han me cast; and I ne kan nor may
> For al this world, withinne myn herte fynde
> To unloven yow a quarter of a day!"   (1695–98)

In a rare moment of self-awareness, Pandarus in Book III raises the question of how an outsider might view his pandaring activities. Troilus attributes to him only the most generous of motives, and in the process enunciates a principle of analysis that might usefully be addressed to Chaucer's poetry as a whole:

> "Departe it so, for wyde-wher is wist
> How that ther is diversite requered
> Bytwixen thynges like, as I have lered."   (III, 404–406)

The ironist, of course, makes his way by asking us to "depart" what is said from its "diverse" and intended meaning in context, to make discriminations that in turn involve moral evaluations. The number of "worthy" men and "good felawes" on the Canterbury pilgrimage would otherwise be statistically unrealistic, if nothing else. But Chaucer's dramatic method often asks for distinctions too fine or produces evidence too ambivalent for confident moralizing. On the question raised by Pandarus, for instance, Troilus's high-minded defense of his friend's activities speaks eloquently for the prince's own character and gives the morally unsuitable go-between the answer he no doubt wishes to hear. Yet the discussion has injected into the moral action of the poem that verdict of "al the world" that was to make his name a common noun. Pandarus has, of course, put the matter in extreme form; it arises from a rhetorical effort to insure Troilus's discretion rather than any deep interest in moral judgments for their own sake. There had never been any question of gold or "ricchesse" as Pandarus well knows. But there are more subtle kinds of covetousness, and Troilus's altruistic interpretation cannot dispel the impression that Pandarus's motives lie somewhere in the murky area between moral extremes, neither as pure as the two believe them to be nor as impure as the reductive popular tradition imputes. Like most human actions whose motives are imprecisely known even to the actor himself, Pandarus's behavior eludes facile moral judgment.

Where the characters fail to complicate judgments sufficiently, the narrator steps in, further muddying the waters. He, as much as anything in the poem, is responsible for those "thynges like" that require our departing. His responses to the characters, though often embarrassingly sympathetic, deliberately simulate a process of evaluation. His admiration of Troilus remains to the end as steadfast as the hero, but his championing of Criseyde proves to be less reliable as a moral barometer, as "sliding" in fact as her own heart. From the time of her "sudden" love for Troilus until she takes up with Diomede, the narrator is continually defending her against detractors whose views need not have intruded so damagingly, if at all, into the action. The last instance is particularly instructive:

I fynde ek in the stories elleswhere,
Whan thorugh the body hurt was Diomede
Of Troilus, tho wepte she many a teere,
Whan that she saugh his wyde wowndes blede;
And that she took, to kepen hym, good hede;
And for to helen hym of his sorwes smerte,
Men seyn—I not—that she yaf hym hire herte.

(V, 1044-50)

The value of this stubborn refusal to condemn is curiously
equivocal. When in the next stanza it becomes clear that there
is no question that Criseyde has "falsed" Troilus and she her-
self admits it, the narrator's doting sentimentality undermines
his authority. This works to Criseyde's disadvantage: one
would like to sympathize but such company makes it difficult.
Then, curiously, the reaction reverses itself. We, like the narra-
tor, have known Criseyde too well not to be compassionate, no
matter how unapproving. The mediation of the narrator be-
tween our sympathies and their object serves as a reminder
of how unreliable human judgment is and how preferable
even blind compassion to unfeeling condemnation. Less ana-
lytically perhaps, one reacts to the mediation itself, to having
judged in part in reaction to another's judgment. Had this
narrator told us, like Henryson's, that she would soon descend
into the common court, our initial reaction might have been
outrage while second thoughts would force us to admit some
justice in calling a whore a whore. But Chaucer's narrators
err on the side of compassion, which is why the reputation
for "humanity" clings to the poet himself and critics argue
over the state of even the Pardoner's soul.

Much of what the narrator does is less ambiguous though
not inconsequential. His intrusions into the consummation
scene prevent monotony and preserve its ideality, as Byron
does in the Haidée episode of *Don Juan*, by concessionary[13]
reminders of a less satisfactory, but more familiar reality. The
pose of twofold vicariousness—as humble servant of the ser-
vants of Love and as mere historian, the unresponsible re-

tailer of second-hand tales—enables the narrator to mingle many realities. The antique world provides the framing history of the Trojan War, a classic pattern of tragedy, but the love story belongs to the high Middle Ages. Criseyde and Pandarus enjoy the colloquial ease of domestic life, but Troilus's uncompromisingly courtly style of loving is explained as antique fashion, and the absolute commitment to temporal love as a locus of comprehensive value is made possible, until the "Epilogue," by the absence of a competing Christian morality. The narrator responds to his story with a comparable double standard, innocently conforming to the simplest of pleasure principles. When he likes what is happening, as in Book III, the historicity disappears; as Love's clerk, he attends to ceremonies of the lovers with the immediacy of a celebrant, fully immersed in the realities of their passion. When things are not going well, however, he becomes detached and bookish. The farther apart the lovers, the more frequent the references to what "the storie telleth us," what "men seyn," to the long perspective on Troy and to historical sources. After Diomede has destroyed all hope of reunion, the narrator removes himself further from the romance, deflecting the genre toward chronicle history with the addition of three lifeless portraits from Joseph of Exeter. When the hero's catastrophe culminates in an unheroic death, "Chaucer" steps out of the fictional world entirely, pushes away his story as though it were no more than a physical manuscript ready to be cut loose from its creator and ripe for scribal bungling; then packing Troilus off to the eighth sphere, he becomes a Christian.

The temptation to take the so-called "Epilogue" as sufficient and comprehensive has proved understandably irresistible to many critics; the position it takes would have pleased any moralist in Chaucer's audience and seemed incontrovertible to even the most sympathetic listener. The appeal to Christian otherworldliness admits no easy rejoinder, especially when supported by the experience of the pagan hero himself. An energetic *contemptus mundi* is certainly one response to

the instability of temporal values, but there is little evidence
that it has been adopted by a sizable number of Christians,
even in the Middle Ages. It is an extreme solution to Troilus's
problem, accessible to the hero only after death and not in-
voked by his metaphysically advantaged narrator any sooner.
It springs dramatically from the narrator's dissatisfaction with
a fictional world that has proved intractable to his making
and consequently not to his liking. In context it need carry
no greater weight than the narrator's invocation of Venus in
Book III. Putting Troilus's tragedy in a Christian perspective
is a bold anachronism that functions on a large scale some-
what like Pandarus's concern for the loss of his reputation.
To follow Troilus's condemnation of "blynde luste" with the
advice to turn one's heart upward and love Christ has a hid-
den illogic that has caused many critics to forget that Troilus
was not a Christian. This extreme and unacceptable evalua-
tion of a hero who has merited so much admiration during
the course of the poem directs our attention not toward the
other world or a platitudinous morality, but back to the es-
sence of the story itself, the tragic condition of temporal life
that cannot hold the ideal in more than a momentary reality.[14]
If the Epilogue relates the poem to any part of the Christian
myth, it is more to the expulsion from Eden than the Re-
demption.

The shape Chaucer has imposed upon Troilus's career does
more than trace the rise and fall of his earthly fortunes; it
affirms in book after book in countless ways the high value
of his love. It would be absurd and pointless to agree that
such testimony may be casually overturned by the Christian
perspective of the Epilogue. The narrator, however, manages
to contrive the illusion that one may do so, by the confusion
of two realities: as an historical figure Troilus exists outside
of Christian sanctions and even his absolute and exalted
style of loving is attributed to his distance in time and place
from "men here." Intermingled with this historicism is what
one might call the existential reality[15] whose tragic dilemmas
are as much a part of the world of Chaucer's audience as

Troilus's erotic behavior and the ambiguously idealized pattern of *fin amor* it subscribes to. The narrator's Troilus is at once a hero of the ancient world and a man of the fourteenth century, hence, by implication, a man of all time.

This double vision allows Chaucer to round off the poem in a way that is formally satisfying without compromising the integrity of his argument. The story remains all the more forcibly a tragedy by the acknowledgment of a Christian perspective that can resolve the basic dilemma, but only by a radical shifting of terms. The narrator's reactions lay down a smoke screen against the Gowers and Strodes, the uncompromising moralists of his audience, and perhaps to some extent against the poet's own religious scruples. The conclusion is dramatically effective because it is psychologically, not intellectually valid. "Man," as a modern analyst has pointed out, "can react to historical contradictions by annulling them through his own action; but he cannot annul existential dichotomies, although he can react to them in different ways. He can appease his mind by soothing and harmonious ideologies."[16] The narrator dismisses the existential torment occasioned by Troilus's fortune, with the comforting hypothesis that it is in fact only an historical problem whose dichotomies may be annulled by ideology. The result is formally and dramatically coherent, but not entirely sound logically.

In pursuing a line of what some might term romantic criticism, I am in no sense questioning the profundity, sincerity, or intellectual responsibility of Chaucer's own Christian faith. But I see no need to mistake the poet for a theologian or dogmatic moralist. Poets deal in the experience of life, and religious doctrine constitutes, even for the medieval, only one facet of the experience of secular existence. Though Christianity undeniably touched every aspect of medieval life, men might yet, without becoming doubters, have found themselves at some level "dissatisfied, anxious, and restless."[17] In spite of the belief in the immortality of the soul and the possibility of its salvation, death in the Middle Ages remained an occasion for grief. The impermanence of earthly satisfactions contin-

ued to be a matter of surprise and sorrow, requiring ever-re-
newed consolation. Indeed one of the triumphs of Christianity
is its recognition of human frailty, acknowledging man's
readiness to be distracted from the cogency of its doctrines, by
ritualizing them into the dynamics of his daily experience.
The great medieval books of consolation, from Boethius on-
ward, gain their impressiveness by working dramatically,
conceding, alongside of the magisterial solutions of dogma or
philosophy, the painful actualities of mortal experience. Re-
cent criticism of Boethius has attempted to do justice to the
"darker side" of the *De Consolatione*, finding the dialogue
"more convincing as a dramatization of the psychological ex-
perience of the attempt, than as an exposition of the means . . .
to the transcendent solution of the problems with which it
deals." Winthrop Wetherbee has characterized Philosophy's
use of poetry and myth as having "the effect of a double ex-
posure of the course she urges. For her, the heroic images she
presents are models of decisive, liberating action, repudiations
of fortune and the ties and fears of earthly life. For the pris-
oner, and for us, they are also images of the difficulty of such
renunciation and transcendence."[18]

Chaucer's *Troilus and Criseyde* is no less a work of its time
for its insistent double vision of human experience. Beside the
formidable truths of transcendent Christianity, it sets a "natural
perspective" on this mortal condition. Man's dilemma is for-
mulated in terms of the apparent conflict between two strong
imperatives, each claiming divine sanction: One requires the
renunciation of this "fair world" in favor of Christ's love; the
other expects that man, as human nature dictates, will figure
forth within his own stratum of the created hierarchy the
holy bond of things that Boethius and Troilus alike celebrate
as the manifestation of divine love. What is possible in the
avian idyll of the *Parliament* is of course doomed in the fallen
actuality of the *Troilus*, but an awareness of the perfect
model makes the attempt seductively tantalizing and even
morally feasible. In thus defining imaginatively the complexi-
ties of mortal experience, Chaucer has distinguished prece-

dent in the poetic philosophers of the twelfth century. The commentaries of Guillaume de Conches on Boethius and Bernardus Silvestris on Martianus Capella discover not the unequivocal Christian "moralitee" of most allegorists, but paradox. One might say of Troilus what has been said of Bernardus's reading of the figure of Vulcan: "At once the embodiment of a subjective view of human experience and an objective exemplum of that experience . . . he testifies to the futility and the inevitability of certain patterns in human behavior—he demands and at the same time suspends moral judgment."[19] Chaucer, more poet than philosopher, lends greater emphasis to the "subjective view" in the five books devoted to Troilus's love than to the "objective exemplum" of the Epilogue, possibly because he could say of that love as did Guillaume of the wisdom of this world, that it is "foolishness with God" (I Cor.), not because God esteems it to be foolishness, but because it is foolishness in comparison with His.[20]

CHAPTER VII

PATIENT GRISELDA:

"BILOVED AND DRAD"

Patience, hard thing!

G. M. HOPKINS

CHAUCER was not moved to exploit Boccaccio's pagan fictions because of a dissatisfaction with orthodox theology; on the contrary, he expresses the philosophic poet's urgent need to examine the ground of human experience that makes the consolation of theology necessary. Putting to canny advantage the pre-Christian setting, Chaucer managed to infuse a vitality into Christian doctrine often denied its explicit pronouncements. His audience, transported imaginatively into that remote world, is invited to discover, or re-discover, the relevance and immediacy of familiar beliefs. If Chaucer's dalliance with antiquity needs justification, it should be on much the same terms Augustine applied to allegory: because of the "darkening" of the surface meaning, the reader is obliged to participate actively in a process of intellectual discovery. But intellection is not all that is involved. Chaucer's philosophic poems recreate the conditions of thought as much as the thought itself, the feelings that provoke inquiry as well as the feel of its process. Hence, while these "pagan" poems may

137

in one way or another compel a Christian resolution, they do not hesitate to acknowledge the often unmerited pain that makes it necessary, as well as the difficulties attending its accomplishment.

The virtues of the pagan setting are even more evident in Chaucer's explicitly religious tales. Of the four such works in the Canterbury collection, the two assigned to the nuns may be classified as devotional exercises. The Second Nun's life of St. Cecilia—more than likely an early work—and the Prioress's legend of the Virgin betray little interest in the problematic aspects of common human experience. The characters, such as they are, have that purity of moral coloring associated with melodrama. Whether they are black or white depends entirely on their acceptance of the religious assumptions of the tale; they exist primarily to celebrate the validity of those assumptions, specifically the existence of a supernatural realm from which emanates the power to effect justice in this world on terms of its own definition. The conflict in these tales is between absolute good and absolute evil, and the action hangs upon a divine intervention into the human realm that confirms the supremacy of the good, on earth as in heaven. Their disposition is unashamedly complaisant, depending entirely on the aquiescence of the audience to their theological and generic assumptions. They comfort while they entertain, by ignoring the doubts and difficulties that are the lot of less than saintly beings.

Much the same kind of thing might be said of the Man of Law's saintly romance,[1] and therein lies its weakness. The conventions of hellenistic romance give the saintly heroine little to do to justify her apparent election, except exude piety and suffer repetitiously. Her efforts at proselytizing have been stripped by Chaucer[2] of the "busyness" of Cecilia, while her adult innocence cannot claim the same indulgence as the Prioress's "little clergeoun." But the greatest weakness of the Tale lies in a generic conflict inherited from its source. Trivet had introduced this pious episode into his lengthy chronicle, a work of historical pretension and continuity. Returning the story of Mauritius's mother to an independent status, the Man of Law nevertheless retains much of the historical aura, most evidently at the conclusion. In spite of the numerous miracles that assist Constance on her journeys, her story ends in an enumeration of the deaths of all concerned, sprinkled over by the narrator with such inappropriate romance sentiments as:

But litel while it lasteth, I yow heete,
Joye of this world, for tyme wol not abyde;
Fro day to nyght it changeth as the tyde.   (1132-34)

This kind of moralization, injected repeatedly by the Man of Law, constitutes a serious breach of generic decorum in the tale as he has fashioned it.[3]

The rhetorical bombast with which Chaucer has endowed his legalistic narrator represents a further unassimilated expansion of his source. Coupled with the increased emphasis on the pitifulness of his passive heroine and the resultant "impression of a curiously childlike naiveté,"[4] the strategy of the adaptation suggests a deliberate attempt at undermining the public pretensions of a solidly secular speaker to establish himself as a "pillar of the church." As such, the *Man of Law's Tale* would belong in the next group of fictions, which are more concerned with the exposure of the narrator than with the apparent intentions of the narrative. But the context of the *Tale* in the manuscripts casts doubt on Chaucer's final purpose. The tale "in prose" promised in the elaborate and devious *Introduction* has been replaced by this rime-royal performance, which may simply have been an earlier work of the poet. Uncertainty in locating the narrative voice of the *Tale* precludes a confident assignment of its failure to the Man of Law. But it remains nonetheless difficult to embrace wholeheartedly the religious elements of the *Tale*,[5] to accept its heroine as a *figura* of the "help of God" image,[6] or to add up the borrowings from Pope Innocent's *De miseria humane conditionis* into a "Christian comedy."[7] The *Prologue* to the *Tale* points unmistakably, I believe, in the other direction. The description of "impatient poverty" might have been ap-

139

propriate to the tale that follows[8] had the narrator chosen to make it so. But the use of material, originally designed to incite a rejection of this world, to praise the comfort and luxury of rich merchants is surely an un-Innocent transition. Then to seize upon the reference to tale-telling merchants as a means of divulging the "source" of the story merely compounds the sin and calls attention to the speciousness of such transitions and the feeble grasp of the narrator on his material. The *contemptus mundi* formulae provide an occasion for secular regret rather than a prelude to otherworldly meditations, and the religious apprehension of the narrator seems as superficially formal as that of the Monk, who adorns his "tragedies" with similar platitudes. Whether or not Chaucer so intended it, the imperfections of the *Man of Law's Tale* cast serious doubt on the perspicacity and piety of its teller.

The Clerk succeeds where the Man of Law fails, by enfolding his romance in the cloak of allegory. The central issue in each tale is much the same: the appropriate human response to testing by adversity, the essential Boethian dilemma once more, but couched in explicitly Christian terms. The Clerk, following Petrarch, glosses his tale from the Epistle of St. James (1149–62). Griselda's perfect virtue, though its fictive historicity remains unaltered, is removed from the contemporary scene, nostalgically set in stronger "olde tymes yoore" (1140), an example for all mankind smarting under the "sharpe scourges of adversitee" (1157). Such trials are sent by God, not as temptations, but as tests of strength, spiritual exercises reasonably demanded of His creatures by the Creator: "For greet skile is, he preeve that he wroghte" (1152). Walter, already God's surrogate as Griselda's temporal lord, becomes the purveyor of her earthly fortunes when he becomes her husband. His double claim to her obedience and authority over her will is legally assented to and solemnized in the contract of marriage. Like the supernatural beings in earlier incarnations of the story, he has the undisputed right to test the wife he has made his, while he retains, within the decorum of the

humanized fiction, the capacity to reward her patient obedi-
ence. Thus, in spite of its historical locale, the Clerk's tale,
unlike the Man of Law's, is able to preserve the structural
pattern of romance postulated by the ideality of its heroine.

Not all readers have found the Clerk's method as persuasive
as I suggest, however. Though many, before and since, have
considered the tale with Muscatine a "connoisseur's poem,"[9]
others have balked at its premises and branded one or both
of its protagonists as monstrous.[10] The temptation has often
proved irresistible to write off the poem's assumptions, theo-
logical or domestic, and its lack of psychological realism, as
an example of "medieval taste."[11] Fortunately, there is evi-
dence that the divergence in critical reception of the story is
not exclusively a modern phenomenon. A letter from Petrarch
to Boccaccio, written at the very end of his life to accompany
his Latin translation of the *Decameron* story, preserves the
response of some early readers to his rendering, which Chau-
cer followed so closely:

> In the first place, I gave it to one of our mutual friends
> in Padua to read, a man of excellent parts and wide attain-
> ments. When scarcely halfway through the composition, he
> was suddenly arrested by a burst of tears. When again,
> after a short pause, he made a manful attempt to continue,
> he was again interrupted by a sob. He then realized that he
> could go no further. How others may view the occurrence
> I cannot, of course, say; for myself, I put a most favorable
> construction upon it; believing that I recognize the indica-
> tions of a most compassionate disposition; a more kindly
> nature, indeed, I never remember to have met. . . . Some
> time after, another friend of ours, from Verona . . . having
> heard of the effect produced by the story in the first in-
> stance, wished to read it for himself. I readily complied, as
> he was not only a good friend, but a man of ability. He
> read the narrative from beginning to end, without stopping
> once. Neither his face nor his voice betrayed the least emo-
> tion, not a tear or a sob escaped him. "I too," he said at

the end, "would have wept, for the subject certainly excites pity, and the style is well adapted to call forth tears, and I am not hard-hearted; but I believed, and still believe, that this is all an invention (nisi quod ficta omnia credidi, et credo)."[12]

One hesitates to interpret too freely the meaning of the dry-eyed Veronese's words, but his consciousness of the fictionality of the work arose apparently from the lack of credible motivation for the actions of the principal characters, their unnatural or "monstrous" behavior.[13] One may infer, moreover, from the numerous small changes he made,[14] that Chaucer too sensed the problem, but his solution was many-faceted. The plausibility of the chief antagonists is heightened, but the manner varies significantly. For Griselda, alongside the austere religious symbolism pointed out by Sledd and others, there is the evident attempt to create dramatic tension. The task would appear virtually impossible, given Griselda's pledge not to show "neither by word ne frownyng contenance" (356) any sign of her will, except in acquiescence to her husband's. But Chaucer has added many touches that serve to define the tremendous resistance of such a will dedicated though it may be to outward passivity; most vivid is the swooning reconciliation with her children when the tension has been released, but there are also telling verbal gestures, such as the reference to their marriage day (852–54) or the caution against tormenting the new bride (1037–43). Even where the Latin or French text is followed closely, the occasional double translation of a phrase contributes subtly to our estimate of the magnitude and humanity of Griselda's character.[15] Whatever else Chaucer may have felt about the tale, he credited wholeheartedly the virtue and nobility of its heroine.

His handling of Walter, on the other hand, saves the tale from sentimentality or facile piety. The young marquis reveals from the beginning all the strengths and limitations of the nobility, and his subjects regard him with appropriate ambivalence—"amor et timor." "Biloved and drad" (69), he wavers between a sense of responsibility to his position and a perverse desire to exert his will, to be free of constraint in order to indulge a "lust present" (80). His coming upon Griselda while hunting portends the typical consequences of the *pastorale*—dalliance and *droits du seigneur*—but instead he gazes upon her beauty and virtue with complementary nobility, "in sad wyse" (237). Unpredictably autocratic or finely noble, Walter's erratic behavior in the opening scenes lays a plausible groundwork for his imposition of a harsh legality on the marriage proposal and anticipates, to some extent, the subsequent testing. But just at the point where many critics have found Walter's humanity difficult to appreciate, where folklorists point to his supernatural antecedents, and where the Clerk prepares his allegory of providential agency, the narrator interjects an unexpectedly strong, disapproving comment. Apparent sympathy for Griselda's plight eventually provokes him to outright disparagement of Walter's character and role-playing; he even goes so far as to question Walter's mental health. Repeatedly, in passages added by Chaucer, the Clerk condemns the gratuitous trials—as evil (459–62), as the wilfulness of lords (581), as the immoderation of husbands (621–23), and finally as an obsessive compulsion:

> But ther been folk of swich condicion
> That whan they have a certein purpos take,
> They kan nat stynte of hire entencion,
> But, right as they were bounden to a stake,
> They wol nat of that firste purpos slake. (701–705)

In effect, what many critics have found intolerably fictional or repugnantly inhuman, the narrator does his best to convince us is morally distasteful but recognizably all too human in its apparent inhumanity.

This extraordinary reaction on the part of the Clerk may do a great deal to help suspend our disbelief, but at the same time Chaucer is taking a very great risk, greater perhaps than when he appends the "Envoy" to the *Tale*. This same abusive narrator will shortly recant with an allegorical reading of the tale in which Walter's role can only be interpreted as figuring the divinity. Of course, the focus of the allegory falls upon Griselda, on the human import of the story, and in any case the narrator is not called upon to account for the inconsistencies accruing from his previous outbursts. Yet the manipulation of the narrative is audacious. Chaucer pays the Clerk the supreme compliment—unparalleled in the *Tales* except in the performance of the Nun's Priest—of complete mastery over the materials of his fiction. Chaucer permits him the luxury, as well as the implied wit and perspicacity, of three different perspectives in his tale—that assumed during the narration, that of the allegorization, and that of the Envoy. The "concessionary" effect of the comic address to the Wife of Bath, so brilliantly defined by Muscatine,[16] has been anticipated in the clash of the earlier perspectives. It is as if Chaucer kept in mind, even as he reworked it, those divergent critical responses the story has elicited since Petrarch's time, then deliberately set about to heighten the double effect. On the one hand he engrosses us in the pity and outrage of the action, on the other he concedes its fictionality by retreating into the safety of allegory.

This complex use of the narrator is reminiscent of the *Troilus* in that it creates a dramatic context that modifies the concluding religious sentiments of the poem. Without questioning the validity of the allegory, the experience of the *Tale* asserts an equally urgent and compelling point of view. It is all very well for the theologian to claim God's right to test His creatures as He chooses, but, from the miserable temporal perspective of the tested, His willingness to do so may easily appear at odds with His claim to love and justice, as unreasonable and intolerable, in fact, as Walter's obsessive behavior. Of course such a reaction depends on the "Boethian" failure to distinguish Providence from Fortune. Yet Walter is indeed identified with the latter until the final moments of the *Tale*.[17] Though the error might be blamed upon a lack of a true metaphysical perspective, failings of this sort are such significant and irreducible constants in common religious experience that theology neglects them at its peril. By maintaining within the fictional construct the "comic" resolution of his romance, the Clerk provides, as the Man of Law does not, the generic correlative for the providential scheme of the Christian order. The enigmatic Walter is transmuted in the end from an agent of Fortune into a divine surrogate; Griselda's final words of reunion with her children confirm the revelation: "God, of his mercy / And youre benyngne fader tendrely / Hath doon yow kept" (1096–98). The *Clerk's Tale*, by virtue of its simple generic fidelity, manages to embody within its stark outlines the eternal vision of divine foreknowledge without sacrificing a painful appreciation of the cost to the human will.[18]

By incorporating both points of view into a single work, a Boethius or a Chaucer gains not only the benefit of dramatic tension but the support of recognizable experience to assure authority to its doctrinally acceptable conclusions. Just as the narrator's unhappiness with Walter's behavior helps to certify the extraordinariness of Griselda's virtue, so allegorically his re-echoing complaints acknowledge the magnitude of faith required by the words of St. James. Griselda's example belongs to "olde tymes yoore," he concedes, and "this world is nat so strong" (1139–40). This sense of temporal mutability underlies all of the Clerk's performance: Taking his cue perhaps from the Host's maxim on "tyme" (6), he begins with a lament for the vanished great of Italian art and wisdom, then generalizes sombrely on the common fate—"and alle shul we dye" (38). Like Theseus, he wrestles with the experiential facts of time and change, fortune and mutability, and, above all, death. But the Clerk is not bound by the metaphysical limitations of the pagan Duke, and the linearity of his narrative structure reflects the confidence with which he can face the consequences of time. To make a virtue of necessity is for him to "lyve in vertuous suffraunce," in perfect assent to the divine will. His conviction proceeds, not from intuitions of the natural order of love, but from the scriptural revelation of God's justice and mercy. After such knowledge, the only possible remedy for the adversities of Fortune can be the absolute submission of a Griselda.

Though the Clerk sets an austere course for the faithful, he does not pretend it will be easy. His imaginative sympathy may aspire to the ideality of a Griselda, but he also concedes the reality of a Wife of Bath. There is a fine humanity in his efforts to mediate between them and, in his storytelling, the quintessential perception of the philosophic poet. Alone among Chaucer's explicitly religious works, the *Clerk's Tale* joins this group of "philosophic" narratives in which human virtues and limitations are scrutinized from a perspective bounded by time and nature. Only a profound intellectual imagination can account for the Clerk's ability to assume for the nonce the point of view of *l'homme moyen philosophique*, for whom the aspect of eternity lies hidden in the mysteries of faith and is, all too often, a "hard thing." The burden, as with all of these philosophic fictions, falls upon its audience: to hear with patience to the end of the narrative is to have won in some measure the virtue and faith of its heroine and its teller.

PSYCHO-LOGICAL FICTIONS:

"REMEMBERAUNCE OF OLD GOOD FELASHIPP"

The most moral writers, after all, are those who do not pretend to inculcate any moral. The professed moralist almost unavoidably degenerates into the partisan of a system; and the philosopher is too apt to warp the evidence to his own purpose. But the painter of manners gives the facts of human nature, and leaves us to draw the inference: if we are not able to do this, or do it ill, at least it is our own fault.

HAZLITT

CHAUCER'S philosophic fictions, as I have distinguished them, are not simply narratives that reproduce thematically a pre-existent system of abstract thought. Still less can they be identified by an explicit "moralitee," though the four works discussed in the preceding section seem to move progressively toward overt statement—from the uncomprehending dreamer of the *Parliament* to the Boethian oration of Theseus, the palinode of the *Troilus* and, finally, the allegorization of the Clerk. In each case, the forthright moralization, whatever its independent value, is qualified, if not radically undermined, by the fiction of which it is a part. The poems are "philosophic" only insofar as whatever ideas they explicitly formulate are tested and implicitly reformulated by the experience of the narrative in which they are contained. Like all great poetry that deserves the epithet, Chaucer's philosophic works resist the facile summation produced by lifting out a few lines that fit neatly onto some prefabricated scheme popularized by the historian of ideas. Their intellectual content is inseparable from the imaginative form; the totality of the fictive experience is the philosophic substance, and its conceptual explicitness is mere accident.

Chaucer's method consistently depends upon a recognizable distinction of the narrative from the narrator. The poetic fiction reproduces dramatically the poet's own creative encounter with another author's work, itself a finished text with its own shape and integrity. The reworking of these established materials always includes and forces on our consciousness an awareness of the shaping imagination. It does not matter if the narrator is merely an unanalytic reporter like the dreamer or a tacit organizer like the Knight, befuddled and ambivalent as in the *Troilus* or a sophisticated manipulator like the Clerk. We are never allowed to become so absorbed in the fiction that we ignore the dynamic interplay of the fictive matter with the control of its shaper. These works have the authenticity of philosophic poetry because Chaucer's adaptations of old authors are dramatic reenactments of the "experience" of "auctoritee."

The consequences of such a procedure are predictable. Though these poems direct our attention primarily to the thematic implications of the reshaped fiction, the usefulness of a narrative persona to achieve the desired "meaning" inevitably suggests further problems and raises other possibilities. If the capacities of the narrator have a significant effect on the thematic import of the narrative, does not this process itself incorporate reservations as to the authenticity of its conclusions? Might one not reverse the formula used to define these fictions and ask what is the authority of experience? Since, after all, most "auctoritee" reflects the experience of some human author, what guarantees its validity in this mutable world whose inhabitants are all by definition fallible? Perhaps the impulse to transmute experience into an organized form may itself be contaminated. The desire to create, or even re-create, fictions, to "make things up," ought, if such is the case, to be cause for suspicion. One cannot tell at what point such a line of reasoning may have occurred to Chaucer, if indeed he ever was consciously moved to such questions. But his major work leaves no doubt that this was the direction followed by the instincts of his imagination, the shift from philosophic to psychological fictions requires only the slightest alteration of emphasis in the balance between narrative and narrator.

The *Canterbury Tales*, to which Chaucer devoted the last half of his poetic career, represents the logical final step in a life-long exploration of the nature and uses of fiction. Incomplete and fragmentary as it is, the work contains, in a confused order, the many stages and divagations of this investigation, but the overall direction is clear. The chronological displacements resulted, I suspect, from conflicting impulses within its creator: One motive was probably an inglorious desire to have something to show, to fatten the manuscript by making use of whatever was at hand—old translations, abandoned tales, pious exercises—in effect, to compete in bulk with that prolific hack, Gower, showing that even after the lackluster *Legend of Good Women* had been abandoned, he could nevertheless produce a massive anthology. But running against this current was the increasing fascination of a new game, inspired by Boccaccio and perhaps Sercambi, but carried to unprecedented dramatic length by Chaucer: the possibility of relating each tale intimately to the voice and character of the teller, quickening the framework with a vigorous interaction among the pilgrims, within as well as outside of their tales. The demands of such a creative endeavor better suited the talents of a poet whose amateur pride and lively dramatic sense made him too impatient to be able to repeat the same kind of story over and over, grinding out couplet after couplet like the "professional" Gower.[1]

The *Tales*, far from complete even in their reduced format, betray Chaucer's working method. The fragments, probably at one time separate quires, often begin with older and unaccommodated material to which is added a new composition that exploits fully the dramatic potential of the frame.[2] The Second Nun-Canon's Yeoman sequence is perhaps the most telling example.³ The competent but spiritless translation of the life of St. Cecilia with its overstuffed prologue seems light years away from the complexities of motive, the frantic attempts at concealment and revelation, which erupt on the scene with the mysterious Canon and his servant. Similarly the *Physician's Tale* does not seem particularized to its teller⁴ and may be an early work, but it elicits an enthusiastic response from the Host, which carries over into his invitation to the Pardoner and perhaps provokes the tortured display of insecure arrogance that follows.⁵ The *Shipman's Tale*, though undoubtedly written for the *Tales*, has been cut loose from its original narrator and reassigned without any adjustment to its new and presumably less feminist speaker. Even the first tale, the Knight's, set in one of the most polished fragments, had, as we have seen, a previous incarnation. To read the *Canterbury Tales* as they have been smoothed out by early scribes and modern editors is to leap back and forth over twenty or perhaps thirty years of Chaucer's career with little external and ambiguous internal evidence to guide us. But in spite of the scrambled impression given by the *Tales* as a whole, there is little reason to doubt that Chaucer's insight into the nature of fiction led him toward the increasing involvement of an identifiable teller in the act of fiction-making.

The first fragment, though it may well pass as a "final version," is an epitome of the stages in Chaucer's experimentation. Beginning with a refurbished "early" work and ending in an apparent decision not to add another fabliau, it sets a pattern for the deepening impression of the teller's psychic nature on the matter of his tale. The implication of such a view of fiction would have been, to the medieval mind, profoundly moral, though nonetheless psychological, because of the primacy granted to ethical considerations. Any moral deficiency exposed in the fictional process could have been interpreted in terms of whatever version of faculty psychology was available, whether neo-Platonic or neo-Aristotelian, as a failure or abrogation of the greatest of man's intellectual resources, his God-given reason. Hence, Chaucer's fictive anatomy of the psychology of fiction uncovers what a recent historian has described as "the blind forces and activities in us which are part of human life as it consciously experiences itself, but are not part of the historical process: sensation as distinct from thought, feelings as distinct from conceptions, appetite as distinct from will."[6] Chaucer's conclusions about the ultimate consequences of this perspective on the uses of fiction will be the subject of this section, but the first chapter will mark the stages of a movement from "philosophic" to "psychological fictions" and examine the ways in which moral evaluation becomes part of the fictive, if not the historical, process.

CHAPTER VIII

THE CANTERBURY EXPERIMENT:

"A SOPER AT OURE ALLER COSTE"

—At supper! Where?
—Not where he eats,
but where 'a is eaten.

HAMLET

*P*ALAMON AND ARCITE, whatever its initial form, was certainly adapted to the Knight. He even anticipates its stoical theme when accepting his lot as first story-teller:

He seyde, "Syn I shal bigynne the game,
What, welcome be the cut, a Goddes name!" (*GP* 853–54)

But as the Knight is an idealized figure, a noble representative of that chivalric tradition that always seems just to have vanished, he has no vices or foibles, no particularizing traits that color his narrative. The proportion of romance elements—more battle and tournament than love—suit him well, as does the serious philosophic inquiry. The tone is generally lofty and well controlled but includes moments of colloquial directness, which may be taken as befitting his maturity and practical wisdom.[1] But, all in all, there is little in the narrative manner of the tale that would require explanation were it excerpted from the Canterbury framework.

Much the same might be said of the *Miller's Tale*, though something would definitely be lost.

The artful parody of the love triangle, the idiom of popular romance,[2] and comic vision of a just universe take their point from the Miller's drunken insistence upon "quiting" the *Knight's Tale*.[3] But the fun is more Chaucer's than the Miller's. The bawdy fabliau structure, the dense particularity accorded the material existence of village life,[4] and the triumph of Alisoun's fresh and lusty animality attach the *Tale* firmly to the brutish cunning Miller of the *Prologue*. But the elegance of its architectonics, its parodic diction, its witty integration of character with plot, and its "just" dénouement—all far exceed any realistic expectation of the capacities of this "janglere," this "goliardeys," even in his soberest moments.[5] Chaucer, not Bacchus, has transformed the Miller's performance into a work of transcendent genius but, in so doing, has taken poetic liberties with the dramatic context. One would not, of course, want it altered in any way; but no more than the *Knight's Tale* is it formed by the peculiarities of its individual teller. It arises from a dramatic collision of generalized social differences—different milieux and life-styles, different genres and their attendant world views. Though the Miller's portrait, unlike the Knight's, assembles many particular details of appearance and behavior, his *Tale* does not pursue their implications by giving specificity to the "quiting."[6] The conflict between the tellers was not in any case a matter of clashing personalities. That is left to the Reeve.

Whereas the Miller was merely parroting drunkenly the Host's little pomposities, the Reeve knows precisely what he means when he sets about to "quite" his predecessor's tale. Though it employs an enriched fabliau technique similar to the Miller's, his *Tale* appears markedly inferior when considered apart from the dramatic context. Admittedly the central conflict is amusingly complicated by misplaced social and intellectual vanity: "Deymous Symkyn's" pride in his haughty wife's high birth makes a double outrage of his daughter's "disparagement" (4271) by Aleyn; and the clerks' naïve frontal assault on the miller's thievery, coupled with their strong Northern accents, makes them appear doubly gullible—

outlandish *and* academic. But on the whole the Reeve's tale lacks the gaiety of the Miller's: it dwells upon the coarse brutishness of its characters and culminates in a bloody free-for-all in a dark room, whereas the foibles of John the Carpenter are climactically exhibited to the light and laughter of the whole town.[7]

The opening portrait of a belligerent Symkyn, a walking armory of violent weapons, establishes the ethos of the piece, but in spite of its obvious similarities to the Miller of the pilgrimage, it represents ultimately less an allusion to his adversary than a revelation of the teller's mental state. In his *Prologue*, the Reeve freely indulges his choleric temperament and describes the outlets it seeks when confined by physical impotence.[8] He embroiders with image after image his sermon on the frustrated passions of dotage. Skillful with language, his is nevertheless not the "sely tonge" (3896). The sexual infirmity he analyzes with such vehemence is obviously a way of coming to terms with his inability to inflict immediate physical damage on the Miller, "bleryng" his eye. He equates sexual "play" with merely speaking of "ribaudye" (2865-66). Indeed, language has now become his only weapon —"avauntyng, liyng" make up half the "sparkles" which heat the "wyl" of old age. But his rhetorical posturing goes beyond using his tongue like the Pardoner to spit out his venom. He assumes, without being fully aware of it, the role of a preacher,[9] lingering over his images,[10] cataloguing vices, sermonizing on death—but all, of course, to invest himself with a moral authority that will strengthen the force of his attack. In spite of the Host's impatience with such role-playing, the Reeve returns automatically to the citation of Scripture in order to justify his tale:

> He kan wel in myn eye seen a stalke,
> But in his owene he kan nat seen a balke. (3919-20)

His application of the proverb from Matthew (7:12), however, seems to suggest that he really means the "bleryng" of "an eye for an eye," unconsciously perhaps conflating the images while deflating the ethic.

The Reeve's desire for vengeance permeates his tale to such an extent that it becomes more than just an exposé of the Miller's vices. His anger turns the performance into a verbal substitute for an act of violence. Everything is sacrificed, even the dignity and well-being of his Northern "heroes," to the Reeve's desire to inflict physical punishment. The contrast with the preceding tale is perfectly captured in the final lines of each. The Miller cheerfully parcels out the just rewards to his several erring characters:

> Thus swyved was this carpenteris wyf,
> For al his kepying and his jalousye;
> And Absolon hath kist hir nether ye;
> And Nicholas is scalded in the towte.　　　(3850–54)

The Reeve, in contrast, heaps ignominy on one man, returns irresistibly to self-righteous sermonizing, and caps the benediction with a self-satisfied reiteration of his one and only purpose:

> Thus is the proude millere wel ybete,
> And hath ylost the gryndynge of the whete,
> And payed for the soper everideel
> Of Aleyn and of John, that bette hym weel.
> His wyf is swyved, and his doghter als.
> Lo, swich it is a millere to be fals!
> And therfore this proverbe is seyd ful sooth,
> "Hym thar nat wene wel that yvele dooth";
> A gylour shal hymself bigyled be.
> And God, that sitteth heighe in magestee,
> Save al this compaignye, grets and smale!
> Thus have I quyt the Millere in my tale.　　　(4313–24)

The Reeve's performance moves beyond the preceding tales in discovering the uses to which a fiction may be put. Though less engaging than the Miller's, his *Tale* has an additional interest, the revelation of the mind and character of the teller

158

by the way he tells the kind of tale he has chosen. What the tale loses in intrinsic value, it gains in dramatic substance as part of the larger fiction of the pilgrimage. The elements of the Reeve's total contribution to the *Canterbury Tales* form a pattern that Chaucer developed and elaborated in many of his well-considered portraits. This pattern tells us a great deal about his understanding of the relationship of fiction to both language and character. A pilgrim's performance will often begin by asserting—in response either to the provocation of another pilgrim or simply to the invitation of the Host—a firm rhetorical posture. In its simplest form, an attitude toward language, expressed or implied, is evoked quite casually. Frequently, however, the rhetorical style employed by the speaker is associated with a literary or subliterary genre that emerges, or is alluded to, in the process. So the Reeve's concentration of extended similes and his somber analytic tone strike the Host as "sermonyng," though he had not in fact spoken as yet "of hooly writ."[11]

The genre appropriated by the pilgrim usually carries with it certain assumptions, certain intellectual, spiritual, or professional pretensions, which are, more often than not, at odds with the vocation or character of the speaker: "The devel made a reve for to preche" (3903). In some cases, though the genre may be professionally in order, its proper function is perverted by the speaker, as when the Friar and Pardoner use the sermon to attack personal enemies. The extent to which this donning of a linguistic pose is a conscious process varies greatly; the range is as wide and subtly shaded as the moral reach of the *General Prologue*. The Pardoner is a self-confessed hypocrite and enjoys defining precisely what he is up to. The Friar, a suave, successful, and vain man, may however, have slipped into the now ingrained habit of identifying the spiritual with the material aspects of his professional activities and feels consequently justified in using the authorized functions of his calling to acquire wealth or abuse the hangers-on of the secular clergy. He offers, in fact, just the kind of model the Reeve is unconsciously imitating when he "docks" his top, tucks his robe about (*GP* 590, 621), and attempts to "authorize" choler by sermonizing. Late medieval society rejoiced in, fostered, and often regulated the public identification of rank and profession, as the *General Prologue* abundantly illustrates. The pilgrims, however, often exhibit an irrepressible hungering after other roles, and Chaucer lets them give voice to the impulse of play-acting in the language and rhetorical modes they assume. The ironic consequences are, of course, generally beyond the speaker's hearing.

The telling of a story deliberately encourages such role-playing. A storyteller sets himself apart from his group, defining all others as "audience." He in turn is defined by the language he uses, lifted and isolated from the casual flow of verbal commerce. His "hwaet," "whilom," or "once upon a time" initiates another kind of discourse, transports his audience to an imagined reality over which he has godlike powers as its only maker. If a professional, he is accorded a special standing, depending on the society: the heroic bard is regarded with respect, at times with awe; the scruffy minstrel, with a mixture of contempt and curiosity. But even the amateur assumes something of a vatic aura when he ventures upon a tale. Chaucer knew well this special status conferred upon one who reads his poems at court; he played against—and with—the position by adopting various narrative personae in the dream-visions and the *Troilus*. The storyteller unavoidably takes a role, but, like the actor's, his success will depend on his ability to make that role acceptable to the audience so that they will not be distractedly conscious of the personality behind it. He may rely upon the anonymity of his professional standing or, like Chaucer, make a tacit contract with the audience to treat a persona as its equivalent. That the consciousness of a narrative persona later played an integral part in the development of the prose novel, yet remains a reluctant "discovery" of recent criticism, is a reminder of the perennial conditioning of audiences to naïve responses.[12]

When the pilgrims begin to tell their tales, they are, whether they are aware of it or not, slipping into a prefabricated role that allows them enormous freedom to magnify and project the most energetic parts of their psychological make-up. Those who have already assumed a posture, like the Reeve, simply transfer its properties to the new role. Oswald finds that the preacher can tell a ribald tale after all, if it is adjusted to serve the single purpose of venting his spleen and exposing the sinful Miller for what he is. But there is an ironic facet to the role of storyteller. The assumption is that anyone can tell a story, and no doubt the medievals were by and large better at it than we. But when the amateur takes up the reins of a story, he may be misled by the newly acquired power into a feeling of absolute freedom. The sense of being released from the weight of his everyday self may tempt him into believing himself perfectly anonymous. For the virtuous or the truly pious, the opportunity presents no danger, but lesser mortals who are pretending to virtue to camouflage enmity, or trumping up piety to increase their public esteem, find themselves, Phaeton-like, burned in their venture. The role of storyteller proves more transparent than they had thought and, as in the case of the Reeve, the psychological underpinnings of their characters stand exposed, more obvious and more dramatically engaging than their conscious intentions. By some such psychological logic as this, many of the *Canterbury Tales*, as has often been noted, tell more about their teller than about their ostensible subject matter.

At times, Chaucer further exploits the seductions of role-playing and fiction-making by releasing thematic currents that run counter to the flow of the narrative and its narrator's desired impression. A second exercise in professional antagonism on the Canterbury pilgrimage and the resulting narrative brick-bats provide two clear but complicated examples.

The Friar enters the scene with a double miscalculation. Presuming no doubt on his previous success with widows, he interrupts the Wife of Bath with what he intends as a lighthearted but learned gesture of impatience: "This is a long preamble of a tale" (*WBP*, 831). The Wife deftly puts him

161

in his place when she begins her tale, but he reckons also without the Summoner, who makes up for his stupidity by the virulence of his resentment of friars and the volume of his abuse. The Summoner promises to be a more formidable adversary than one would have expected from his portrait, vowing in his turn to "telle tales two or thre / Of freres" (*WBP*, 846-47)—which he more or less does. But the Friar takes him on, and with surprisingly unhappy consequences.

The Friar's method is to assert his dignity, or "honestee" (1267), pointedly ignoring the Summoner and ingratiating himself with the Wife by a hypocritical compliment to the difficulty of her "scole-matere." He begins his attack on summoners by pretending to substitute "game" (1276, 1279) for "auctoritees," the proper domain of preachers and "clergye," but once his fun begins, even the Host finds him less than "hende." The tale proper is preceded by a jeremiad against the secular clergy in the persons of the archdeacon and his master-spy of a summoner. The Summoner interposes vehemently but the Friar continues high-handedly, wittily punning and turning elegant phrases at the expense of his "invisible" opponent.[13] The fiction hardly covers his first seventy-five lines of fulsome, relentless attack, the most extensively explicit piece of vilification during the journey. Yet the Friar superciliously ignores his obstreperous victim, relishing a complacent superiority over such inconsequential vulgarity and ignorance. The tone carries over into the delineation of the fictive summoner's literal- and material-mindedness, which leads to his entrapment. Again, at the conclusion of his narrative, when he adopts the pious formulae of the sermon, the Friar pointedly ignores the presence of the Summoner, hypocritically asking his audience to pray for the man's repentance and escape from the clutches of the fiend. The Friar throughout is superbly confident that his quick wit and social prestige make him invulnerable to his adversary's powers of rejoinder.

His tale, like his surrounding remarks, is enjoyably pert, intelligent, and replete with sprightly ironies. Constructed on the old tag, *intentio judicat hominem*, it sets about to confound its summoner by pitting his single-minded, unscrupulous "entente"[14] against the clever frankness of a highly learned devil who has no trouble binding the dull fellow closer to him the more he reveals about his infernal condition. The theme and ironic method are deliberately obvious, designed to focus attention on the tone of urbane, toying condescension shared by the Friar and his alter ego, the yeoman in green. The snare in which the summoner damns himself is replicated in the greater fiction as Chaucer allows his teller to condemn himself by enthusiastic endorsement of the character and methods of the fiend. The net is secured by a firm interlacement of verbal echoes and "reasonable rhymes,"[15] which reach back to the *General Prologue* and forward to the Summoner's riposte. The persistence and omnipresence of fraternal busyness, which annoys the Summoner and the Wife of Bath, accounts for the emphasis on the verb in the couplet from the Friar's portrait:

> Yet wolde he have a ferthyng, er he wente.
> His purchas was wel bettre than his rente.　　　(255–56)

The second line will be mockingly echoed by the Friar's fiend, bewailing his apparent frustration:

> My purchas is th'effect of al my rente.
> Looke how thou rydest for the same entente.　　(1451–52)

By this point in the *Tale*, however, the rhyme has been deliberately used by the narrator to yoke his estimate of the Summoner's purposes with the man's own eager self-confession:

> And for that was the fruyt of al his rente,
> Therfore on it he sette al his entente.　　　　(1373–74)

> "Heere faste by," quod he, "is myn entente
> To ryden, for to reysen up a rente . . ."　　　(1389–90)

The carter's example, as interpreted by the fiend ("It is nat his entente," 1556), makes clear the theological import of the climactic exchange in which the old woman's curse is qualified by "but he wol hym repente!" and the Summoner hastily replies, "That is nat myn entente!" (1629-30), thus insuring his damnation. But the ultimate authority over infernal powers, the limitations on their bailiwick that associate them as much with "lymytours" as with summoners, has already been expressed by this knowledgeable fiend in a couplet that introduces a new rhyme and a new dimension of metaphysical consequence to these mundane intentions. God brings the good of salvation out of the apparent evil of their temptations,

> Al be it that it was nat oure entente
> He sholde be sauf, but that we wolde hym hente.
>
> (1499-1500)

The Friar finishes off his performance with a homiletic exhortation, rung to a close with yet another combination of the now familiar rhymes:

> And prayeth that thise somonours hem repente
> Of hir mysdedes, er that the feend hem hente!   (1663-64)

Clearly, the authority the Friar arrogates to himself in the act of preaching has less to do with divine sanction than with what has been defined as the satanic privilege of extorting what one can by whatever license has been conceded to one's "order." Despite his superior mentality, the academic jests and pretensions, the refinement of witty discourse in which he takes such pride himself, the Friar emerges from the *Tale* as surely damned as his fictional summoner in his eagerness to put the privileges of his profession to personal and unseemly uses. The *Tale* confirms the *Prologue* portrait[16] of the one whose attractive social assets may induce many weak-minded souls to approach his spiritual suppers with too short a spoon.

The Summoner's rejoinder also has ironies that redound upon the teller, but they are far less damaging. Primarily, there is the comic prospect of the enraged narrator, so mad that "lyk an aspen leef he quook for ire" (1667), telling of a friar who, after preaching against anger, falls into a self-defeating rage himself.[17] The ironies against the teller virtually force themselves upon our notice, and the appropriateness of matter and method of attack to the churlish, low-minded Summoner are equally self-evident. It is as if Chaucer were deliberately calling attention to his procedure of carving out a tale to suit his teller and then undercutting him with the same stroke. Yet the artfully refined portrait of the unctuously pompous friar, like those in the *Miller's Tale*, exceeds the realistic capacities of the teller, while its comic riches absorb the opprobrium attached to the Summoner's wrathful motive, amply justified as it is in the first place.

The story itself combines a parody of the Canterbury Friar's style and a paradigm of his victim's revenge. The friar of the *Tale* flaunts his sensuality and hypocrisy before the ignorant rustics whom he feels confident of overwhelming with his "glosynge." Just when he expects to reap the fruits of his labor, he receives a vulgar affront that puts him in a fury of outraged dignity. One cannot help translating the event back into the Canterbury fiction, where the Friar is repaid for his haughtiness by the Summoner's double-barreled riposte of anal anecdotes. This is the kind of attack for which neither friar has adequate defense.

The final humiliation of the friar proves to be once more beyond the genius of the Summoner, but devastatingly appropriate to the Friar. The central event is laced with ingenious puns[18] that anticipate the offensive gift, the most notable of which—"to grope tendrely a conscience" (1817) and "What is a ferthying worth parted in twelve?" (1967)—support the justice of the outcome by reminding us of the Friar's perversion of the sacrament of penance into an occasion for financial gain (*GP* 221-32). The Summoner's friar, by his own choice of words, charges the atmosphere of the scene with a pervasive reduction of symbol and sacrament to base *materialia* so that even the ignorant Thomas can pick his cue for revenge, as it were, out of the verbal air. The friar's language is not so much anticipatory irony as it is a logical consequence of his proudly confessed attitude toward the Word. He finds in

Scripture, albeit "in a maner glose" (1920), justification for his vows of poverty, though the blessed poor he cites are ironically so "in spirit" (1923). The friar's "chast" estate he associates with Eden, scrupulously recording that man was "out chaced for his glotonye" (1916), while devising with hypocritical abstemiousness a gourmet dinner for himself. Even the venerability of his order is attested "in charitee" by its origin with "Elye . . . or Elise" (2115ff.), prophets who entered into Paradise without awaiting Resurrection. The key to his learned approach to Scripture is revealed by his choice of theme for his sermons, "nat al after the text of hooly writ" but "al the glose." "Glosynge is a glorious thyng, certeyn" is his motto, and even for this he has scriptural authority in the Pauline phrase, "For lettre sleeth" (1789–94; 2 Cor. 3:6). This systematic inversion of the Word of God fills the sick room with a linguistic odor associated with devils, who traditionally in Dante's phrase "make a trumpet of their nether parts."[19] The fart is metaphorically present in the scene long before the irate Thomas provides the objective correlative, and the Summoner's friar himself confirms that "Freres and feendes been but lyte asonder" (1674), just as the Canterbury Friar had inadvertently done in his own *Tale*.

The framing of this central episode by two panels of ingenious iconographic parody only adds insult to the friar's self-generated injury. The *Prologue* anecdote scatologically inverts an established fraternal fiction in which an eschatological vision discovers the celestial members of the order comfortably wrapped in the mantle of the Blessed Virgin, the "Mater Misericordia."[20] The corresponding panel of the triptych, set apart by Chaucer's addition of the scene at the village "court" with its "internal audience,"[21] parodies even more precisely the friars' intellectual pretensions: the squire's solution for the "departynge of the fart" is, as Alan Levitan has indisputably shown,[22] modeled on a Pentecostal image for the "spreading of the Word" (see 1882). The extraordinary ingenuity that graces these low "japes" of the Summoner extends in either direction the perversion of language and learning for material gain disclosed in the central panel; the commonplaces of antifraternal satire are realized in repulsive icons of irrepressible "subtiltee / And heigh wit" (2290–91), which accurately depict their metaphysical dimension. In response to the self-serving "honestee" of the Friar, Chaucer has transformed the irate Summoner into a churl who at least has the *honesty* to curse the Friar to his face (1707). While carefully insisting on the dramatic propriety of the performance, he has invested the *Summoner's Tale* with a surprisingly generous artfulness, which, though it may not diminish the unredeemable odiousness of the Summoner himself, reveals the greater distaste the poet shared with moral theologians for intellectual and spiritual presumption of any kind.

Fortunately one need not debate with Dantesque precision the infernal futures of these two reprehensible figures,[23] but Chaucer's dramatic art, by elaborating the suggestive *Prologue* portraits into complex narrative performances, inevitably prompts such moral questions. The social acceptability, the evident "honestee" of the Friar to which the Host testifies, presents a more pernicious, spiritual threat to society than the Summoner's crude extortion. By allowing the learned "maister" to condescend to the provocation of his low antagonist, Chaucer permits his audience to participate in a moral evaluation that proceeds from his revealing behavior. The Friar's rhetorical mode, his choice of narrative and its implied values discharge a foulness of mind and spirit that the Summoner's rebuttal efficiently relegates to a suitable moral dung heap. The obliquity of judgment is consonant with Chaucer's method elsewhere—in the satiric techniques of the *General Prologue*[24] and the dialectical use of the narrator in the *Troilus*—and points to his highly developed sense of that interdependence of psychology and morality that characterized medieval thought since Augustine.[25] With the infinitely varied possibilities of the Canterbury format, Chaucer realized a means of arriving at moral discriminations as subtly nuanced and accurate as the capacities of his audience.[26]

CHAPTER IX

THE PARDONER AND THE CANON'S YEOMAN:

"GYLOUR BIGYLED"

Folly *often goes beyond her bounds; but* Impudence *knowes none.*

JONSON

Self-contemplation is infallibly the symptom of a disease, be it or be it not the cure.

CARLYLE

HE Pardoner's performance constitutes one of the most complete and explicit illustrations of the dramatic formulae set forth in the preceding chapter. Like the Wife of Bath, his greatest rival in self-revelation, he enjoys talking; like her, he finds it the only available weapon against a hostile world of masculine supremacy. His defense, like hers, is a strong offense, but a verbal assault delivered not so much to wound as to distract. Yet, like the criminal anxious to safeguard his secret, the Pardoner cannot resist seeking out his enemy and overplaying his role. Consequently, whatever lingering questions one may have about his motivation at various points in the *Tale*, there is no denying that the dramatic occasion has struck a raw nerve, and the performance that follows only increases the tension.

The convolutions of the Pardoner's behavior need not be set forth in great detail; the groundwork of Kittredge,[1] qualified by Sedgewick,[2] expanded by Lumiansky,[3] and updated by Halverson,[4] has provided a convincing account.[5] The sexually deficient Pardoner senses his true antagonist in the Host, who we are told in the *General Prologue* "of manhood . . . lakkede right naught" (756). But Harry's fawning enthusiasm for the Physician's pathetic story and his absurd malapropisms lull the "noble ecclesiaste" into a feeling of self-confident superiority. He counters the Host's ironic epithet, "thou beel amy," with a pointed repetition of the latter's boisterous oath on that presumed patron of kidneys, "Seynt Ronyan," but secretly hopes to make capital of the Host's habitual display of bonhommie by shoring up his virile, tavern-haunting image with a ribald tale. The rebuff of the assembled "gentils" forces him to change his tactic and widen his attack.

In his *Prologue* the Pardoner defines his characteristic rhetorical posturing with a thoroughness that stems from his delight in flaunting its hypocrisy.[6] He details with relish everything from his physical gestures and favorite "gaudes" for entrapping the yokels, to a perverse analysis of his underlying motives. By insisting on his own viciousness, he strives to stun his pilgrim audience into accepting his confessional pose as final. His eagerness to force them to take avarice as his ruling passion has the combined motivation of, first, his revenge on the naïveté of those "gentils" who assume that the mere telling of "some moral thyng" carries independent authority, conducive to moral improvement and, second, a desperate concern to have even them concur in his well-fortified pose as one who desires money to indulge in the sins of the flesh, to "drynke licour of the vyne, / And have a joly wenche in every toun" (452–53). After his enormously powerful tale,[7] he appears to be riding high and either as a further taunt to his impressed audience or in hope that they will be carried along by the audacity of his wit, he again equates the pilgrims with his usual rustic congregation, singles out the Host to acknowledge his triumphantly moral immorality, and finds himself brutally attacked on precisely the physical grounds he had thought well obscured by his cynical revelations. It requires the Knight to restore the equanimity of the social compact, but his careful distinction of pronouns and the ironic imposition of a kiss of peace leave no doubt that the Pardoner is still very much the loser.

The *Pardoner's Tale* bears a somewhat different relation to the whole of the teller's performance from those discussed previously. As an example of the "secondary pose"—the authoritative role of preacher that this speaker is consciously exploding—it absorbs the generic allusion usually found in the pilgrim's prefatory maneuvers. The Pardoner merely rehearses his customary hypocrisy licensed by his profession, and his *Prologue* sets the intra-fictional stage. Whereas the Reeve and the Friar turn to homiletic formulae to reinforce their claims to moral superiority over a single pilgrim, the Pardoner inverts his usual procedure and theirs, by taking the pilgrims backstage to disabuse them of such fictive illusions. He invites them to accept him in a new role, guiding them into the dressing-rooms of motive and intention, forcing them to acknowledge a kinship in all such performing, which they, as story-tellers and perhaps as everyday actors in the play of morality, share with him.[8]

The *Pardoner's Tale* owes little to the format of the learned sermon,[9] but touches upon a number of its components in such a way that the dominant exemplum (to suit the Canterbury context) still seems in accord with his usual, and necessarily less than academic, bill of fare. The overblown rhetoric of the statement, division, and résumé of the theme—the sins of the tavern—and the ambivalent benediction testify to the Pardoner's competence as a preacher, while the subject matter reinforces his "primary pose" as a "riotour" himself. The proffered moral of the exemplum—sin is its own undoing, especially if that sin is the "radix malorum"—also attempts to be comfortably self-serving. Better to be damned for material cupidity than known for what he is, one obsessed by physical eunuchry to the point of blindness to its spiritual dimension.[10] But while the Pardoner may feel himself to be as supremely in control of his tale as of his audience, other currents in his story-telling prove just as damaging to him as his miscalculation of the Host's response and in fact elucidate the difficulties he finds himself in when he attempts his final "gaude."

The first of these "submerged" motifs is that of fellowship. The "riotours" have assembled with a common goal: "a compagnie / Of yonge folk that haunteden folye, / As riot, hasard, stywes, and tavernes" (463–65). They enjoy an easy commerce in vice—"ech of hem at otheres synne loughe" (476)—and pride themselves on their sense of community. Outraged by the fate of an "old felawe" of theirs, they band together to avenge his death, solemnly if drunkenly swearing brotherhood:

Togidres han thise thre hir trouthes plight
To lyve and dyen ech of hem for oother,
As though he were his owene ybore brother.   (702–704)

But their compact covers only one goal and presumably one age group, for their first act is to abuse the old man they encounter. When he rebukes their discourtesy, citing Leviticus on the respect due the aged, they intensify their threats against those who hate "us yonge folk." The old man's directions to the tree at the end of a "croked way" may be taken realistically as a response of fearful evasion before such gratuitous hostility. The dissolution of their goal, to seek Death, results in the dismemberment of their fellowship and brotherhood (cf. esp. 808 and 832). The Pardoner perorates on the ensuing acts of homicide and avarice as he did on the swearing of blasphemous oaths (472ff.), finding their unifying theme in the exemplification of the rending of man's common brotherhood in Christ:

Allas! mankynde, how may it bitide
That to thy creatour, which that the wroghte,
And with his precious herte-blood thee boghte,
Thou art so fals and so unkynde, allas?   (900–903)

This gratuitous moral redounds grimly on the Pardoner him-

172

self; having appeared on the Canterbury scene in perverted fellowship with the Summoner,[11] he can salve his social ego only by spitting out his tale with "venym" on the entire company. By disassociating himself from the brotherhood of Christ, he, like the "riotours," has torn the bonds of earthly fellowship, for which the pilgrimage was meant to be a religious model. The Knight's attempt to reestablish the communion of gladness and good cheer can only precariously include a man whose own spiritual perversity prevents his forthright participation in a Christian community.

The old man, whose appearance in the tale seems unnecessarily expanded and obtrusive, further points up the fundamental deficiency in the Pardoner's character. A puzzle to generations of critics, this mysterious figure brings into focus a generic ambiguity that is the source of much of the story's power. On the one hand he is a pathetic creature whose lamentations against his unhappily extended life may be taken realistically; on the other, his highly colored, elegiac language[12] and his uncanny provision of a fitting directive to the "riotours" smack of the dense symbolism of parable, if not true allegory. The range of critical interpretations testifies to his modal slipperiness; every possibility has been put forward from merely a realistic old man, to the Wandering Jew, or the "old Adam" of St. Paul's typology, or an agent of God's providential economy, to such obvious allegorical labels as Death itself, physical or spiritual, or "Elde," its harbinger.[13] None of these suggestions lacks some justification, but, equally, none convinces. An almost deliberate ambiguity about the figure resists generic categorization. Like the story as a whole, the old man exists in a world firmly anchored in earthly conditions yet mysteriously subjected to spiritual directives.

The initial scene, in which the "riotours" learn of their companion's death, moves imperceptibly, through the agency of an innocent child, from recognizable actuality to something increasingly symbolic. The drunken literal-mindedness of a determination to seek out this "privee theef men clepeth Deeth" appears at first absurd bravado but soon turns into grim ferocity. When the narrator expresses their "grisly ooth" in the line, "Deeth shal be deed, if that they may hym hente!" (710), the metaphysical overtones are unmistakable. The "riotours" have animated Death, an unsubstantial act of physical negation, and in seeking to destroy the "privee theef" have put themselves in the company of Christ. But whereas His sacrifice was to overcome spiritual death, they merely wish to extend physical life. The logical consequence of such a wish they will soon meet, embodied literally in the old man.

The "riotours'" drunken oaths predicate a moral condition in which there is no reality beyond the physical, no abstraction divorced from concrete form. Paradoxically they create for themselves a world of allegory, though their motive is not to explore spiritual dimensions but to deny them. Their fate has a poetic and moral logic when Death takes the concrete shape of eight bushels of solid gold florins. Part of the old man's purpose in the tale is to push them further along a way in which blindness to the metaphorical and blindness to the metaphysical prove to be related. The generic confusion, brought into focus by the old man's speeches, is a function of the moral miasma that pervades the tale. It is the literary correlative to that state of sin that the "riotours" have made into a fellowship, a perverse fraternity of spiritual vacuity in which the Pardoner devoutly seeks a charter membership.[14]

As a "noble ecclesiaste," the Pardoner seems to have consecrated his life to turning symbols into empty signs. The false relics he peddles as a sideline, the dubious pardons he sells, the specious bulls on which he rests his authority, the rote sermon he declaims hypocritically—all objectify that compulsive spiritual depravity that urges him to espouse publicly a mortal sin in a recklessly flamboyant attempt to distract attention from a physical deficiency. And of course his eunuchry itself, in this literary context, is not the cause but the manifestation of his spiritual condition. Taking his cue from the Host's malapropism, he embarks upon a performance in which verbal authority is consistently undermined. While he pretends to a clear-minded distinction between physical objects and consecrated symbols, between commercial exchange and sacramental penitence, between what he says and what he intends, between one audience and another, and between Death and the lust for gold, his conscious efforts are all directed toward obscuring such distinction. Like the cooks of his diatribe on gluttony, he is devoted to turning substance into accidence. His condition is best described by Augustine's caution against the failure to recognize figurative language as "a miserable servitude of the spirit in this habit of taking signs for things, so that one is not able to raise the eye of the mind above things that are corporal and created to drink in eternal light."[15] His retribution comes when he fails to set a limit to the process.

The Pardoner's performance culminates in his own version of the overweening bravado his "riotours" displayed.[16] The Host, whom he thinks to bully with his superior wit, becomes his "old man," and his reward is to have his carefully disguised secret held up to public ridicule, enshrined in the metaphor of those relics he had so smugly exposed for the worthless things they are.[17] Punished aptly by the Host's coarse rhetoric, the Pardoner finds his world reduced to the pitiful physicality he had tried to gloss over with a pretension to youthful animality. The *Tale* in which he takes such pride presages his undoing by the spiritual realm whose directives he had deliberately chosen to ignore. His well-filed tongue stilled by rage, the Host's kiss burning his cheek, he is left to proceed, weaponless and exposed, spiritually, physically, and morally impotent, among a community of pilgrims whom he had thought to domineer.

The Canon and his Yeoman, defined at their introduction as outsiders to the pilgrimage, offer intricate variations on the theme of deception and self-deception. Thoroughgoing outcasts of society, their outward appearance only gradually yields its true character. The narrator has difficulty identifying the master's canonical garb, but it is the Host once again, with his blunt and unswerving insistence on observable realities, who frustrates the Yeoman's practiced attempt to "set up" the Canon.[18] By pointedly questioning his lord's "sluttish" appearance, their dwelling among thieves, and finally the discoloration of his own face, the Host wears out the Yeoman's already over-taxed faith in his ability to maintain the fictions by which these two are bound together in a program of deception to finance their self-deception. The Canon's suspicious nature quickly propels him from the scene, but the Yeoman stays on in a pathetic effort of mingled self-justification and simplistic recrimination.

Whereas the Pardoner conducts a one-man operation of consummate skill and audacity, the Yeoman contributes little more to the Canon's exploits than a pair of strong lungs and a parrot's memory. What brute cunning he possesses is pressed into service by gullibility and greed, but finds itself repeatedly undermined by a self-protective instinct of common sense and folk wisdom. Muscatine[19] has aptly characterized the Yeoman's "rugged dramatic idiom," as a "blind materialism" reflected in the breathless outpouring of technical catalogues—lists of alchemical materials and laboratory apparatus, the processes and their secret names—all punctuated by the "dully repetitious" commentary on the frustration of this "slidynge science." The *prima pars* of the *Yeoman's Tale*, with uncanny dramatic acumen, portrays an untutored mind in the act of trying to come to terms with its own folly, anxious to recover self-respect by disassociating itself from the Canon's "cursed craft," but unwilling to sacrifice the possible esteem to be gained from the display of arcane information, no matter how mindlessly retailed by this self-confessedly "lewed man." This alternation between breast-beating and swagger carries over to the "broken pot" episode.[20] On the one hand, the Yeoman enjoys relegating his master and company to "that ilke shrewe," the fiend, but at the same time one catches the note of pride on the part of a man who, even in a subservient role, played his role in this supremely dangerous game. The psychology is that of the confirmed gambler, one who knows better but cannot resist the seductions of yet another try:

We faille of that which that we wolden have,
And in oure madnesse everemore we rave.
And when we been togidres everichoon,
Every man semeth a Salomon.   (958–61)

Though this final line is meant sardonically, the irony quickly
ensnares the Yeoman himself. As he moralizes his vision of
the dark satanic world of alchemy, he needs to assert his su-
periority to his former self and the others caught in their il-
lusions of wealth-producing wisdom. But the old king's name
triggers off an exhibition of what had come to be known vul-
garly as "Solomonic lore."[21] This pathetically commonplace,
proverbial wisdom—"all that glitters is not gold," etc.—is trot-
ted out as the resounding moral conclusion to his confused
confession. The tangles of moral complicity—the Canon's
and his own—are reduced to the simplest intellectual terms.
All the complexities of fanatical belief and doubt, hope and
despair, true knowledge and misleading practice, are reduced
to nothing more than thievery and false-seeming. Such a
judgment, of course, conveniently absolves the Yeoman of
primary guilt. In the *secunda pars*, he has a "true" tale to put
forward that will elaborately support such a verdict.

The two parts of what is called the *Yeoman's Tale* differ
strikingly in dramatic idiom and rhetorical stance as well as
in moral vision. One or two narrative quirks, however, en-
courage the sense of continuity: the flat repetitive commentary
of Part I—"Al is in veyn" (843)—is echoed in the recurrent
"it dulleth me" in Part II, while we are invited to recall the
unnatural antisocial coloring of the pot-breaking scene by the
rhetorical frill (1341–49) that suddenly intrudes an ironic as-
sociation of the priest's greedy gladness with the joyful songs
of birds and lords and ladies loving. The world of alchemical
addiction, the Yeoman would have us believe, is both un-
natural and a bore. But these are trivial connectives, when set
against the large contrast of the muddled discourse and con-
fused action in Part I with the clarity and precision in the
handling of Part II's intricate narrative. The complicated se-

quence of deceptive experiments is managed with deftness and even some subtlety,[22] while the moral perspective is conversely narrowed to the point that it may properly disgust the narrator. The Yeoman insists that the false canon portrayed in Part II is not his master, and while some are tempted to doubt him,[23] there is reason to take him at his word here. The Canon we glimpse in the *Prologue* and Part I is furtive and willing to deceive, but never displays the brazen self-assurance of Part II's con-man. Furthermore, there is good evidence that he shares the Yeoman's seduction by alchemical experimentation, practicing deception primarily to finance his addiction.[24] He clearly possesses considerable arcane learning, some of which has been passed on to the Yeoman in garbled form to be used in their deceptions. The canon of Part II is a quick-trick artist who lives well by moving on quickly. He is a clear scoundrel on whom the Yeoman can settle his guilt and shameful stupidity without having to perpetrate the further deception that his own Canon is quite such a simple case. The psychological and moral obscurities of his master's behavior and his own responses are quite beyond the Yeoman's analytic powers, but by creating this scapegoat, made up of familiar satiric stereotypes, he cuts the Gordian knot, fixing the guilt on the Canon vicariously, while freeing himself, publicly at least, from the complicity he shared against his better judgment but with full consent of his greedy will.

The Yeoman winds up his self-serving revelations with a peroration that has been most puzzling of all to interpreters. Once again he cannot resist the display of exotic information.[25] After some cautionary proverbs against pecuniary loss (1402–25), he trots out "what philosophres seyn in this mateere" (1427). The wisdom of Arnold of Villanova consists in a "Hermetic" explication of the mysterious fraternization between sulphur and mercury, "the dragon and his brother." The conclusion, however, is that the art of mortification is best left to those who share "th'entencioun and speche / Of philosophres" (1443–44), for it is the "secree of secrees, pardee" (1447).[26] The charming anecdote in which "Plato" enlightens his disciple *"ignotum per ignocius"* regarding the name of the "privee stoon" (1448ff.) also leads to the revelation that philosophers are the only guardians of such knowledge:

> For unto Crist it is so lief and deere
> That he wol nat that it discovered bee,
> But where it liketh to his deitee
> Men for t' enspire, and eek for to deffende
> Whom that hym liketh; lo, this is the ende.   (1467-71)

Note that the Yeoman's final caution—against making God one's adversary—is by no means the absolute trump-card it has been taken to be.[27] It certainly forbids lesser mortals from the practice of alchemy, but the door is left open for a few divinely inspired philosophers (as well as, one assumes, those who can afford to purchase, by money or service, access to the "science" and "konning" of the elect). Clearly this line of patter could have been useful in the past for "setting up" his own master, whatever his actual philosophic qualifications. The Yeoman now dispenses these exempla to distance himself further from the impoverishing sins of alchemy, but he still manages to bolster his own ego with this ostentatiously learned mumbo-jumbo. The patent inconclusiveness of his anecdotes, intended though they may be to round out his anti-alchemical argument with unimpeachable authority, subversively implies that he is not quite as free as he would like to have others believe from the lure of "philosophic" profit.

The Canon's Yeoman shares with the Pardoner a talent for deception combined with an uncontrollable propensity for self-deception. Each has at his disposal an overstuffed bag of well-rehearsed rhetorical tricks by which he hopes to impose on the cheerful will and customary morality of the pilgrim company. Each begins by conceding the ill use he has made of his verbal abilities, then follows with a moral tale that is as self-serving as it is ultimately self-defeating. What the Yeoman lacks of the Pardoner's intelligence, quick wit, and primary knowledge of his material redounds upon his moral state as well. Not bright enough for the sustained, aggressive

179

hypocrisy of the Pardoner, he continues to be trapped by the limits of his previous verbal experience, ready to submit to whatever authority comes along, whether it be the true gold of the Word or the glittering verbiage of uncertain mortification.

CHAPTER X

THE MONK AND THE PRIORESS:

"CRAFT IS AL"

The rhetorician would deceive his neighbors,
The sentimentalist himself;
while art
Is but a vision of reality.

YEATS

THE linguistic miasma that pervades the discourse of those loosely attached to the secular Church might also be expected of the regulars if the performance of the witty Friar is any indication. But there are instructive variations and even surprises. In the *General Prologue* the three members of the regular clergy are grouped together, an impressively well-dressed trio whose social inclinations have successfully laid to rest their vows of poverty. Though all three are satirically inspected and found vocationally wanting, important differences in tone and method reflect significant moral distinctions. The Prioress is all manner and manners, from her singing to her table etiquette; her "tendre herte" has the same misplaced extravagance and superficiality as her rosary. But while she may not be much of a nun, she makes an impressive heroine of romance; the "hidden" source for the portrait in the *Roman de la Rose* deflects the satire toward amused indulgence—a discreet and inoffensive joke, befitting a woman innocently unconscious of her failings, unaware that her worldly attainments may be thought less than appropriately ornamental to her high calling. The Monk, on the other hand, equally luxurious and self-indulgent, flouts the restrictive rules of his order, and his self-assured, pompous tone is echoed by the enthusiasm of the easily persuaded narrator—"And I seyde his opinion was good" (183). By his open and calculated disregard for the vows of his *regula*, the Monk places himself in spiritual jeopardy, but the danger is at least confined to his own salvation. If he appears more culpable than the Prioress in consequence of the full deliberation and consent of his will, he seems less injurious than the Friar, who extorts from the poor, seduces the young, and perverts the sacrament of penance for his personal pleasure and greed. The Friar's contempt for others, as well as the material and spiritual harm he inflicts upon them, justifies the low methods of the Summoner.[1] The Host, we recall, is far too taken in by the Friar's smooth appearance to do more than caution him to be "curteys, as a man of youre estaat" (III, 1287). Useless as a moral index, Harry Bailly judges his fellows by their contribution to the look and conviviality of the social scene, as his miscalculation with the Monk demonstrates.

"Worthy," in the Host's estimate, to have followed the Knight in the first place, the Monk comes again to mind after the tale of Melibeus and Dame Prudence has set Harry thinking about his own wife's brawny impatience. The transition is so casual as to seem unrelated, but after complimenting the Monk on his fair skin and masterful air of command, Harry settles into a "man-to-man" mock lament over the loss to the species caused by the removal from the sexual game of such a fine "trede-fowel" as this religious specimen. While the Monk may pride himself on his manliness, his sporting life, and well-fed appearance, his dignity will not admit these barnyard analogies, particularly after the *Shipman's Tale* has recently spelled out their consequences. There is a hint of his discomfort in Harry's "be nat wrooth" (1963), but his reply strives with studied patience to reassert his "honestee." The Host with his simple "master of ceremonies" notion of variety had been pressing for a lusty turn to follow the sententious *Melibeus*, but the Monk decides that his dignity will best be served by a display of monastic learning, a saint's life or some of the hundred tragedies he has in his cell—presumably to encourage a suitable *contemptus mundi*. To emphasize that there will be no nonsense about these proceedings, he prefaces his tale with a scholarly definition that includes not only the now classic structural description but also remarks on the metrical form and some fuss over the proper chronology of his tragedies. Hardly what Harry expected, the *Monk's Tale* does not entirely fulfill its teller's intentions either.

The opening of the *Tale* repeats the description of tragedy, but this time it stretches itself out into the eight-line stanza to which the *Tale* has given its name. There have long been suspicions that what follows is an early work.[2] The stanza, unlike rime-royale, is uncongenial to narrative or is made to seem so here: its stuffing is so consistently flat,[3] dull, and uninspired, so restricted by its formal confines that the stories are reduced to lists of incidents or at best a sequence of minimally elaborated events. The lack of spirit would seem to be quite unChaucerian were it not for the mechanical stretches of the *House of Fame*, Book III, and the lackluster *Legend*. But these other unfinished and presumably abandoned works are not so ponderously self-defeating. One is tempted to say of the Monk's tragedies, as did Keynes of *Sir Thopas*, they are so bad that only "supreme craftsmanship" could have produced them, were it not that they lack the romance burlesque's splendid economy. Whether they are in fact an abortive early exercise or whether Chaucer merely nodded and unwittingly committed a fallacy of imitative form, these tragedies are eminently suitable to the Monk and extend into the fiction-making the pompous tone and tedious pedantry of his initial rhetorical stance.

The opening definition affirms the exemplary value of tragedy ("Be war by thise ensamples trewe and olde," 1998), but concurrently attributes to Fortune the fall from prosperity

183

("Ther may no man the cours of hire withholde," 1996).
These two statements determine the ethical limitations of the
performance and ultimately undermine the teller's attempt to
establish his monkly dignity. The organizing principle seems
to be an interminable parade of tragic heroes, marching two-
by-two. After Lucifer and Adam, the great originals, come the
two strong men betrayed by women, followed by two royal
idolators. The order is interrupted when the imperial pair,
Zenobia and Nero, are separated to introduce some modern
instances, the two betrayed Peters and the two imprisoned
Italian nobles. But the sequence concludes with two powerful
enemies of the Hebrews and the "grete conqueroures two,"
Caesar and Alexander, leaving Croesus to find his dreaming
mate in Chauntecleer. This assemblage of biblical, pagan, and
modern figures stems from the same impulse as the "Nine
Worthies" tradition, though less tidily limited. Historical and
encyclopedic, the *Monk's Tale* pretends to what will pass for
scholarship with the popular audience. But it also lays claim
to a religious purpose, and on this score it betrays its teller.

The glaring inadequacy of the medieval definition of trag-
edy, for modern critics, is the omission of the hero's complic-
ity.[4] The Monk's exemplars range from the supremely guilty
Lucifer, through "human fiends" such as Nero, Holofernes,
Nebuchadnezzar, and some interestingly flawed heroes such
as Sampson, to the virtuous Zenobia and the admirable world
conquerors and pitiable modern unfortunates. There is re-
markably little effort to associate these tragic falls with the
moral estate of the heroes, and equally little concern to relate
the activities of Fortune to Divine Providence except where
it is already part of the biblical narrative.[5] For most of the
pagan figures, with the obvious exception of Nero, the Monk's
admiration waxes warmly enthusiastic, finding worldly power
and governance on an imperial level more impressive than
virtue. The death of Alexander elicits his most extravagant
rhetoric, filling an entire stanza with a bathetic revelation of
direction of the teller's true feelings:

Who shal me yeven teeris to compleyne
The deeth of gentillesse and of franchise,
That al the world weelded in his demeyne,
And yet hym thoughte it myghte nat suffise?
So ful was his corage of heigh emprise.
Allas! who shal me helpe to endite
False Fortune, and poyson to despise,
The whiche two of al this wo I wyte? (2663-70)

One can see why the Monk and the Knight attract one an-
other in a magnetic field of dramatic opposition. Though the
Monk is prevented from "quiting" the *Knight's Tale*, the
Knight appears to be the only one with sufficient prestige to
say quit to the Monk's filibuster.[6] Even though his critical
remarks are on the same naïve level as the Monk's definitions,
the Knight has proved in his *Tale* his right to oppose the
"greet disese" (2771) of tragedy. Not merely in its qualified
optimism, but in the richness of its philosophic reflection and
sophisticated art of its presentation, the Knight's performance
stands in revealing contrast. The Monk's attempt to reassert
his solemn dignity has only emphasized his penchant for the
good life and administrative power that had initially prompted
the Host to reinterpret in his own terms the essence of the
man's character. He does not suffer the kind of attack the
Friar invited, but his mask of respectability is doubly affronted
when Harry asks for another tale—"somwhat of huntyng"
(2805). His huffy refusal to "pleye" absents him not only
from the genial graces of the Host but also from the efforts of
the Knight to maintain a truly gentle fellowship. In spite of
the overextended tediousness of his tragedies, the Monk's per-
formance is admirably conceived to explore the personality of
a man whose lust for power and material pleasure has found
comfortable expression in a vocation regrettably intended to
serve other purposes.

The Prioress, though also guilty of infractions of the rule, is
not apparently wilful in her disobedience. She is portrayed

185

indulgently in the *General Prologue*[7] and treated with such respect by the Host that he almost loses himself in deferential qualifiers when he requests a tale. Her simple reply of "gladly" sets her apart from the masculine regulars who embroil themselves to their discredit with their fellow pilgrims. Only she and her "chapeleyne" among the religious travelers are given tales of unmistakable devotional piety. If, as Marie Hamilton has suggested,[8] the Prioress's performance owes much to the Mass of the Innocents, it may be taken as further indication that, whatever her flaws and whatever the limitations of her narrative, Chaucer intended to portray a fundamentally innocent nature. While I do not wish to dispute the justice of critiques that associate the Prioress's fondness for her "litel clergeon" with that "conscience" which lavished expensive food on small dogs, and "tendre herte" on trapped mice, her child-like humility is not, I believe, without redemptive value. Though such public professions of modest devotion inevitably appear suspect to modern audiences, Chaucer has endowed the language of her *Tale* with an economy and structural elegance that translates the courtly manners of her portrait into a positive source of spiritual enhancement.[9]

The brief *Prologue*, which sets the rhetorical tone for the performance, is a gem of construction. The first of the five rime-royale stanzas versifies the opening of the eighth Psalm: "out of the mouth of babes and sucklings," a text singularly appropriate to the *Tale*, which is organized around the song of a child—his greatest joy, the cause of his murder and of its discovery, and, finally, the accompaniment of his glorification, at which point (607–608) the verse is re-echoed. The remaining stanzas are devoted to the Virgin, a fitting object of veneration and model for this most feminine of narrators, but also, in a sense, the chief actor in the narrative. The act of praise is structured in several ways. The most evident is the accumulation of attributes concentrated densely in the three central stanzas: "honour," "root of bountee," "soules boote," "humblesse," "bountee," "magnificence," "vertu," "grete humylitee," "benyngnytee," "grete worthynesse." Penetrating this simple quantitative definition is a movement of chronological progression. The Marian invocations allude distinctively, in four successive stanzas, to her various iconic designations, leading from the humble and temporal to the regal and eternal: Virgin, Mother, Lady, Queen. Thus the static abstractions are related to that active spirituality which is in reality their source.

A distinction of emphasis between the Virgin in stanza two and the Mother in stanza three is proposed in traditional iconographic figures. The "white lylye flour" (461) expresses the fact of virginity, "a mayde alway" (462), while Moses's bush, "brennynge" yet "unbrent," focuses upon the paradox of the virgin Mother: "O mooder Mayde! o mayde Mooder free" (467). The force and efficacy of Mary's many virtues, which had made possible this paradoxical state, are made fully apparent by the inversion of subject and object for the verb, "ravyshedest" (469), making her the active partner in the Conception. It was her "humblesse" that "enticed," or "charmed," the Holy Ghost to descend, her capacity as handmaid that made possible the Incarnation.

With the allusion to the descent of the Spirit, at the exact center of the lyric, a new theme is inaugurated that contributes to another kind of formal organization, circular rather than linear, joining the end of the *Prologue* to its beginning. When the Holy Spirit "alighte" (470) in the Virgin, "conceyved was the Fadres sapience" (472). The reference to the Second Person of the Trinity, the Son and *Sapientia* of the Father becomes, by poetic implication or ellipsis, the Wisdom conceived in Mary that she retains as a permanent possession. In the preceding line, He "thyn herte lighte," means either that He "lightened" her heart, that is, caused her to be light-hearted and joyous, or that He "enlightened" her by conferring on her that "great light," such wisdom and virtue which no earthly "science" (476) might expound, the illumination that presages her supernatural roles of Lady and Queen. It is specifically through this initial access to light, through her place in the Incarnation, that her eternal office of Intercessor or Media-

trix receives its theological justification. She may now antici-
pate the prayers of men

> And getest us the lyght, of thy preyere,
> To gyden us unto thy Sone so deere.   (479–80)

Mary, by virtue of her wise humility, became the recipient
vessel of divine Wisdom, lighting in and enlightening her
heart. Having been on earth the gate through which divine
Light passed to take human form, she now in heaven may
be the way by which human prayers, if humbly wise, ascend
to the divine Wisdom, her Son. But she is more than a simple
intermediary. Her ultimate benignity is to go "biforn," "er
men praye to thee" (477), to obtain the light that guides the
prayer and the petitioner; hers is the inspiration and the wis-
dom that insures the efficacy of prayer by enfolding it at its
origin in the light of divine Wisdom. The function of the
Prioress's striking use of "ravyshedest" becomes richly conno-
tative. What is being stressed is Mary's active participation,
then as now. Just as the Virgin's "humblesse" called forth, or
anticipated, the descent of divine Wisdom to abide in her, so
her present wisdom sends forth divine Light to any man on
earth exhibiting that humility which is the proper setting for
prayer.[10] The apt verbal ambiguities and the elegant word-
play reveal at the center of the *Prologue* a refined sense of
analogy and nice theological distinctions, all displayed with
apparent ease and graceful simplicity.

In the final stanza, the circular, unifying movement of the
invocation draws tight. The volume of praise due the Queen
of Heaven is more, suggests the Prioress, than a weak vessel
such as she can contain. Modestly yet artfully, she claims to
speak as "a child of twelf month oold, or lesse, / That kan
unnethes any word expresse" (484–85). But through the simile
we are reminded that such physical weakness may be sup-
planted by spiritual strength, if the Guide is present; "Ex ore
infantium et lactentium perfecisti laudem. . . ." We have re-
turned to the opening stanza. By accumulation, progression,
and finally by closing the circle, the Prioress has accomplished

her praise of the Virgin in the very act of invoking aid for its performance. The initial text, which seemed to reach forward to the *Tale*, now is seen to include the teller; and the *Prologue* itself prefigures by the mingling of art and divinity the miracle of the Virgin which it heralds. Perhaps Chaucer wished to suggest that the Prioress, in spite of all her childishness, was equally a potential vessel of grace, since he lavished on her initial utterance his most sophisticated art.[11]

The *Tale* that follows is by no means inferior in elegance or economy. The story itself was a popular one in both senses of the term. The numerous analogues testify to its wide dissemination,[12] while its direct emotional appeal and innocent belief mark it as of the people, the property originally of the minstrel or the common preacher. But here the handling of the material is entirely in keeping with its dignified narrator— "estatlich of manere." It is, as Preston has aptly put it, the kind of "treatment that might be given to a folk song by a very distinguished composer."[13] The tale is purified of its vulgarity by a deft, formal manipulation of character and setting.[14]

In this narrative, which greatly strains credulity, contact with the actual is made through the three slight human figures. The schoolboys and the mother are sketched with quick but telling strokes of realism that fix them within the bounds of the known world; the dogged, serious industry of the seven-year-old and his joy of accomplishment; the anxious vigil of the mother and her agonized search; and finally, the scene, with its canny sense of psychology and dramatic placement, between the two school fellows, in which the older reveals both frustration and desire to swagger in the splendid line, "I lerne song, I kan but smal grammeere" (536). But these are merely tokens of the actual world, designed only to charm, identify, and convince, not to be over-valued for their realism in a poem that draws upon several kinds of value and very different generic conventions.

The other human figures are merely public functionaries— the provost and the abbot with his "convent"—while the supernatural actors account for the real conflict of the piece. On the one hand there is the Blessed Virgin, whose careful attendance on the child is presented with tactful indirection through the mouth of the martyr. Poised against this delicacy is the bold handling of the Jews, clearly the inhuman agents of the supernatural forces of evil. It is the "serpent Sathanas" (558) who urges them on from his "waspes nest" stationed in their heart. They are lineal descendants of the archetypal slaughterer of innocents, the "cursed folk of Herodes al newe" (574). They work with savagery and bestiality and are punished in like fashion, but within the *Tale* are not conceded the human actuality thàt would allow the charge of anti-semitism, as we now think of it, to obtain.[15] Earthly pawns in a cosmic play, as much victims of their allegiance as the "litel clergeon" himself, they are realized typically rather than naturalistically and do not invite conventional moral judgment; they inhabit the legendary world.

This striking contrast in the depiction of character is correlated with the curious amalgam of the physical and the spiritual in the central action of the poem. Speirs has pointed out that "the wholehearted acceptance of the supernatural involves in the mediaeval mind no rejection of the natural body."[16] Ideally, the body becomes the passive instrument of spiritual forces, the perfect vessel through which the Deity performs His praise. Hence, as Speirs notes, the peculiar value of the idiom, "it (the song) passed thurgh his throte" (549) and the strong element of physical ritual involved in the placement and removal of the "greyn." A miracle, the dramatic handling of the *Prioress's Tale* reminds us, is an intrusion of the divine into the human world, a manipulation of the physical by the spiritual. The true action of the *Tale* is revealed only by the martyred boy's testimony; significant action available to ocular proof takes shape only as ritual.

This quality of symbolic or ritual action is skillfully reinforced by artful selectivity in the definition of setting. The contrasts of good and evil, natural and supernatural, found among the *dramatis personae* are unobtrusively given iconic form in the "resting places" accorded the murdered child. The

Jewish "homycide" is said to cast the boy into a pit, but the narrator continues with vehement specificity:

> I seye that in a wardrobe they him threwe
> Where as thise Jewes purgen hire entraille.   (572–73)

Yet in the final lines of the poem, his little body achieves a fitting repose "in a tombe of marbul stones cleere" (681). Thus his earthly progress images the passage from the abyss of foul humiliation to a noble exaltation. But immediately after his murder we had been informed of a still more glorious and permanent placement that will be his by virtue of his innocence and virginity. He will join that troop of the blessed, the Prioress affirms (581), which St. John envisions in the Apocalypse, those who follow the "white Lamb celestial" and "synge a song al newe" (589). The heavenly reward will reflect his terrestrial activities as well as his virtues; music and purity united in perfect praise. These three foci—the privy, the marble tomb, and the procession of the Lamb—clearly operate, like the mansions of the Corpus Christi plays, on a figural as much as a literal level, reflecting respectively the savagery of the Jews, the earthly veneration of the martyr, and the final dispensation of the spiritual forces. As settings they support the values attached to the characters who perform within their frame.[17]

These individual foci of action and value are placed within a narrative pattern that contributes significantly to the elevation of the story to the level of an archetype. The *Tale* is set in a distant Asian city, far from verifiable experience. But the scene is specifically a street, through which "men myghte ride or wende, / For it was free and open at eyther ende" (493–94). Along this street the action of the poem shuttles its way, for the little school is "doun at the ferther ende" (496) from the homes of the schoolboys. As the child passes twice a day "to scoleward and homward" (550), this "weye" begins to acquire a special resonance. It traverses, of course, the Jewry; it is a straight path the deviations from which are alleys that lead to the "wardrobe," the embraces of the "serpent Sathanas." The structure of the *Tale* is sufficiently stylized to catch reverberations of the *mythos* most fully explicit in such major examples of Christian "quest-literature" as *The Divine Comedy* and *Pilgrim's Progress*.[18] The passage of the "clergeon" along this distinctive way comes to suggest the progress of the Christian soul through the temporal world. Beset on every side by the agents of "oure firste foo" (558), even the innocent are not free from harm, and the only recourse is to prepare for things eternal by making oneself an instrument of God's praise.

By such economical yet suggestive manipulation of scene, character, and action, Chaucer has refined the tale of much of its gross sentimentality and popular superstition. The essence of the miraculous is sharply clarified against the dark mysteries of good and evil, while the fate of the innocent is enlarged in such a way as to record the universal human dilemma. The artistic effort involved is not unlike that of the medieval craftsman trained to perpetuate his revelations in stained glass, fine needlework, or illuminated manuscripts.[19] In the late Middle Ages, as C. S. Lewis has remarked,

> Neither the poets nor artists were much interested in the strict illusionism of later periods. The relative size of objects in the visible arts is determined more by the emphasis the artist wished to lay upon them than by their size in the real world or by their distance.[20]

Something of this non-illusionistic craftsmanship is to be found in the structural organization of the *Prioress's Tale*: a juxtaposition of the exquisite and the grotesque, rigorous selection and magnification of detail, and a sophisticated stylistic technique that, while it refers to what may be seen, is so deployed that the invisible world may shine through.

This is not to say that the work of the Prioress satisfies the demands of great art.[21] Like her "litel clergeon" who willingly neglects his primer to learn by rote an antiphon "in reverence / Of Cristes mooder" (537-38), she imparts to her tale the finest technical skill she commands. She offers her humble song as the best instrument of praise in her spiritual possession. Hers is not the theological intellect to distinguish between the Old Testament justice accorded the Jews in her tale and the higher law of Christian forgiveness and mercy. Her text, like that of the Pearl, has nonetheless Gospel authority:

> Do way, let chylder vnto me tyght,
> To suche is heuenryche arrayed. (*Pearl*, 718–19)

She allies herself with the "babes and sucklings" of the Psalm, with "Seint Nicholas" who "so yong to Crist dide reverence" (514–15), and with the innocent child of her *Tale*. Hers is a devotion so fine no theological controversy ever disturbed it. The emphasis of monastic life she represents is at the opposite extreme from the Monk's, and she benefits from the lack of intellectual presumption. Her modesty, though as artful as her table manners, has at least the right model in the typology of the Virgin, who became in her innocence and humility a vessel of divine wisdom.

Obviously there are dangers in such a reading of the Prioress's performance. For many critics, her failure to exercise her reason becomes mere childishness, an extension of the delight in pretty things and pretty ways emphasized in the portrait. Unlike her little "clergeon" she has reached the age when rational choices and self-knowledge are expected of her. Thus, her simple faith is distinguished only by its veniality from the vicious abuse of reason exhibited in other pilgrims. The moral problem that surfaces in the *Tale* is in fact not her failure to choose, but our inability to estimate the sincerity and profundity of her choice. The evaluation of individual faith is in reality impossible to all but God, and the literary context that might have given us divine insight is vexed by the ambiguity of the historical and generic evidence. One cannot entirely dismiss the charges of anti-semitism and sentimentality on the grounds of their ubiquity in miraculous legends of this sort, yet after the *General Prologue*, one cannot feel certain of Chaucer's complicity.[22] In the face of such a dilemma it seems wisest to test the purely literary evidence, to evaluate the formal care and rhetorical economy Chaucer has invested in this provocative performance.

P. M. Kean has astutely pointed out the tendency in medieval devotional poetry to substitute "a formal device for any thematic development," and in the Prioress's *Prologue* in particular, "the absolute quality of Chaucer's religious writing, in contrast to his more contextual use of philosophical material."[23] Perhaps, then, the medieval artisan provides the safest analogy for the Prioress's performance—the worker in stone or paint or words who demonstrates his faith by the exquisite application of his skill to a "program" supplied by those with greater learning. Lacking the overpowering force of original genius or intellect, she does her best, with the appropriately submissive technique of the "illuminator."[24] The gold leaf she applies to her *Tale* may be ambiguously secular, but it is intended to shine with the radiance of an otherworldly light. While her narrative is certainly restricted by its conventionality and its emotional appeal, the hard finish and deft strokes accorded its telling prevent it from becoming simply trite or maudlin. This is, of course, precisely the kind of incongruity one was led to expect of its teller, one who dissipates her feelings on small creatures and devotes her mind to the elegant accomplishments of the aristocratic world.[25] The Prioress, though limited in the scope of her "conscience and tendre herte," has in her exquisite *Prologue* and formalized *Tale* "peyned hire to countrefete" not only the "cheere of court" but also the finesse of its most skillful craftsmen. Through her *Tale* and her way of telling it, Chaucer has extended her tantalizingly ambiguous portrait. She remains an engaging complex of innocence and elegant surface, piety and high polish.[26]

CHAPTER XI

THE FRANKLIN AND THE MERCHANT:

"WE SEKEN FASTE AFTER FELICITEE"

If words be not an incarnation of the thought, but only a clothing for it, then surely will they prove an ill gift ... Language, if it do not uphold, and feed, and leave in quiet, like the power of gravitation or the air we breathe, is a counter-spirit, unremittingly and noiselessly at work, to subvert, to lay waste, to vitiate, and to dissolve.

WORDSWORTH

THE three substantial members of the regular clergy are followed in the *General Prologue* by three imposing men of a monied class that in the fourteenth century was beginning to nibble at the prestige and power of the nobility. In spite of their obvious social prominence and professional expertise, a certain coolness descends on these portraits; the narrator gives little sense of the human personalities that animate this merchant, lawyer, and professional host and officeholder. They are, with the possible exception of the Franklin, "seemers," men who view their occupations as necessitating a certain amount of ostentation and subterfuge. In many ways "modern men," they anticipate a capitalistic society that has scarcely heard that there were once, for such professions, Christian ideals of the kind Piers Plowman enunciates. The houses with enclosed pleasure gardens figuring symptomatically in several of their tales (as well as the Shipman's story of a "merchant of St. Denis") look forward to our suburban villa with its requisite swimming pool. Men almost obsessively conscious

195

of the risks of their professions, they are used to playing their cards close to the table. What they give away of their private lives is confined to brief prologues of provoked, painful, and almost unwitting admission. They prefer the "anonymity" of the story-teller but are in varying ways betrayed by what their tales manifest of deep-seated anxieties and unquestioningly secularized ethical standards.

The Man of Law's performance survives in a tentative condition, and any comment must be correspondingly approximate. A "sargeant" in the *General Prologue*, he appears to have been used in the *Introduction* to his *Tale* for some comic self-advertisement by Chaucer and perhaps a jibe at his friendly competitor, Gower. But while his literary critical remarks[1] might be taken as an oblique preface to the story of Constance (known for its incestuous beginning,[2] familiar perhaps to Chaucer's audience in "moral" Gower's version), the Man of Law's pointed eschewal of verse cannot. The inconsistencies of the sequence prohibit confident dramatic analysis, but the weaknesses of his *Tale*, discussed above in relation to the Clerk's, invite conjecture. While the motives Chaucer might have ultimately intended the Lawyer to betray must remain hypothetical, the treatment accorded others in his class (including the Physician) suggests that the piety he wishes to express is to be taken as less deep-seated than his love of "courtroom" oratory and respect for those values of the merchant class extolled in his *Prologue*.

The *Franklin's Tale*,[3] on the other hand, avoids such pitfalls by limiting its "moralitee" to the secular aspects of married life and such aristocratic views of love and honor that may have seemed fitting, like those of the *Parliament*'s seed-fowl, to his status in society. His performance, moreover, has an integrity in the manuscripts and a clear identification with the speaker, denied the Man of Law. The only textual problem lies in the incompleteness of the *Squire's Tale*, which has raised some critical question as to the quality of that youthful production[4] and the possibility that the Franklin's comments constitute an interruption.[5] In spite of the relative comprehensiveness of the evidence, however, the Franklin's character has been the subject of ceaseless dispute throughout this century, since Kittredge defined the "Marriage Debate" and determined that the Franklin carried it "to a triumphant conclusion by solving the problem."[6] But this cordial reception did not prevent another American scholar from comparing the pilgrim's social status to that of "a Toledo oil-magnate" bewailing "the vicious tendencies of the son whom he is lavishly maintaining at Yale or Harvard,"[7] or a later English critic from placing him within the university walls in the person of "a comfortable don of an ancient college, careful to be wise and not too serious, and telling his story with mellow vinous satisfaction."[8] Such opposing estimates will no doubt continue to provide Chaucerians with an arena in which to exercise their jousting skills. A consideration of the Franklin in proximity to the company he keeps in the *General Prologue*, by his own choice as well as Chaucer's, may help (though I hold out no great hope) to sway the outcome.

Like his fellow travelers on the pilgrimage, the Franklin cannot resist the temptation of an obtrusive and self-conscious manipulation of language, but unlike his predecessor, the Merchant, he bends over backwards not to offend his audience or, indeed, anyone. His performance starts off with some rather effusive comments on the young Squire's abilities, and he even defers meekly to the brusque reassertion of authority by the Host. Yet the moment he begins his *Prologue* he returns to his earlier theme of the connection between *gentillesse* and the deployment of fine language. Like the Merchant he gives us a glimpse into the unhappiness of his family life, but in his *Prologue* and *Tale* he addresses himself to general matters far removed from his private concerns. Yet his desire to speak a definitive word on "trouthe" and "fredom," as well as marriage, may be taken as part and parcel of the yearning for social acceptability in aristocratic circles that has made him want his son "To comune with any gentil wight / Where he myghte lerne gentillesse aright" (693–94). In both instances, there seems to be an unstated assumption that the moral ca-

197

pacities of the nobility are something that can be learned and then donned like the cloak of rhetoric.

The Franklin's storytelling, like his fabled hospitality, is characterized throughout by self-conscious bustling and ostentatious display. He makes a point of the genre of his tale and its aristocratic pedigree (709ff.), but in spite of some resemblance to the Breton *lai*, the story most likely came to Chaucer from Italian sources.[9] The coating of archaic proper names and the Breton locale seems to have been applied arbitrarily to emphasize social pretension and what Laura Hibbard Loomis called "the noble but old fashioned tastes of the whitebearded Franklin."[10] Whether or not the vogue of the Breton *lai* lasted into Chaucer's time has been disputed,[11] but there can be no question that the Franklin associates the genre with the kind of aristocratic manner his tale attempts to define and he would be happy to have attributed to himself and his family.

The imitation of noble ways is equally apparent in the Franklin's adoption of the Squire's rhetoric. He patterns the style of his *Prologue* on the "eloquence"—or "vertu" as he calls it (680)[12]—of the young man, appropriating one of his favorite devices, "affected modesty."[13] The pose of the plain, blunt man—"Thyng that I speke, it moot be bare and pleyn" (720)—will serve to pacify the Host and such other "lewed" men who will take it literally, but it is also calculated to appeal to the "gentils" who will recognize the sophistication of his disclaimers, his learned references, and the witty play on the rhetorical term, "colours." An obtrusive reliance on rhetorical flourishes distinguishes the art of his *Tale* as well, as it had those of his social equals, the Man of Law and the Merchant. The Franklin's motives seem relatively innocent, however, and his skill, for the most part, proves equal to the high purpose of the occasion. There are curious instances nevertheless when he seems to resist his subject matter—grumbling over the "supersticious cursednesse" of "astrology," for example (1273-93)—and others when he seems to give up on the high style itself:

But sodeynly bigonne revel newe
Til that the brighte sonne loste his hewe;
For th' orisonte hath reft the sonne his lyght,—
This is as muche to seye as it was nyght!   (1015-18)

However one interprets these particular narrative intrusions, there are a sufficient number of such peccadillos to insinuate that the narrator is not entirely at home with the chosen subject of his tale or the elegant manner with which he aspires to grace it. His feelings—personal as well as narrative—are rescued by the pervasive good will of his sanguine disposition, but this does not prevent there being a gentle irony to his conventional disclaimer: "My spirit feeleth nought of swich mateere" (727).

The Franklin's most serious rhetorical blunder, for which Chaucer has taken most of the blame and some faint praise, is the "Complaint" of Dorigen (1364-1456). Manly, one of the first critics to elaborate on the aesthetic import of rhetorical schooling, at first considered that this long speech "nearly spoiled" an otherwise "finely told" story,[14] then later tried to salvage it as a parody, "a *reductio ad absurdum* of the use of exempla."[15] Absurd though the performance may be, the humor seems less likely to lie in a misplaced and unsuccessful burlesque of rhetorical fulsomeness than in the Franklin's inability to bring off an Ovidian aria, displaying the antique virtue of his noble heroine. Looking at Chaucer's handling of his source material in St. Jerome's list of pagan exemplars, Germaine Dempster has uncovered "a degree of *negligence* and *rape*, of which we find very few other instances in his works."[16] Chaucer may well have been amused as he went through the list several times, adding exemplum after exemplum, until he reached a point of bathetic inconsistency with Dorigen's immediate dilemma. But his audience could only have participated in the comedy through the dramatic context, watching Dorigen's high resolve become eroded by garrulity, as she postpones action again and again by mustering up yet another troop of exempla. As she becomes more desperate, the exempla become less detailed until she breathlessly concludes with three in one couplet: "The same thyng I seye of Bilyea, / Of Rodogone, and eek Valeria" (1455–56). Lest there be any question of tone here, one need only recall Dempster's description of the magnificent irrelevance of these histories to Dorigen's situation:

> Valeria's glory had consisted in refusing to remarry, Rhodagune's in killing her nurse, and Bilia's in never remarking on the smell of her husband's breath.

Where the Franklin had intended to give us the elevated style of a noble lady faced with a tragic dilemma, a peek over Chaucer's shoulder confirms that he has produced a much more human and engaging, if somewhat hysterical and even occasionally silly woman.

Dorigen, from the beginning, in spite of Arveragus's deference, is a dependent, self-indulgent woman, quick to melodramatic excesses. Her grief at her husband's departure elicits a rather perfunctory description from the practical-minded Franklin:

> For his absence wepeth she and siketh,
> As doon thise noble wyves whan hem liketh.
> She moorneth, waketh, wayleth, fasteth, pleyneth. (817–19)

Such exhibitions are merely the useless prerogative of a leisure class, he seems unintentionally to imply, but certainly do fill up one's time. Measured against the sensible social behavior of her good friends, the monumental "hevyness" of Dorigen appears less than truly dignified, somewhat too much in the "proper manner," and ultimately foolish. Her treatment of the squire Aurelius reveals the full scope of her impetuous, almost giddy femininity. At first stunned and forcibly shocked into acknowledging his existence, she then takes revenge on his importunity with her rash oath. Her promise is not only self-contradictory, it is also maliciously parodic of the "daungerous" courtly mistress—professing to be motivated by pity

("Syn I you se so pitously complayne"), but pitiless in its seeming impossibility. Her final words, suddenly ignorant of the conventions of courtly service that had paved the way for her marriage, ring with the moral indignation of a franklin:

> Lat swiche folies out of youre herte slyde.
> What deyntee sholde a man han in his lyf
> For to go love another mannes wyf,
> That hath hir body whan so that hym liketh? (1002–1005)

The gratuitous dilemma inflicted on the hapless squire, left to face a "sodeyn deth horrible," justifies our enjoyment of the comic spectacle of this obsessed and haughty woman writhing in turn through her exempla-ridden complaint.

The inadequacies of the Franklin's risible attempts at characterizing nobility in action detach his narrative from its "serious" concerns. Aurelius is little more than a rag-bag of courtly clichés, echoes of the *Knight's Tale* and the *Troilus*. He loves, moans, suffers, pines, and wastes away in tactful silence, according to the rules, and never insults his lady by doing any of these things for a shorter period than two years. Arveragus is equally businesslike about his knighthood, balancing "a year and more" of "blisful lyf" in marriage with "a year or tweyne" (809) of service at arms. The Franklin seems to feel that the demands upon a knight would be regulated as strictly as for a businessman; when most needed by his wife, "out of towne was goon Arveragus" (1351). His *gentillesse*, too, is all propriety and good form. He responds to his lady's shattering news with "Is ther ought elles, Dorigen, but this?" (1469), not out of suspicion it seems, but with "glad chiere in freendly wyse" (1467). His stern decision, buttressed with his crucial *sententia* on "trouthe," is unhesitatingly aristocratic in its gentility, but his ensuing collapse into bitter tears betokens a more recognizable humanity combined with the less than noble desire to preserve secrecy (upon threat of death) and keep up appearances. His feelings are efficiently compartmentalized; his stiffly principled nobility and his real but less exalted emotions never quite meet.[17] But the bravado of his *gen-*

tillesse is more than its own reward: it releases a cascade of imitation and provokes the *embarras de gentillesse* in which the tale tumbles to its conclusion.[18]

Behind the elegant but artificial puppets assembled by the Franklin from bits of faded romance, clichés of character, and conventions of courtly manner, lurks a reality that is not their own but that of their narrator. It reveals a sensibility perhaps less refined and idly extravagant in emotion and ideal, but more practical, prejudiced in favor of the common morality and the familiar virtues of Holy Church, and above all, more fundamentally human. It is this reality, the ever-present personality of the Franklin, that gives the lie to the posturing and self-conscious nobility of his characters. It effects, moreover, a double vision of the action that has amusing thematic consequences. Whereas the Franklin's noble drama attempts to see clearly in one direction, the high comedy Chaucer pieced together from his lapses, points obliquely in another.

The Franklin's intentions are not difficult to isolate. They are twofold and part of the drama of ideas in the sequence of tales initiated by the Wife of Bath. The Franklin begins his tale with an explicit exposition of his concept of the perfect marriage. In response to the antithetical views of the Wife and Clerk, but passing over the Squire's indisputably "courtly" ideals, the Franklin proposes a compromise of mutual obedience and equal mastery.[19] The initial success of the experiment, the "blisse" and "solas" (802) of Arveragus and Dorigen, is then prescribed as an antidote to the grim cynicism of the Merchant's view of marriage, "wepyng and waylyng, care and oother sorwe" (IV, 1213).

But as the story unfolds, a second, less explicit purpose reveals itself—a working definition of the noble ideal of *gentillesse*. Here again, the Franklin takes his cue from the Wife of Bath, who had devoted much of her tale to a digression on that "verray gentillesse" that comes not of birth but of God's grace alone (III, 1162ff.). The Squire, too, by reviving Chaucer's favorite line (V, 479), provides a model in Canacee for that "pitee" that Aurelius must learn in order to achieve true nobility. To exemplify this aristocratic theme, the Franklin drags his characters through all the absurdities of his plot, from the rash promise to the magical illusions, merely to set up a dilemma that can be resolved only by the gracious working of *gentillesse*, specifically of its two vital components, "trouthe" and "fredom." Arveragus's conviction that "trouthe is the hyeste thyng that man may kepe" (1479) enables him to exercise the equally fundamental virtue of "fredom" by generously sacrificing what is most precious to him, his wife's purity, that she may be true to her word.[20] Aurelius and the "Orliens" clerk follow suit in making what obviously seem to the Franklin equally great sacrifices, demonstrating that "gentil" virtues are not the exclusive prerogatives of knighthood. The structural weight of the concluding *demande*, "Which was the mooste fre, as thynketh you?" (1622), confirms that the notion of an ideal marriage has been replaced by a broader but no less idealistic theme.

That "gentillesse," "trouthe," and "fredom" were in reality serious, valid ideals for Chaucer's audience and for the poet himself need hardly be argued, given their prominence in the Knight's portrait (*GP* 146). But the *Wife of Bath's Tale*, with its ungainly digressions and ill-mannered "gentil" squire, offers equally strong precedent for their misappropriation by a socially unqualified narrator. And the *Squire's Tale* has just depicted an impeccably proper courtly lady, who, like Dorigen, never having heard "speke of apparence" (V, 1602), turns hysterically to suicide when faced by a disparity between her high ideals and the truth of appearance; but the Squire's heroine is—somewhat unfortunately for the elevated tone—a bird. Yet just as the Franklin's noble actors come much nearer to meeting the demands of the form than the grotesque efforts of the Wife, so, too, his handling of these abstractions proves to be more artful and complex, and surpasses easily the Squire's school-boy idealizations. A comparison with the Knight's philosophic romance,[21] however, which also makes do with

203

flat, representational characters, calls attention to the narrowness of the Franklin's philosophic vision, its bondage to the dramatic context and the character of the teller. In contrast, its themes, like the Wife's, seem more self-serving, the result of personal concerns rather than objective inquiry. What holds for his quixotic ideal of marriage conceived in courtly love is equally true of his notion of "fredom" that in effect equates Arveragus's complaisance to adultery with the loss of a thousand pounds.

The isolation of the Franklin's notion of what his tale is about should make it immediately apparent that his two themes are not adequate to cover all the substantial embellishments of his narrative. The elaborate "prayers" of Dorigen and Aurelius are structurally inconsequential to the plot; the removal of the rocks is effected by magical illusion with no suggestion of the assistance of the invoked deities. The two petitions (identical in request but conflicting in purpose) and the irony of their fulfillment seem to belong to another narrative structure, one, for example, like the *Knight's Tale*, where the conclusion clearly depends upon the intervention of the gods and the philosophical issues raised by the interaction of humanity and divinity. The *Franklin's Tale*, as far as its given themes of marriage and *gentillesse* are concerned, could well have dispensed with such metaphysical implications.

Dorigen's prayer, or first "complaint," stems from her excessive grief, but her hysteria leads her to absurdities that are certainly beyond the scope of the tale as the Franklin envisions it. Challenging the order of the Universe and the reasonableness of Creation, she turns the amorous problem into a metaphysical one. She invokes an unmistakably Christian God rather than the pagan pantheon of the rest of the poem: "Eterne God, that thurgh thy purveiaunce" (865). While all things are reputed to have a purpose, she can find nothing in the black rocks except "a foul confusion of werk" (869–79), a source of misery to all the orders of Creation, threatening its fairest creature, man. She acknowledges, of course, that there is another way of looking at things:

I woot wel clerkes wol seyn as hem leste,
By argumentz, that al is for the beste,
Though I ne kan the causes nat yknowe.　　　(885–87)

But in her wild protest she throws disputation of clerks to the
winds and demands that the rocks be sunk into hell for her
husband's sake. Her last words, "thise rokkes sleen myn herte
for the feere" (893) betray, however, a grief that is basically
self-centered and wilful. Thus the complaint is turned into
more than just a noble wife's lament. A piece of metaphysical
foolishness, it contains within it the theological reply to such
protests. The adversities of Nature as of Fortune can be over-
come not by violent rebellion against the order of things, but
by faith in divine purveyance and a patient acceptance of the
world as we find it.[22]

For Aurelius, too, the rocks come to represent the sole ob-
stacle to personal happiness, but his prayer is more devious.
He avoids calling directly upon the chaste goddess of the moon
to aid his lustful cause; going over her head, he calls upon
Apollo to lead her astray in an incestuous, cosmic intrigue that
will draw the earth's waters above the rocks. The powers in-
voked in these two prayers correspond to both the nature of
the cause and the justice of the complaint: Dorigen's love is
sanctified and respectable; Aurelius's adulterous and pagan.
Dorigen inveighs against an unjust divine Providence; Aure-
lius, his pitiful amorous fate. But in each case the intense dis-
taste for the black rocks is loosed by a dissatisfaction with
things as they are and a concurrent inability to suffer patiently
the trials of adversity. An unconscious awareness of the meta-
physical implications of these protests is hinted at in the punc-
tuation of their conversation with oaths invoking God in his
office of Creator: "by God that this world made" (967), "by
thilke God that yaf me soule and lyf" (983), "by that Lord . . .
that maked me" (1000). We are made forcibly aware that the
universal order of things is being inadvertently questioned and
tested by this feverish wife and her pathetically doting squire.
It is now evident why we must remain detached from them as

characters and why they are allowed to seem so stiffly comic and absurd. They have, in fact, muddled themselves into foolish metaphysical depositions, which will be repented at leisure in the web of events spun by their prayers. The grief and distressful obligation consequent on the granting of their petitions will far exceed those that preceded them.

Yet, although the implications of the story are to be taken seriously, never are the actions or characters endowed with a tragic seriousness. They are mannered in a style of high comedy unintentionally conferred upon them by their overreaching narrator. The Franklin himself is ironically allowed to voice what will be the submerged theme of his *Tale* when, in his early disquisition on love and "maistrye," he indulges in a brief admonition to patience. Its words apply equally to the more comprehensive implications of the virtue which Dorigen had so impetuously ignored:

> Pacience is an heigh vertu, certeyn,
> For it venquysseth, as thise clerkes seyn,
> Thynges that rigour sholde nevere atteyne.
> For every word men may nat chide or pleyne.
> Lerneth to suffre, or elles, so moot I goon,
> Ye shul it lerne, wher so ye wole or noon.   (773-78)

So indeed Dorigen learns to suffer against her will, because the Franklin, in the hope of dramatizing the nobility of her married love, has yielded to rhetorical temptation and permitted her to voice her passion with an intemperance that sets her will against the will of God.

Had Dorigen, or her narrator, been more conscious of the supernatural rather than the social ethos of her story, her complaint might have echoed Arcite's:

> Allas, why pleynen folk so in commune
> On purveiaunce of God, or of Fortune,
> That yeveth hem ful ofte in many a gyse
> Well bettre than they kan hemself devyse?   (I, 1251-54)

But the Franklin himself has indicated that he is not entirely easy with the gifts of Fortune he has received, abundant though they are. If I am correct in my estimation of the Franklin's character and of the submerged theme of his tale, the connection between the two will be immediately apparent. The nagging concern for *gentillesse*, for rank and position, may be seen as but another variety of dissatisfaction with things as they are.[23] Like Dorigen, he places immediate happiness above a patient submission to the established order. But he is clearly not a vicious man, and accordingly the tone of the tale and the exposure of his limitations are tolerantly indulgent. The underlying theme of the *Tale*, which recoils upon the teller, is not a deadly sin—as in the tales of the Merchant or the Pardoner—but an imperfect virtue. A severe moral stance forces us to admit that there is something foolish and misdirected in the actions of the Franklin and his heroine, but the comic method gracefully acknowledges that "Pacience is an *heigh* vertue, certeyn."

The *Merchant's Tale* has only recently occasioned critical controversy.[24] It has been proposed that the *Tale* antecedes its *Prologue*, and that its sardonic tone and mordant irony are an illusion of unmedieval emphases on psychology and dramatic propriety. The Merchant's confession to a bitterly unhappy marriage is indeed brief and probably a late addition,[25] but I find it impossible to imagine that the tale that follows is not meant to complement the confession dramatically.[26] The tale begins in conscious parody of the Clerk's story of a wealthy Italian nobleman in the process of choosing a wife, but the conjunction of two distinct generic units quickly turns the simple fabliau into a penetrating, if sardonic, analysis of the masculine psychology that produces the stereotypical January–May marriage. The mock debate permits the central character to reveal in a generalizing intellectual context the fatuities of his mind, those foibles and vanities that warp and misdirect the mental processes. The fable, on the other hand, transmutes

207

these qualities into symbolic action, not simply as the conse-
quence of decisions taken, but in an imaginative projection of
these moral and psychological quirks onto the narrative proc-
ess itself. This mode of imagining, as much if not more than
specific actions themselves, defines the narrator's attitude to-
ward his hero.

January's character is by no means difficult to describe; the
mastery of the *Merchant's Tale* lies in the detailed wealth of
its development. A monstrous egotist, this "worthy knight" has
lived a life of unchecked wilfulness. Finding himself too old
for his former exploits, he decides upon marriage to simplify
and regulate the boundaries of his sexual games. His pride and
lust earn him the epithet of "hastif" January, but it is the
rationalizing piety he insists upon affecting that proves his
comic undoing. He translates his desire into elaborate encomia
on the wedded state, and the narrator expands his rhetorical
pretensions unmercifully with arguments that consistently
work against themselves, undercut by mordant irony. The de-
bate between the two brothers, following on January's deci-
sion, provokes only irritation in the impatient lecher. He asks
merely that they assent to his will (1468) and conceives of his
council as a mirror to his own thoughts, his own ego writ
large. Placebo, who ingeniously turns Solomon's precepts to
his own purposes, fills the bill perfectly, while Justinus's Sene-
can authority and personal experience offer unpalatable cau-
tion and precipitate the sudden rising of the session. The dis-
covery of May intensifies January's fatuousness; the "assoiling"
of his question about his heaven on earth provides Justinus
with the needed opportunity to vent his hatred of this "folye."
His "japerye" begins with the promise of an earthly purga-
tory instead and concludes with the advice to consult the Wife
of Bath. This sequence of debates, a long preamble to the tale
proper, has enabled the narrator and his judicious mouthpiece
to set themselves aloof from January's absurdities with ironic
mockery, while the husband-to-be gives them outrageous proof
of the extravagance of his dotage.

The irrationality of his unexamined impulses finds an apt

correlative when January's "heigh fantasye and curious busy-
nesse" (1378ff.) is defined by the simile of a "mirour, polisshed
bryght" set up in the marketplace to catch the fair images as
they go by.[27] Impotent lust has short-circuited his intellectual
faculties; now he exists wholly in a fantasy world, cut off from
reason; his self-reflecting vision of things has become his only
reality. A mirror of his mind is what he has made of his coun-
cil, in spite of Justinus's fractiousness, and a flat, impenetrable
surface is the appropriate image for January's mental state:
deaf to irony, blinded by lust, determined to transform the ex-
ternal world into a reproduction of his will.

The mirror is not the only image in the debate scene that
has resonance far beyond its immediate context. Charles Owen,
in a seminal article on Chaucerian irony,[28] has admirably de-
scribed the process by which the figural components in Janu-
ary's mind—especially, the enclosed garden, the paradise of
marital bliss, and the blindness of love—materialize literally,
and with an ironic backlash, in the fabliau. The actual garden
he creates, like Eden, has a serpent in it, while his physical
blindness is miraculously lifted at the end of the tale only to
be replaced by another kind, which by the grace of Proserpine
keeps foolish old husbands dotingly deceived. Love's blindness
is the narrator's image (1598), and its various actualizations
are appropriately imposed first by external Fortune, then by
the presiding deities of the garden. The images of January's
besotted fancy, on the other hand, take shape under his own
direction. It is as if the lordly power he exercises by projecting
his will on the members of his court proves capable of literal
extension onto the physical world about him. He constructs
a fantasy marriage in his mind, then realizes both the marriage
and the fantasy in his pleasure garden and, in spite of some
buffets from Fortune, achieves at the end of the tale his ex-
pected paradise on earth, furnished with a youthful helpmate,
restored sight, and even the promise of an heir. That this bliss-
ful future may be Justinus's idea of purgatory is a perspective
afforded by the narrator, but January remains secure in his il-
lusion to the bitter end. He exists in a world of his own de-

vising, a world in which the wilful imagination has deprived him of both sense and judgment. No longer physically blind, his sensory apparatus is nonetheless prevented from providing him with true images, just as his reason has from the beginning failed to discriminate within his imagination. Cut off in either direction, he becomes the total picture of "heigh fantasye."

The profile of January's mind, ingeniously worked out by the Merchant's fiction, yields easily to a modern psychological understanding of the delusive powers of the fantasy as well as to the medieval formulation of the abuse of reason. The Merchant's ironic conclusion allows us to read January's fate from either perspective: pitifully disabled by a self-inflicted blindness or, more sardonically, having attained the happiness he deserves. For curiously, though the Merchant is unrelenting in his contemptuous excoriation of January, this old cuckold—unlike John the Carpenter—holds center stage throughout and cannot help but elicit an occasional flicker of sympathy, however inadvertent and morally misplaced.

The reason for this ambivalence is, as many have noted,[29] that the Merchant, in spite of his careful extravagance of characterization and his smugly superior stance, has more in common with January than he cares to acknowledge. It is not merely that they are fellow sufferers at the hands of calculating wives or that January in any specific detail reproduces the Merchant's former unenlightened state, but that they share a limitation of mental vision that underlies the Merchant's ability to create January's world with such intuitive precision. The failure to observe the distinction between the literal and the symbolic extends far beyond the activities of the hero of the *Tale*. I have already mentioned that when the narrator chooses to have Fortune intervene, he does so by actualizing a commonplace image. But in fact throughout the *Tale*, he deliberately violates the decorums of rhetoric and fiction and does so obtrusively, with a cynical relish that is meant for comic effect, but becomes a revealing measure of value.

On a simple level, the Merchant neglects the more obvious

duties of a narrator, taking no consistent point of view toward his characters. January is treated, indiscriminately, with effusive sympathy at one moment, withering disdain at the next. In regard to the minor characters, whose full minds we are not privy to, the contrasts are even sharper. May is presumably to be pitied when faced with the wedding night spectacle of her old cock of a husband shaking "the slakke skyn aboute his nekke" (1849), but when she disposes of Damian's love note in the "pryvee" and proceeds to rationalize like some great lady the taking of an impecunious lover, the irony of the familiar "lo, pitee renneth soone" in this context disposes of all compassion quickly. Damian's case shows how unrelated to the character's behavior the narrator's comments can be. When the squire's love is kindled, moral outrage erupts apostrophically:

> O perilous fyr, that in the bedstraw bredeth!
> O famulier foo, that his servyce bedeth!
> O servant traytour, false hoomly hewe,
> Lyk to the naddre in bosom sly untrewe,
> God shilde us alle from youre aqueyntaunce!   (1783–87)

But when the woeful youth next appears, languishing for love, the Merchant falls over himself with sympathetic concern:

> Therfore I speke to hym in this manere:
> I seye "O sely Damyan, allas!
> Andswere to my demaunde, as in this cas.
> How shaltow to thy lady, fresshe May,
> Telle thy wo? She wole alwey seye nay.
> Eek if thou speke, she wol thy wo biwreye.
> God be thyn helpe! I kan no bettre seye."   (1868–74)

It is not that the characters suffer a change of fortune or moral integrity, or that the narrator, like *Troilus and Criseyde*'s, has heightened sensibilities. The formulae of narrative commentary are applied with such cynical irresponsibility and studied lack of sympathy as to repudiate all question of motive or inclination to morality.

As with the characters, so it is with every system of value touched on. "Courtly love" wends one of its seamiest courses —from the billet-doux thrown into the "pryvee" to fornication in the pear tree. Other political and social rituals fare no better at January's court; but the attack on marriage is the most devastating. And with marriage fall many things religious, from the authority of Holy Scripture to the sacrament itself. The narrator's ironic praise is laced with double-edged biblical allusions, from analogy of the terrestrial paradise and its provision of a wife as "Goddes yifte" (1311) to the culminating and exquisitely inappropriate exempla typifying women of wise counsel (1362ff.) taken from a radically different context in the *Melibeus*, where their advice is indeed exemplary but not necessarily in the best interest of their husbands. The most explicit deflation of sacred text is the narrator's comment on January's long paraphrase of the Song of Songs to entice his wife into the garden: "Swich olde lewed wordes used he" (2149). The full force of the statement depends on the fact that the words indeed are literally erotic if not "lewed," but such meanings had been long submerged under such allegorical interpretations as Christ's love for his Church.[30] The fatuity of January's rhetoric becomes something close to blasphemy on the Merchant's part.

So, too, the sacrament of marriage is depicted by a perfunctory list of external details, finished off by the priest's making "al siker ynough with hoolynesse" (1708). The ceremony becomes a sequence of discrete acts that despiritualize its components—from the "stole" about the priest's neck to the concept of "hoolynesse"—to mere concrete objects, empty but tangible counters that can be manipulated at will. The sacrament makes everything secure, like the stamp of a seal the priest affixes to what for January is in any case little more than "legalized prostitution" (cf. 1841).[31] The Merchant would apply the same treatment to all systems of value: allegorical or spiritual levels of meaning are ruthlessly crushed onto a flat, literal plane; symbolic objects are left only their naked physicality;

and abstractions such as "love" and "holiness" suffer systematic reification.

Paradoxically, this flattening process contributes much of the rhetorical vividness and narrative color to the *Tale*. The Merchant's disregard for the decorous observance of traditional value extends to the formal and stylistic aspects of his performance as well, yet in this case his iconoclasm generates a good deal of humor and verbal excitement. The use of classical deities provides the most striking examples here. The passage describing the wedding festivities (1709ff.) begins with extravagant yet recognizably figurative comparisons—the musical instruments better than those of Orpheus, etc.—but with the introduction of Bacchus and Venus, the style changes. We are no longer given rhetorical heightening, but literal fact: Bacchus actually is the sommelier, and Venus provides a kind of exotic floor-show, dancing about "with hire fyrbrond in hire hand" (1727)—somewhat indiscriminately it would appear, for we later discover that she has also "hurt" poor Damian in the process. It is not quite clear what kind of rhetorical or fictional world we are in here. When we are further told that "Ymeneus, that god of weddyng is, / Saugh, nevere his lyf so myrie a wedded man" (1730–31), are we to assume this is another high-flown comparison or that Hymen is in fact a guest looking on? The conflation of modes, the persistent flattening of metaphoric comparison, seems to be confirmed when the Merchant chooses a literary analogue for this event: *The Marriage of Mercury and Philology*, an allegorical venture that also mixed abstractions and symbolic divinities, is as remote as possible in style and purpose from the fabliau antics of this occasion, where the eager husband hastens his guests' departure while gulping aphrodisiacs. Yet the reference to Martianus's celestial marriage sets up the multiple ironies of the lines: "Whan tendre youthe hath wedded stoupyng age, / Ther is swich myrthe that it may nat be writen" (1738–39). It may also remind us of the easily forgotten, quasi-allegorical cast to the names of the type figures in this often grossly naturalistic production. The stylistic and even generic confusion pointed up in this passage tells us something about the general meaning the Merchant intends his tale to imply. His characters and action, like the allegorical, belong to a realm of universal and permanent truth, but a realm which has been totally emptied of the sacred. January's marriage is a heaven on earth, if the gods are there, but it is a heaven of lust, deception, and blindness, which many will prefer to associate with another place.

Pluto and Proserpine extend onto a larger narrative plane[32] the stylistic manipulation of classical and literary deities found in the wedding scene. Nothing much is said of their customary domain; we are merely referred to Claudian. The infernal—or, if one prefers to stay with Justinus, purgatorial—implications are developed quite obliquely. Introduced as from a very unclassical "fayerye," once they open their mouths, they give away their true origin as thoroughly bourgeois inhabitants of a milieu common to the fabliau, with all of its domestic bickering and clichés of sexual role-playing. Their miraculous powers are less significant in the action than those of the divinities in the crude analogues that scholarship has unearthed for the *Tale*.[33] Their wonder-working gestures are already part of the metaphoric fabric of the narrative, and in this tale metaphor becomes actuality with predictable regularity. Their miracles are absorbed in a demythologizing process, just as their divinity has been swallowed up in a mundanity worthy of the Wife of Bath. The Merchant's depiction of the marriage rite gives a fairly strong indication of his metaphysical assumptions; his refusal to accord a distinct mode of being to the classical deities—neither figures of speech nor properly otherworldly—is the literary complement to his disrespect for spiritual realities. What begins in January's notion of marriage as a paradise-on-earth sets off a chain reaction of ironic short-circuits that affect all metphysical and fictional assumptions of a reality beyond the barest, most literal, grossly physical existence.

As one last example of the Merchant's refusal to acknowledge separate levels of being, one should note Justinus's reference, which shocked some early critics, to the Wife of Bath as an authority on marriage. Chaucer himself engages in a similar witticism in his "Envoy à Bukton," which should remind us that the Merchant's cynicism and its casual disrespect for symbolic modes and fictional levels is a ready-made pose and easy source of amusement. The manner keeps its audience off balance and provokes quick, if somewhat uneasy, laughter. The attitude also has a tendency to be self-generating: once set in this mode, a narrator as anxious to appear authoritative as is the Merchant cannot easily change course, stabilize the tone, or suspend the ironies. One must grant, with Bronson and others, that the Merchant does produce a tale with some good farcical moments and considerable wit, however black the comedy. The kind of pose he adopts, however, may be understood psychologically as an over-reaction to his personal difficulties and a kind of self-protection in a time of crisis, like his anonymity in the pilgrimage.[34] One need not speak of a "frenzy of contempt and self-hatred"[35] or overstress the "bitterness (that) betrays him";[36] such critiques have merely propelled other critics in the opposite direction. But the imaginative coherence of the *Tale* bespeaks a dramatic creation of psychological consistency.

This is not to say that the "bitterness" and "self-hatred" are not there. The very zest with which the Merchant indulges his cynical wit and reifying imagination confirms a pain of disillusionment—presumably with himself, if we believe his *Prologue*, but projected onto the world around him—and a coordinate instinct for salvaging something from the ruins. "He who despises himself," Nietzsche has said, "nevertheless esteems himself as a self-despiser." One senses the Merchant's self-esteem not only in the ironic superiority to his fictional hero but also in the delight he takes in imposing his will on his audience through a fictional mode that by implication squashes their multileveled universe to a plane as flat as the road to Canterbury. Though he may momentarily reveal his inner torment, the Merchant is not one to wallow in self-pity or self-laceration. He is quite practiced, the *General Prologue* tells

215

us, in putting his words to good use: "His resons he spak ful solempnely, / Sownynge alwey th'encrees of his wynnyng" (274–75), and he is not averse to using fiction skillfully to demonstrate how much he has profited from his own experience, how greatly his knowledge of the world has increased. To this end he creates a fictional world in which language determines the final reality and words may be manipulated at will; no symbolic value haunts their empty signification. The Merchant is a professional man, long familiar, presumably, with the hollowness of rhetoric; in his *Tale* he demonstrates that even the hollowness may be put to useful purpose. For, as he says of another cynical deceiver, "Craft is al, whoso that do it kan" (2016).

CHAPTER XII

THE WIFE
OF BATH AND
THE NUN'S
PRIEST:

"OUT OF
OLDE BOKES"

*In imaginative fiction of
any depth, there has always
to be a delicate balance
between the writer's intui-
tive penetration into his
characters and the nesci-
ence which he must con-
fess to sharing before the
frontiers of their final
mystery.*

J.I.M. STEWART

AS a fiction maker, the Wife of Bath ambles down the Canterbury road virtually without a peer. She puts to shame her nearest rival, the Pardoner, by virtue of the spontaneity and agility of her fertile imagination. Yet as a storyteller in the conventional sense, she is pretty much of a disaster, her *Tale* being in many ways the least independent of its dramatic context. Though the story does not lack intrinsic interest, her narration, removed from the Canterbury framework, would seem a conundrum of ungainly digressions and misshapen materials: it can only be understood in terms of its teller, a speaker who rides roughshod across the boundary between ordinary discourse and storytelling. If the Wife of Bath appears to conceal herself less in the role of narrator than do most of the other pilgrims, it is because her whole life is given over to creating of fictions. Or, to put it more accurately, she expends apparently unlimited verbal energy in assembling the single story, endlessly fascinating, but elusive and incomplete, of her own existence. Less restricted than her fellow performers by a fixed pose or rhetorical stance, she tirelessly revises and recreates her account of a reality that refuses to hold long any shape she tries to put on it. Spurred by her dissatisfaction into an unflagging performance, she becomes her own supreme fiction.

The image Alisoun creates of herself is full of contradiction, obscurity, and illogicality, and has steadfastly resisted the efforts of early critics to fix it with a label from astrology or the deadly sins.[1] She has been called everything from an agent of the devil to a life-force of Falstaffian magnitude.[2] Like all the "great" characters of literature, she retains something of that essential mysteriousness of the human personality that is detected in a more than superficial analysis and can be reproduced in art only by a comparably profound act of imagining. If one can trust R. A. Pratt's reconstruction of the process,[3] however, she began rather simply. The narrator of the *Shipman's Tale* is little more than an animation of the anti-feminists' cliché, a familiar alliance of sensuous desires with the quick wit necessary to finance them. As a type she recurs—mythically and allegorically, one might say—in Proserpine and May of the Merchant's fabliau. But Chaucer was not content to leave the Wife of Bath to that extent "unrealized." The sections of her *Prologue* accumulated: the three old husbands (from "Theophrastus"), the two young husbands and the tale of Jankyn's book, the opening argument (from Jerome), the astrological passage, and the various interruptions. In the process her portrait in the *General Prologue* was revised accordingly and a new tale provided. Some of the manuscript glosses may even indicate, Pratt conjectures, that Chaucer contemplated further embellishments. The invention of centuries of anti-feminist satire,[4] the Wife of Bath obviously proved irresistible to her creator's imagining, as she in turn developed into a creation possessing fertile, though self-absorbed imagination.

In spite of its apparent contradictions and multiple poses, the Wife of Bath's performance exhibits underlying consistency. In psychological terms, hers is a "battered" personality. Everything she does is an attempt to assert her independent reality in a world where masculine dominance claimed authority over her mind, body, and spirit. Legally, the terms of marriage reduced her to the status of chattel, body and all. As a woman and wife, she was depicted in the allegorization of the Fall of Man, repeated by the Parson on this very pilgrimage (321ff.), as not only the cause of man's woe but, in the personified guise of "Sensuality," as the eternal inferior to male "Reason." She was preserved illiterate, allowed only the puny weapon of her own "experience" to contend against an armory of masculine "auctoritee." No wonder, then, that the Wife uses any strategy that comes to hand to establish and defend her identity. No wonder, either, that she finds herself uncomfortably contrary, consistently obliged to assume the very posture she is opposing. Though she pretends to rejoice in her horoscope (609ff.), it is the most transparent of her fictions. The conjunction of Mars and Venus ought to bring about the disarming of Mars (as in the proem to Book III of the *Troilus*); but she prefers to construe her temperament as a projection of the arming of Venus. Nevertheless, despite her conscious resistance, it is very much the tempering power of Venus that, before the Wife's performance is completed, emerges as the determining, though imperfectly acknowledged, force in her personal mythology.

The Wife's first assault takes on the intellectual establishment. Turning Jerome's rebuttal of Jovinian inside out, Chaucer creates for her a pseudo-scholastic tour-de-force that rivals that of the anti-feminists themselves in its combination of scriptural recall and logical absurdity. Arguing the pros and cons of question upon question,[5] she leads the inquiry away from any damaging moral issues and affirms her right to use her blessed "instrument" as she sees fit. Chaucer no doubt relished this satiric exercise in the manner of the "scoles," creating the dramatic pretext of marital "scoleiyng" in which doctrinal "auctoritee" wars with an "auctor"-infested experience. But behind the flat-footed confidence of the Wife's tone, one begins to sense the battering that had provoked such belligerence, the smugly superior clerics who "devyne and glosen up and doun" (26) and assume that by holding a monopoly on the written word they confirm their virile authority. For all of its comic irrationality, this part of the Wife's *Prologue* takes an accurate, if oblique, measure of her opposition, for even Jerome indulges in less than cogent argumentation such as hers. In the process, one glimpses the underlying pathos of her situation.

The next section, equally literary in origin and equally "up so doun," gives the Wife a distinct edge on her adversaries, though the antagonists in her three January–May marriages were more evenly matched to begin with. Chaucer's accommodation of Theophrastus's diatribe against young wives to the voice of just such a wife may weaken her moral stand, but it tempers the husband's charges with a lively respect for the verbal energy and quick-witted ingenuity of this Wife who has, in this primary school, learned a great deal about the best defense. The easy triumph over her three rashers of old bacon leaves Alisoun a comfortable young widow, hardened to rapid offensive action against men, but less immoral perhaps than confused about the connection between money and sex, and poignantly ignorant of love. The formative years have taught her how to survive, how to create the kind of self that will withstand the Januaries of her world: she has become a thoroughgoing professional; like the Merchant and Lawyer, she has acquired competence in a job that gives her command over the *temporalia*, the material aspects of her existence. Her cloth-making vocation, mentioned only in the *General Prologue*, recedes into little more than a symbolic means of associating her with Eve, the originator of female "deceite, wepyng, spynnyng" (401).[6] The Wife of Bath is, by natural profession, a Woman.

With the fourth husband, everything changes. There seems to be no literary source for this passage, and the narrative loses the assured control that characterized the reminiscing voice to this point. Initially a marriage of sexual attraction, the new battle succumbs to the frustration of other attractions and survives as an armed truce. Of the man we learn nothing but that he was occasionally out of town (550) during the long years of the marriage. For the Wife, too, this was a period of travel, of those famous pilgrimages listed in the *General Prologue*. But in the context of this domestic unhappiness, the "wandrynge by the weye" (*GP*, 467) appears less satisfactorily pleasurable than most commentators have assumed. It seems to have been a time in which the old fiction no longer worked; with the passing of youth, a new self had to be forged out of the fragments. A renewed aggressiveness eventually emerges, but the process is neither quick nor easy. The narration loses continuity: the unpalatable reality of the fourth marriage, the brutal fact of rejection, is submerged in assertions of sexual vigor, nostalgia for lost youth, feeble claims of revenge, and the preparations for a new mate. Underlying the discourse, however, is a feeling of dislocation that causes even this most confidently garrulous of women to lose track of her thought (585-86).

With Jankyn the clerk, we arrive at the immediate source of provocation for the Wife's initial clerkly discourse and are even treated to a reading from the famous book that no doubt supplied much of her learned ammunition. From Jankyn, too, she acquired the basic method of bludgeoning her opponents with texts and examples, a masculine technique which Chauntecleer, too, knows well. But we are also introduced early on to the Wife's alternate means of coping with this new but equally refractory masculine world—what may be called her "venerien" mode. The first hint of this approach appears in the dream she recounts to her intended victim, this young and available scholar, half her age, but with irresistible legs. Girlishly, she admits the falsity of the story; a piece of maternal advice on capturing a man, she claims—"my dames loore" (583). Moreover, she seems to concur with the proffered interpretation of her death at his hands on the blood-stained bed: the seductive promise of wealth to the impoverished student, "for blood bitokeneth gold, as me was taught" (581). But one need not await Freudian analysis to recognize that the false

221

dream is equally a fantasy offer of virginity made by an aging woman unwilling to accept herself in the role of one buying a husband.

Fantasy also accounts for the Wife's effort to frame the recounting of the fifth marriage with the language of romance. In spite of the unpleasant reality of the "cursed book" that dominates this representative episode, the story begins with the revealing line identifying the young husband to whom she gave all her "lond and fee" as "this joly clerk, Jankyn, that was so hende" (628)—the very idiom of popular romance that Chaucer had exploited so effectively in the *Miller's Tale*. Jankyn's book now becomes a new and unexpected symbol of male domination, and though she cannot yet attack its intellectual methods, she is sufficiently provoked to assault its material form and, after an exchange of blows with its owner, she succeeds in getting it burned as the heretical thing it is. But this is not her only triumph over this new challenge. She manages first to regain control of her property and retain the desirable husband, after which she can then wrap up the package for her pilgrim audience with the rhetorical ribbons of pure romantic fantasy:

> After that day we hadden never debaat.
> God helpe me so, I was to hym as kynde
> As any wyf from Denmark unto Ynde,
> And also trewe, and so was he to me. (822–25)

Her earlier marital tactics have given way to "venerien" wiles. With the shop-worn formulae of feminine consolation, the Wife brings her sequence of marital exploits to a self-satisfactory conclusion. Safely embalmed in the topos "they lived happily ever after," her latest fling is carefully preserved from reality and refutation alike.

If the Wife of Bath's *Prologue* concludes in patently fictionalized autobiography, her *Tale* is just as clearly autobiographical fiction. On the one hand, there are reminders of the "marcien" combativeness and coarseness of tone that dominate the *Prologue*: the putting of the Friar in his place, the digression

of Midas's wife (courtesy of Jankyn's book?), the characteri-
zation of the "lusty bachelor" and his fitting punishment abed,
and again in the final lines of the *Tale*, the irresistible tempta-
tion to round things off with a display of sexual bravado. On
the other hand, the strong element of wish-fulfillment trans-
forms not only the old hag but the dénouement of the story
as well into a more comprehensive reworking of the fantasy
by which she accommodated the uneasy marriage with Jankyn
to her need for self-respect as a desirable woman. Though she
wears the role of storyteller lightly, the plunge into fiction
nevertheless frees her to put forward romanticized self-con-
ceptions she would not otherwise dare to admit.

It is possible that we are meant to take the hag's long speech
on *gentillesse* and poverty as part of the same impulse. One
could account for her scholarly utterances here as one does
for the rest of the Wife's learning—gleanings from Jankyn's
books[7] (though not the one on "wikked wyves"), readings per-
haps that formed part of the poor, low-born scholar's self-
justification to his materially and even "socially" superior wife.
As part of the hag's character, however, they suggest a surpris-
ing extension of the Wife's fantasy to include refined senti-
ments and immaterial values. Perhaps Chaucer, with the in-
stinct of dramatic genius, having established the "rules" of the
Wife's character, deliberately set about to break them here.
Paradoxically, a dramatic character achieves a certain magni-
tude and validity by the reach of its contradictions. Like senti-
mentality and violence in the Prioress, the materialistic sensu-
ality and "gentil" romanticism of the Wife are two sides of a
single coin, the unassimilated fictive extremes through which
she had attempted to negotiate a world that seemed perpetu-
ally to threaten her identity. The old hag's sermon permits her
to voice ideals she could not easily appropriate to her public
self. The shock of her unexpected *gentillesse* merely testifies to
the thoroughness with which she had imposed the opposing
fiction on a conventionally minded, willing audience.

The Wife of Bath's performance, then, compels our atten-
tion because its imaginative reach penetrates those depths of

223

the human personality where contrarieties coexist in oxymoronic tolerance, defying logical judgment and eluding facile moral analysis. As a dramatic—as opposed to novelistic—character, the Wife is presented in terms of her own ambivalent self-conceptions, the fictions she creates to outface the faces she meets. We know more about the Wife than about the other pilgrims; hers is the only prologue that exceeds the length of the tale, forming a continuum of exploratory tones and developing personal concerns. Hers is also the only performance that offers, instead of a settled rhetorical stance, a history of those fictions by which she chooses to view herself and be viewed by others in turn.

In its genesis, the character of the Wife of Bath proves equally fascinating. In spite of the intervening centuries since her creation, we can conjecture as safely about the origin of her character as about most of the great "archetypal" figures of our literature. From Falstaff down to Leopold Bloom, the "larger-than-life" characters who achieve independence of their particular fictive contexts and become part of our literary mythology, have had "makers" who for the most part covered their tracks better than did Chaucer with his Dame Alys. We have considerable information about his sources—especially for the extended *Prologue*—because Chaucer himself has provided it. The originals are not only unmistakably there in section after section—Jerome, "Theophrastus," and many others—but they are also gathered up and identified in the table of contents to Jankyn's "book of wykked wyves" (669ff.). It seems more than likely that Chaucer had some such manuscript anthology of the anti-feminist tradition in his library and that he returned to it again and again in developing his archfeminist's personality. But Chaucer differs from most of the great shapers of fictional characters in that the written source, the "auctoritee," remained a conscious part of the imaginative process. One can reconstruct the creative conflict between the words on those manuscript pages—addressed to different audiences with very different purposes and methods, often deadly serious (Jerome), and at best minimally animated by character and narrative ("Theophrastus")—and, on the other hand, the freshly minted drama of the Wife's performance, uncognizant in its naïve "reality" of its origins elsewhere. This tension between new experience and old authority not only informs the conscious thought of Chaucer's character from the first line on, but profoundly affects the imagined nature and imaginative status he accords the characterization.

The first aspect of this process has been the subject of this section on "Psychological Fictions." Chaucer imagined the fictive characters of the Canterbury pilgrimage as themselves fiction-makers—not merely storytellers, but makers of fictive selves that condition the language and rhetorical methods within and without the tales they tell. The Wife of Bath is a supreme fiction-maker, not because her character is derived from the several fictions (if one may so dignify them) of Jankyn's book, but because of the insight Chaucer had gained into the nature of human character from his understanding of the nature of fiction. Just as the distinction between experience and authority becomes hopelessly blurred when the written arguments of learned anti-feminists become part of the marital education of an illiterate "archwife," so too the difference between fiction and reality becomes meaningfully obscured in a work like the *Canterbury Tales*: structured in terms of fictions within a fiction it develops the proposition that these fictional levels are as interpenetrating, as cross-referential as the pilgrimage framework is to the "real world" out of which it was made. The consciousness that she was created out of old books remains part of the imagining of the Wife of Bath. More than a reflection on Chaucer's professed love of his library and his obvious delight in hidden literary allusions, it is a reflex of his sure dramatic instinct, his intuitive knowledge of the workings of the human mind and psyche, which could create in a fictional being, compounded of fictions, a character that transcends the limits of its own fictive universe.

Chaucer himself testifies to this sense of the Wife's transcendence. She makes her appearance as an authority on marriage in the separate fictional world of the *Merchant's Tale* and, in the "Envoy à Bukton," escapes even the confines of reality fixed by the *Canterbury Tales*. But, the Wife's *Prologue* itself contains the definitive proposition of Chaucer's "metaphysics of fiction," an imaginative statement that teases the critical faculties much as the Moebius strip and Klein bottle do our intuitive sense of dimensionality. When the Wife of Bath describes in detail the contents of Jankyn's treasured volume, we, having reconstructed the genesis of her *Prologue* as Chaucer in the privacy of his library must have felt it, become aware that this book that confers a potent authority on its learned possessor but appears to her senses as stubborn material object, this book is in fact the source of her reality, the origin of her being. When she attacks its three pages, it is as if she were trying to extinguish the reality of which she is made and step through some dark hole into another spatial continuum. The fictional *jeu d'esprit* that Chaucer perpetrates here requires some such science-fictional description, according to which one supra-physical dimension turning itself inside out becomes the new physical reality. Such feats of imagination are, of course, not uncommon to the Christian mind, accustomed as it is to thinking in terms of more than one mode of being and many correspondent planes of temporal and spatial reality.[8] Aesthetically, this sort of mentality contributes that "multiconsciousness" required, according to Muscatine,[9] of the reader of *Troilus*, that "simultaneous awareness of different and opposite planes of reality," which was a condition of fourteenth-century life. It is also responsible for the multidimensional clarity of the kind of allegory that has proved to be coeval with a vigorous Christian theology, in contrast, say to the truly "dark" parables of Kafka.

But Chaucer's casual inversion of fictive time and space in the Wife of Bath's *Prologue* is more complex than is suggested by a hierarchy of allegorical levels extending to the anagogical, the literary analogue of an anthropocentric cosmology for which human experience provides the focal point or literal plane. Medieval Christianity had inherited, through Macrobius and Boethius, another cosmic model also figured by concentric circles, but exactly reversing the center and outer circumference of the Ptolemaic model. Its focal point was the Providential Divinity, the Unmoved Mover; its outer limits, our world of mutable fortune and the limited capacities of fallen man. These two interlocking sets of spheres, like a variation on Yeats' gyres, enabled one to perceive in two directions at once. *From* Earth, man could look up "at a sky not only melodious, sunlit, and splendidly inhabited, but also incessantly active."[10] But it was also possible, by a leap of the theological imagination, to look down through the Empyrean *to* Earth, assuming the perspective of the Final Cause contemplating His created effect. This is also the vantage point of the imitative creator or poet, who peers down at his manuscripts through sphere within sphere of fictive activity. When the Wife of Bath attacks Jankyn's book, which is both her enemy and the source of her being, it is as if she were usurping the role of creator, destroying the "original" so that she might recast herself in her own image. With this audacious overturning of structured hierarchies, she achieves an apocalypse of fantasy, which, drawing upon her deepest personal needs, brings in a new heaven of romance. With this gesture, too, Chaucer perhaps was unconsciously signaling the loss of control over his fictive creature, or perhaps he was merely playing the puckish hidden god, inverting realities at his will. Whatever its motive, the gesture, like all of Chaucer's great comic moments, persuades with the truth of its imaginative implication. The interpenetration of fiction and reality, so astonishingly embodied by the Wife of Bath, serves as a timeless insight into the nature of literary creativity and, like Dame Alys herself, transcends the limits of Chaucer's self-effacing art.

When Chaucer the pilgrim, after the Host's peremptory dismissal of *Sir Thopas*, introduces his translation of the *Livre de Melibée et de Dame Prudence* into the Canterbury sequence, we cannot be certain how the poet meant us to understand the dramatic validity of this "litel tretys." But this reworking

227

of an important source for his own works reminds us of the essential duality of his creative imagination. On the one hand we assume that Chaucer the thinker was genuinely interested in the counsel and consolation that are the subject matter of Albertano's pale imitation of Boethius. But as a mimetic artist he could not help but be sensitive to the comic possibilities of its sketchy narrative and the argumentative tones of its characters. It is no wonder that bits and pieces of this serious tale find their way into the tales of the "Marriage Debate"—often verbatim but always with an ironic relocation. The *Melibeus* provides one of the best examples of Chaucer's ability to take a double view of such sober volumes of moral suasion, responding both in earnest and in game.

But the debate between Dame Prudence and her unfortunate husband finds its way most evidently and immediately into the *Nun's Priest's Tale*, that virtually anonymous performance that is in so many ways a recapitulation of the various themes and narrative devices of the tales that precede it in the fragment. All that we hear of the Nun's Priest outside of his *Tale* is the enthusiasm ("Yis, yis," 2816) with which he agrees to tell a merry tale after the Monk has refused further play. We are, therefore, little prepared for the satiric agility with which he picks up the fallen torch of monastic edification. Not only does he tell of another proud reign threatened by an "unwar strook" of Fortune (2764), prophesied, like Croesus's fall, in a dream, but he invests it first with tragic import—a "sovereyn notabilitee" (3209), as the Monk too might have said[11]— then gives it a comic dénouement, satisfying both the Knight and the Host with his generic legerdemain. Yet it is the *Melibeus* that clearly stands behind the debate over the nature of dreams, a debate that takes up more than half of the *Tale* and establishes the thematic basis for the satiric self-consciousness that pervades the telling of the fable proper.

The contention between Chauntecleer and Pertelote involves more than the interpretation of a single dream. It opposes two radically different theories on the significance of dreams in general, as Curry demonstrated long ago,[12] and at a further level of generalization, draws in those familiar antagonists, experience and authority. Pertelote, speaking for practical, bourgeois experience, cites only Cato and considers all dreams to be an imbalance of "humours" easily remedied by a good laxative. An overly enthusiastic exponent of the "pickles and milk" school, she prescribes a remedy that R. D. French once called a "veritable depth bomb." But Pertelote is not Dame Prudence, nor is she allowed the last word. Instead, the issue that Prudence must get out of the way before she can begin to advise Melibeus on his real problem, the question of "wommennes conseils" (that "been ful ofte colde," 3256), becomes the center of contention in the barnyard. Chauntecleer repudiates her interpretation *and* her theory, her one authority *and* her method of proof, and, above all, her prescription. He does so, however, with smug and supercilious condescension to his illiterate female companion. He begins with Gallic courtliness ("Madame, graunt mercy of youre loore," 2970) and ends in an unshared cackle over mistranslated Latin. Behind this display of masculine scholarliness lurks the strutting "trede fowel" whose manhood has been questioned (2920), and behind him, a small boy who doesn't want to take a laxative:

> . . . and I seye forthermoor,
> That I ne telle of laxatyves no stoor,
> For they been venymous, I woot it weel;
> I hem diffye, I love hem never a deel!   (3153-56)

The upshot of this *hominis confusio* is that he disregards his own argument and his own oracular wisdom, so that he may further show off his virile superiority by an athletic exhibition of sexual prowess—with leonine ferocity and princely pride (3179-84). Underneath the surface of this high-minded debate, then, lie the petty realities of human personality, the recognizable foibles and vanities so noticeably absent from the cardboard allegories of the *Melibeus*. The source of friction between Chauntecleer and Pertelote is larger than opposing dream theories or methods of argumentation, larger even than the sexual difference that assumes such prominence; it is a basic human pride energetically puffed up by the threatened ego, that familiar personalizing vice that hardens the determined positions and quickens aggressive reactions in all such controversies.

Such an analysis of these barnyard arguments is obviously a satiric reflex of the abuses of rhetoric and those self-imposed fictions that characterize so many of the Canterbury performances. It may at first seem needlessly reductive. It is not difficult to find pride or cupidity at the basis of all but the most saintly human behavior, but to do so usually means lowering criticism to the common denominators of moral preaching and ignoring the specific verbal texture. In the case of Chauntecleer and Pertelote, however, we are dealing with characters who represent, by generic definition, abstractions of human behavior, and the debate scene is so structured as to direct our attention away from the pontificated arguments to the obtrusively absurd motivations. Chauntecleer is, after all, introduced in such a way that everything that is most human about him is bound to be most ridiculous: his appearance and deportment, couched in heraldic color and the aristocratic diction of courtly romance, contrast at every point with the chiaroscuro but exemplary model of patient poverty, the widow and "maner deye" who happens to be his keeper. All of the admirable comic strokes in the first half of the *Tale* depend on the sudden reminders that this puffed-up language and passionate egotism, so unmistakable in its human foolishness, has been incarnated in a scarlet-eyed hen and a loud-crowing cock. What we laugh at in their performance is not the chickens, of course, but the generically distilled essence of prideful humanity, specifically (for, as the narrator reminds us, these are *talking* birds, 2880–81) the ingenious verbal smokescreens the human animal pours out to defend his vanity.

Chauntecleer's personality also governs the remainder of the *Tale*—not just the small deposit of Aesopian action that springs from his susceptibility to flattery, but also the manner of the telling. The narrator puffs forth so much rhetorical smoke that the story is ludicrously enveloped by it and almost disappears from sight. The structure of the *Nun's Priest's Tale* recalls that of the Merchant—debate followed by fable—but whereas the Merchant concentrates on projecting one man's imagination out of the debate into the symbolic literalism of the story, the Nun's Priest is more general and abstract. Just as Chauntecleer has no specific satiric referent, so too the manner of telling the tale is related to no particular pilgrim (least of all its virtually anonymous narrator), but to the general impulse of tale-telling itself, the abstract idea of man's tireless manufacture of self-assuring and self-inflating fictions.

E. Talbot Donaldson has touched on this aspect of the *Tale* with his penetrating comments on the way its satire of rhetorical practice alerts us to the motives that lurk beneath what is often dismissed as "a kind of cosmetic art." Rhetoric, he suggests, is "something more than language or adornment; it is, in fact, a powerful weapon of survival in a vast and alien universe. In our own times, as in the Middle Ages and in the Age of Homer, rhetoric has served to satisfy man's need for security and to provide a sense of the importance of his own existence and that of the whole human enterprise."[13] The Nun's Priest's rhetorical devices, too numerous to catalogue exhaustively, are of two kinds: first, the heroic-historical, beginning with the setting of the occasion in a time sequence that starts with the Creation, saffroning the high points with apostrophes and epic similes, and culminating with a chase in which Chauntecleer's fall proves to have the "cosmic reverberations" required by epic standards; and second, the more peculiarly medieval references to authority, from the lengthy and not especially relevant discussion of theologians on free will to such brief citations as the "Phisiologus" on the "mermayde." Above all, as a climax to the series of high-toned apostrophes, there is the authoritative "Gaufred," the master Geoffrey of Vinsauf himself, on the "sentence" and "loore" required to illuminate the cosmic irony of this Friday catastrophe befalling a servant of Venus on her day. This final appeal, to "that most formidable and dullest of medieval rhetoricians" in Donaldson's estimate,[14] is another of Chaucer's wittily audacious inversions of the modes of literary discourse. Placing the authority on rhetoric on the same figurative plane as "Destinee" and "Venus," implies their coequal reality. The manner of the telling—its verbal strategies—is on a par with the causal factors in a providentially governed universe. Hence, the forces of fictive manner—namely rhetoric with all its inflations and amplifications—assume an implied governance over the fictive matter, here the bare events of the Aesopian fable. To put it another way, the form, not free will or destiny, becomes the content or, to use the narrator's own jargon, the "chaf" becomes the "fruyt."[15]

The conclusion of the *Tale* gives us Aesop with a vengeance. "Taketh the moralite, goode men," says the Nun's Priest blithely, after presenting three formulations of a moral—one by the cock, one by the fox, and one of his own—none of which answers to the fable that has just been told *in the way it has been told*. In a literary work, "intellectual content, dianoia, thought, can be understood in two ways," according to Northrop Frye, "as a moral attached to a fable or as the structure of the fable itself."[16] But this modern critical commonplace would not have seemed obvious to a medieval audience, especially to the pilgrims whose Parson would tell them that fables are "draf," "wretcchednesse" retailed by "them that weyven soothfastnesse." At the least, a fable must offer a suitable "moralitee" that will permit the winnowing of all the chaff that goes into the telling.[17] But the *Nun's Priest's Tale* testifies to a creative instinct on Chaucer's part, however obliquely revealed, that stands outside the critical strictures of his age and rejects the deathly separation of form and meaning, the body and soul of literature. Yet, paradoxically, in so doing he offers the Parson a "meaning" very much to his taste. The true "moralitee" of the *Nun's Priest's Tale* extends the incidental abuses of language, "jangling" and "flaterye," to puncture all the inflation of human discourse by means of rhetoric and fictions as, in essence, a striving after wind.

Finally, what then is one to make of these concluding remarks of the Nun's Priest in which he seems to be bringing the ready-made formulae of contemporary preachers satirically to bear on an outrageously over-blown fable? They begin, "But ye that holden this tale a folye" (because it is about talking animals). This is not the introduction to an apology for the genre, as it would seem, but a way of raising questions about it that we might not have otherwise bothered to ask. In fact, one might not worry at all about the inadequacy of the "moralitee," were it not that the Nun's Priest insists that it justifies all that has gone before, all this folly of a tale: After all, "Seint Paul seith that al that writen is, / To oure doctrine, it is ywrite, ywis" (3441–42). Perhaps we do get a fitting moral for the *Tale*, but not from the narrator or the hero, but from the one who learns well by losing the most:

> "Nay," quod the fox, "but God yeve hym meschaunce,
> That is so undiscreet of governaunce
> That jangleth whan he sholde holde his pees."   (3433–35)

One might indeed say that the *Tale* is about "jangling," talking too much when one should hold one's peace. The tale is about that point at which the abuse of language touches upon the abuse of reason, when language separates itself from thought and takes on a meaning of its own. Chauntecleer abuses language, not only when he mistranslates Latin but when he uses his book-learning, his knowledge of dream theory and of argumentation, for purposes he finally and foolishly considers less important than satisfying his sexual vanity. The narrator pays him the dubious compliment of telling his story with a similar abuse—of authorities, or rhetoric, of literary genre and mode.

The narrator's mock-serious inflation of the tale ties the general abuse of language to the uses of fiction, or the process of fiction-making, thus commenting most appositely on the rationale of the *Canterbury Tales* themselves as a fictional construct. Certainly the Parson would agree that most of the pilgrims have been jangling when they should have held their peace, keeping their minds on the spiritual goal of the pilgrimage. And even most modern critics are willing to admit that many of the pilgrims have in the very act of story-telling revealed that about themselves which would have been better remedied by making peace with their Maker. The *Manciple's Prologue*, in which the Host accedes to the cynical treatment of the Cook and declares Bacchus the presiding genius of the pilgrimage, gives a rather grim indication of how far the goodly fellowship could degenerate. The tone seems to call for the Parson's uncompromising view of fiction-making to put things right.

But the *Nun's Priest's Tale* has already revealed Chaucer's radical ambivalence toward the rationale of fiction, though in a quintessentially Chaucerian fashion, by the elusively indirect logic of the imagination. On the one hand, the fable may seem to imply that the act of fiction-making is nothing but "worldly vanitee," a hubristic imitation of his Creator by fallen man, doomed from the start to authenticate little more than the authority of authorial pride. On the other hand, even such a self-deflating moral as this can only be properly expressed by the *experience* of fiction.

THE USES
OF FICTION:

"I WOOT AS
WEL AS YE"

*In poetry there is always
fallacy, and sometimes
fiction.*

SCOTT

THE Nun's Priest's splendidly ambiguous citation of a famous passage from St. Paul is, for all its comic exaggeration, typical of the medieval attitude to authority. Even the divine inspiration of Scripture did not prevent the wresting of a verse or phrase out of its biblical context, putting it to other and often quite contrary purposes. In this case, St. Paul, having just referred to a text from the Psalms (68:9), has only the Jewish scriptures in mind, when he interjects:

> Quaecumque enim scripta sunt, ad nostram doctrinam scripta sunt, ut per patientiam et consolationem Scripturarum, spem habeamus. (Rom 15:4)

Writing to Timothy, the Apostle is equally unambiguous about the kind of written word he considers useful to a perfecting of the faith:

> Omnis Scriptura divinitus inspirata, utilis est ad docendum . . . ut perfectus sit homo Dei, ad omne opus bonum instructus. (2 Tim. 3:16–17)

Robinson, rather misleadingly, glosses with this reference Chau-

235

cer's second recourse to the Pauline tag in what the Ellesmere rubric calls the "makere's" leave-taking of his book.

> And if ther be any thyng that displese hem, I preye hem also that they arrette it to the defaute of myn unkonnynge, and nat to my wyl, that wolde ful fayn have seyd bettre if I hadde had konnynge. / For oure book seith, "Al that is writen is writen for oure doctrine," and that is myn entente. (*ParsT*, 1082–83)

A sharp contrast to the Nun's Priest's playful moralizings, the sober piety of the "Retraction," whether we take it to be Chaucer's own or not, testifies to the range of tone and intention that one author could invest in a single scriptural commonplace. Both citations, however, show how far the passage had been removed from St. Paul's original purpose.

The liberalization of the Apostle's uncompromising view can be attributed to a long tradition of Christian humanism, apparent as early as Augustine but flowering in the twelfth century. Its basic doctrine, Professor Robertson tells us, was often stated "bluntly and emphatically":

> Thus St. Augustine wrote, "Every good and true Christian should understand that wherever he may find truth, it is his Lord's." A similar very broad view is expressed by John of Salisbury (*Policrat.* 7.10): "It is probable that all writings are to be read (except those that are forbidden), for not only all things written but all things done are believed to have been instituted for the utility of man, even though they are sometimes abused."[1]

A similar adaptation of Romans 15:4 is applied by Bersuire in the introduction to his *Reductorium Morale* and in the *Ovide Moralisée*.[2] In a still more secular context, Ralph Higden used the tag to equivocate on the veracity of his historical material:

> Wherfore in the writynge of this storie I take nought uppon me to aferme for sooth all that I write, but such as I have seie and i-rad in dyverse bookes, I gadere and write

with oute envie, and comoun to othere men. For the apostel seith nought, "All that is write to oure lore is sooth," but he seith "Al that is i-write to oure lore it is i-write."[3]

If Pauline authority could be used to justify historical "witness" that was no more than *fama diuturna*, "olde fame longe durynge," why not fables as well? Indeed, Robertson admits that, though St. Paul's epistles to Timothy and Titus constituted "the classical source of Apostolic instruction concerning preaching," the reproof of fable-mongers cited by the Parson in his *Prologue* (31–34) "was taken during the Middle Ages as applying to fables without any meaning or to fables whose meaning was heretical."[4] But the *Nun's Priest's Tale*, while certainly not heretical, undercuts its explicit "moralitee" by implicating the narrator in the "folye" of its characters. The antic disposition of the fable raises questions, however indirectly, about the meaning of "meaning." A logical extension of its imaginative vision would appear to join with the Parson in casting doubt on this so-called humanistic tradition and welcoming a return to the more strictly historical interpretation of St. Paul's injunctions. Such an illiberal view of the uses of fiction necessarily rules out tales that by the narrowest standards of "lollard" piety "sownen into synne." However inimical it may seem to the creative impulses that determined most of Chaucer's poetic activity, however destructive it in fact is to the entire canon of his most valued works, only a perverse exercise in critical casuistry[5] can dismiss the clear evidence that this was the position Chaucer took in his farewell to fiction.

Of course, the lot of the poet has never been an easy one. Attacks on the makers of fictions as little better than liars did not end with Plato. Their currency in the high Middle Ages is apparent in numerous incidental apologies for poetry, long before Boccaccio mounted his famous defense in the *De genealogia* against those who "say poetry is absolutely of no account, and the making of poetry a useless and absurd craft; that poets are tale-mongers, or, in lower terms, liars."[6] The

237

Natura of Alain de Lille had reviled "the dreamy fancies of
the poets" and their "naked falsehoods," but only to allow
that at times "in the shallow exterior of literature the poetic
lyre sounds a false note, but within speaks to its hearers the
mystery of loftier understanding, so that, the waste of outer
falsity cast aside, the reader finds, in secret within, the sweeter
kernel of truth."[7] Even Boethius's Lady Philosophy, though
she initially dismisses the meretricious muses of false consola-
tion, adorns her loftier discourse with their trumpery when
she intersperses harsh prose with elegant meters and indulges
in rhetorical role-playing. Nor has the suspicion of fiction-
makers been confined to the Middle Ages. In the eighteenth
century, Defoe had to contend with one young reader who
declared that "fictious stories" were "not fit they should be
read at all; nay that it was a Sin and that, as the making and
writing of them was criminal in itself, being, as she explained
it, what the Scripture meant by *making a lye*; so no pretended
Use that might be made of it, could justify the Action."[8] The
novelist's means of evading such strictures—to hide behind
specious historicity and a fictitious narrator—revivified those
transparent devices used centuries earlier by many medieval
poets, including Chaucer and his countless imitators.

But Chaucer's own progress as a fiction-maker led with an
inevitable logic toward the "Retraction." Paradoxically, while
from the beginning he exploited the evasive figure of the per-
sona and the authenticating potential of the dream-vision and,
later, of the second-hand narrative, the "olde bokes," he pressed
the logical implications of these techniques until they inverted
themselves, reversing the defense of fiction they had been in-
vented to support. This *volte face* represents an almost pre-
dictable consequence of the linking, in Chaucer's imaginative
reasoning, of his fictional apparatus with the problem of "ex-
perience and auctoritee." Consistently in Chaucer's works, a
substantial part of the significant action takes place in the en-
counter between the narrator and his narrative matter. It may
be a disjunction of the dreamer from the experience of his
dream or a conflict between the story-teller and his pre-estab-

lished story. Though the ascriptions vary, one pole in this drama of pseudo-creativity comes to be associated with experience, the other with authority. The tension between them unavoidably draws into the poem some of the epistemological issues that attach themselves to the terms in philosophic discourse.

But the polarization of experience and authority—alternative ways of apprehending what is in principle a single truth—proves in the fiction, as in philosophy, to be a misleading dichotomy. True wisdom utilizes all the resources at its command. The Chaucerian fiction exhibits a comprehensive epistemology by containing within its unitary structure bipartite elements that seem to be in opposition but interpenetrate imaginatively. Whether in a single character or in a conflict of interests, in the assumptions of a single genre or in a formal resolution of contrasting patterns, Chaucer records with extraordinary dramatic ingenuity the follies of man's search for knowledge.

The binary structure of Chaucer's imagining is apparent at every stage of his poetic development and in every aspect of his fictional enterprise. At times, he dramatizes the conflict within a fiction, as in the lectures of the Eagle, or the Friar's devil, who can tease the summoner about gaining professorial authority through his future experience. The devil, of course, as a fallen angel, still has direct access to knowledge unavailable to man; human epistemological distinctions are irrelevant to him. Chaucer also constructs debate scenes where the conflict is personified: Chauntecleer and Pertelote or Pluto and Proserpine are pure examples, the principles they represent are abstracted from the particularities of common mortal argumentation. The debate in the *Merchant's Tale* is complicated by January's "internal sense"; his faulty *vis cogitativa* is more like an animal lust and better described as a *vis aestimativa*—he knows what he likes. Placebo refuses the use of his higher faculties, but perversely cites authority for doing so, and Justinus alone argues from both received authority and his personal experiment in marriage.

But these fictional enactments are less significant than the formal consequences of Chaucer's epistemological imagination. The dream-visions with which he began his career have a built-in affirmation of the value of experience, which Chaucer handily exploits by making his dreamer a confirmed authoritarian or bookworm. Dreams afford access experientially to veridical knowledge, which the dreamer may simply record as in the *Book of the Duchess* or pass over as in the *Parliament of Fowls*. It may discover the truth about the fundamental unreliability of earthly judgments as in the *House of Fame*, but it may also emulate the unimpeachable revelations of visionary experience as in the *Prologue* to the *Legend of Good Women*. However it functioned, the dream-vision undoubtedly shaped, at a formative period, the structure of Chaucer's formal imagination and his sense of the inescapable epistemological problems inherent in the making of fictions.

This influence is everywhere apparent in Chaucer's first attempts at non-visionary narrative. Even the short exercises that compose the *Legend of Good Women* were taken by one early critic who read them satirically, as a "powerful protest against the domination of authority, a defense of experience as the only ultimately valid basis for knowledge."[9] More convincingly, many critics have argued that the formal architectonics of the *Knight's Tale* supports the thesis that Theseus alleges only by experience (3000–3001) but is in fact supported by authority, a thesis moreover in apparent contradiction to the experience of the lesser mortals in the *Tale*. *Troilus and Criseyde*, however, complicates the narrative process by incorporating a narrator who alternately represents the authority of the established chronicle and the experience of the sympathetic witness. The evaluation of the characters is further discriminated by their proper abilities to translate experience into approximations of Boethian authority, which makes it possible to see Troilus's "conversion" and quest for an absolute in love as an inclination toward the Christian experience, so disjunctively articulated in the "Epilogue."[10]

The *Canterbury Tales* projects this binary structure onto a larger fictional screen. The dramatic device of "quiting" another pilgrim's tale might be described as a means of responding to the unpalatable "authority" of the predecessor by the transmutation of the speaker's own experience into a fictional authority of comparable validity. The principle is obtrusive in the personal and professional flitings of the Miller-Reeve and the Friar-Summoner, and somewhat less explicit but unmistakable in the "Marriage Group." It operates also in what Barney calls the "anti-tales," those used as "foils for adjacent tales" (the Physician's and Second Nun's) or as "general parodies of certain literary excesses" (*Sir Thopas* and possibly the *Monk's Tale*).[11]

Internally, many of the *Tales* reflect a similar "bipartite structure or pace," the first part of which might be labeled " 'auctoritee' and is followed by 'plot machine.' "[12] The strict division into debate and fable or fabliau (the Nun's Priest and the Merchant) is formally the most apparent manifestation of such structures. The authority of a Chauntecleer or a January is actualized in the experience of the tale, in the latter case by the reification of those images by which he attempts to transform experience, in the former by the appropriation of the cock's rhetorical posturing into the conduct of the narrative. Other tales (the Physician's and the Manciple's) begin with authoritative sententiousness and are followed by experiential exemplification, which proves to be dubiously pertinent. The Pardoner constructs his sermon in this way, hypocritically but with a sharp eye for relevance, and the Summoner provides a dramatic setting for the whole of his friar's sermon, but follows it with realization of the man's theme in his own rage and its subsequent public exposure and analysis.

The structure of the *Summoner's Tale*, more graphically than some of the others, comments on the nature of man in general. Confined within a body of brutish physicality, the human spirit is dependent on its external senses for experiential knowledge. But the *intellectus agens*, the image of God within man, attempts to confirm its divine origin by the disciplines of mind that in rational discourse commune with universals. By

241

investing oneself with philosophic authority, one may rise to the status of an Angelic Doctor of the Church. But one may equally well follow the path of Lucifer and hear his pretensions to moral authority answered by the scientific ingenuity of an impertinent young squire. Again and again within the *Tales*, the pilgrims' attempts to raise experience to the level of fictional authority are refuted by a higher authority. So Justinus exposes the folly of January. So, too, the Pardoner condemns himself with the Scripture from his own filed tongue, and the Wife of Bath fails to bring the counsel of true "gentillesse" out of her fiction into her life. The true authority may lie outside the tale, tacitly evoked by its own actions or precepts. So the Reeve chooses to ignore, "Vengeance is mine, saith the Lord," and the Prioress forgets Matthew's injunction to turn the other cheek. But as a community of fictive authorities, the pilgrims behave much like the philosophers of old and the Fathers of the Church, who, in Roger Bacon's view, by correcting the errors of their predecessors, confirm the fallibility of all human knowledge.

Whether one wishes to call him a skeptical fideist or not, Chaucer's understanding of the uses of fiction is profoundly Christian. The creation of a fictive universe assumes an analogy of human invention to the transcendent power of Nature, whose divine authorization transmutes the disparities of human experience into an accordant whole. The dramatic interplay between experience and authority conforms to the Boethian view of Nature set forth in the *Parliament*—a unity of diverse and contentious oppositions, a harmony inaudible to mortal ear though composed of human discordance and elemental strife. Thus, one perspective on the Christian imagination encourages the poet to contemplate his fictions as an art which mends and even changes nature "but the art itself is nature."

Another, less promising analogy may, however, suggest itself for this fictive translation of the base material of experience into the purer forms of poetic authority. The temptations of the Canon's Yeoman's "sliding science" may, from another point of view, seem to attend the literary process as well. Like the alchemical, fictional experimentation remains firmly within the bounds of the experiential world, and its rationale, too, is flimsily built upon linguistic ambiguities. The vitality of the created world is deduced from the immanence of its divine Author, while the transforming power of the human creator or scientist depends upon his ability to alter or reorient the dynamic energies of nature, either human or material. The appeal of such terms as "maker" and "auctoritee" is seductive but double-edged, like the jargon of alchemy. As the Yeoman discovers, "multiplication" may bring one's good to naught, and "mortification," instead of shaving the "quick" of quicksilver, only succeeds in mortifying the experimentalist. The illusion of imitating divinity may be a "derke fantasye" like Dorigen's intemperate obsession or January's self-reflecting imagination. The very words of verbal fictions, like the terms for its practitioner, are slippery, full of what Criseyde calls "amphibologies."

The problems inherent in language itself, since they further complicate the authority of the fiction, predictably come to the fore in the *Canterbury Tales*. The Manciple anticipates the Parson when he asserts that, not only fables, but the words of which they are constructed may lie. "Capitayn" and "theef" can have a common moral referent, and a whore is a whore, whether a "wenche" or a "lady." As in the *General Prologue*, social and professional considerations discolor the precision of ethical terminology. Conversely, "Death" in the *Pardoner's Tale* can mean a "privy theef" or eight bushels of gold as well as the inexplicit abstractions and moral processes discovered in the dramatic irony. In the *Merchant's Tale* the verbal images of the hero's imagination acquire a material substance, while the demands of the Franklin's heroine, by a chain of agencies, cause things to disappear. Moral responsibility depends on language; "the word moot nede accorde with the dede," says the Manciple (208), only to conclude that the wisest course is to say nothing at all.

If words are unreliable, the fable, an aggregate of words,

243

compounds the falsehood by multiplying the lies. The thematic logic of the Manciple's comments links his Fragment strongly to the animadversions of the Parson and the "Retraction." "The wordes moote be cosyn to the dede" is the narrator's rationale in the *General Prologue* (742) for reporting the precise words of his fellow pilgrims. But not even the authority of a "Plato" can obscure the reminder of how far we have been removed from whatever reality words may be thought to designate. Whereas the Manciple had shown that words "fictionalize" moral values by supplying misleading labels, here the narrator compromises language by proclaiming its kinship to ficticious deeds in the name of an idealist linguistic theory. The poet, posing as a mere reporter, claims to be reproducing accurately the words of fictive pilgrims as they produce fictions of their own, yet the equation between sign and thing is expected to hold as true as it did for "Plato" or Augustine. The irony depends upon the juxtaposition of a straightforward mirror image against what appears to be an infinite regression—mirror reflecting mirror *ad infinitum*. The linguistic hero seems to be, not some Neoplatonic theorist, but Ockham: reasoning has become the property of signs.

But, of course, the reasoning itself is fictive. To find Ockham here is to mistake the nature of the object. "Fiction is not philosophy" would, in fact, be one way of glossing the irony of the narrator's citation of "Plato." Chaucer draws much of his irony from just such a mistake in kind—mistaking experience for authority or vice versa, mistaking one fictive level for another or for another mode of discourse or even another reality. While this characteristic mode of irony is what enables one to extract theoretical inferences from his fictions, it is also essential to his comic spirit. The irony is both critical and sustaining; it allows Chaucer to entertain the viciousness of fictions in the very process of creating them. Hence, the "Retraction" can be the logical conclusion to a work that is no more deterred by man's literary sins than his deadly ones from taking genial delight in recreating them. Chaucer's is a human not a divine comedy; in its limitations lie its riches.

NOTES

Table of Abbreviations

AJP	American Journal of Philology
AnM	Annuale Mediaevale
CE	College English
ChauR	Chaucer Review
Crit	Criticism
CritQ	Critical Quarterly
EIC	Essays in Criticism
ELH	English Literary History
ES	English Studies
JEGP	Journal of English and Germanic Philology
JHI	Journal of the History of Ideas
MÆ	Medium Ævum
Med Stud	Mediaeval Studies
MLN	Modern Language Notes
MLQ	Modern Language Quarterly
MP	Modern Philology
Neophil	Neophilologus
NM	Neuphilologische Mitteilungen
NQ	Notes and Queries
PMLA	Publications of the Modern Language Association of America
PQ	Philological Quarterly
RES	Review of English Studies

SP Studies in Philology
Spec Speculum
TSL Tennessee Studies in Literature
TSLL Texas Studies in Literature and Language
UTQ University of Toronto Quarterly

Experience and Authority

1. Jill Mann, *Chaucer and the Medieval Estates Satire* (Cambridge, Cambridge University Press, 1973), has produced the most subtle analysis of Chaucer's ironic method.

2. For the general medieval context of the terms see Ernst Robert Curtius, *European Literature and the Latin Middle Ages*, trans. Willard R. Trask (New York, Pantheon Books, 1963), Excursus IV.

3. See Horace, *Ars Poetica*, 343–44, and compare Sidney, *The Defense of Poesie, Prose Works*, ed. A. Feuillerat (Cambridge, Cambridge University Press, 1968), III, p. 10.

4. See *Middle English Dictionary*, ed. Hans Kurath and Sherman M. Kuhn (Ann Arbor, University of Michigan Press, 1954–), s. v. *auctorite*, 4(b).

5. For a convenient summary of the attitudes toward the veracity of fiction before the Renaissance, see William Nelson, "The Boundaries of Fiction in the Renaissance: A Treaty between Truth and Falsehood," *ELH* 36 (1969), reprinted in *Fact or Fiction: The Dilemma of the Renaissance Storyteller* (Cambridge, Mass., Harvard University Press, 1973).

6. M.-D. Chenu, *Toward Understanding St. Thomas*, trans. Albert M. Landry and Dominic Hughes (Chicago, Henry Regnery Company, 1964), pp. 130–31. See also his article, "Auctor, Actor, Autor," *Archivum latinitatis medii aevi*, 3–4 (1927–28), 81–86.

7. *Toward Understanding*, p. 129.

8. See Etienne Gilson, *Reason and Revelation in the Middle Ages*, the Richards Lectures in the University of Virginia (New York, Charles Scribner's Sons, 1938). See also Guy de Broglie, *Revelation and Reason*, trans. Mark Pontifex (New York, Hawthorn Books, 1965) and C.R.S. Harris, *Duns Scotus* (Oxford, The Clarendon Press, 1927), I, ch. 2.

9. *Reason and Revelation*, p. 32.

10. See D. W. Robertson, Jr.'s introduction to his translation of *On Christian Doctrine* (Indianapolis, Bobbs-Merrill, 1958).

11. *The Soliloquies of St. Augustine*, trans. Thomas F. Gilligan (New York, Cosmopolitan Science and Art Service Co., Inc., 1943), pp. 104–5.

12. *Periphyseon (De diuisione naturae), Liber Primus*, ed. and trans. J. P. Sheldon-Williams, Scriptores Latini Hiberniae (Dublin, Dublin Institute for Advanced Studies, 1968), p. 189. I owe this reference to Donald Duclow.

13. Trans. Douglas M. Moffat (New Haven, Yale University Press, 1908), p. 30.

14. Gordon Leff, *Medieval Thought from Saint Augustine to Ockham* (Baltimore, Penguin Books, 1958), p. 258.

15. Ibid., p. 271. On the other hand he asserted that "a genuine metaphysical principle" is never "contradicted in individual instances. One criterion of its truth is its agreement with experience" (The word is not Scotus', however). See Roy R. Eifler, *John Duns Scotus and the Principle "Omne quod movetur ab alio movetur."* (St. Bonaventure, New York, The Franciscan Institute, 1962), p. 94.

16. Leff, *Medieval Thought*, pp. 282–83.

17. Ibid., p. 282, quoting from the *Sentences*, Bk. I, Prologue. See *Scriptum in librum primum sententiarum ordinatio*, ed. Gedeon Gal (St. Bonaventure, New York, The Franciscan Institute, 1967), I, 30–38.

18. Leff, *Medieval Thought*, p. 291.

19. *Chaucer's House of Fame: The Poetics of Skeptical Fideism* (Chicago and London, University of Chicago Press, 1972). Skepticism itself is a symptom of Chaucer's interest in epistemology; like logic, according to Aristotle, it is a propaedeutic study.

20. Leff, *Medieval Thought*, pp. 297, 299.

21. *Select English Works of John Wyclif*, ed. Thomas Arnold (Oxford, The Clarendon Press, 1871), III, 508.

22. The word, of course, does not mean "reason," but "demonstration" (in this case, literary exempla), yet it is closer to the vocabulary of logic than "experience." Lawlor uses "pref" instead of the ubiquitous "experience" in his *Chaucer*; see esp. p. 45, where he equates it with "what we may know from our own experience (and, if only tentatively, apply to others)." See also the *Squire's Tale*, 482, where "werk" is opposed to "auctoritee."

A possible exception is *SNT*, 15, where "by resoun" is used where one would expect "experience," since it is sensory observation of the physical manifestations of sloth—sleeping and eating—which is at issue, not the spiritual dimension of the vice, which is understood by a higher faculty, or perhaps by faith as in the preceding stanza.

23. Karl Lehmann in his article on "Experience," *Sacramentum Mundi* (New York, Herder and Herder, 1968).

24. Robert Edward Brennan, *Thomistic Psychology* (New York,

Macmillan, 1941), p. 378. See also Murray Wright Bundy, *The Theory of Imagination in Classical and Medieval Thought*, University of Illinois Studies in Language and Literature, Vol. XII, Nos. 2–3 (Urbana, The University of Illinois Press, 1927) and Charles Aloysius Hart, *The Thomistic Concept of Mental Faculty* (Washington, D.C., The Catholic University of America, 1930), pp. 6–24, for a more complete summary of the pre-medieval faculty theories.

25. For this summary, I am indebted to the works cited in note 24 and to Rudolf Allers, "Intellectual Cognition," *Essays in Thomism*, ed. Robert E. Brennan (New York, Sheed and Ward, 1942), pp. 39–62.

26. Ibid., 46.

27. Brennan, *Thomistic Psychology*, p. 134.

28. Ibid., 145.

29. *Commentary on the Posterior Analytics of Aristotle*, trans. F. R. Larcher (Albany, Magi Books, 1970), p. 237.

30. Cited by J. Peghaire, *Intellectus et Ratio selon S. Thomas d'Aquin* (Paris, Vrin, 1936), p. 187.

31. For a brief summary of the "Origins of Latin Aristotelianism," see Fernand van Steenberghen, *Aristotle in the West*, trans. Leonard Johnston (Louvain, E. Nauwelaerts, 1955).

32. A. C. Crombie, "Grosseteste's Position in the History of Science," *Robert Grosseteste*, ed. D. A. Callus (Oxford, The Clarendon Press, 1955), p. 100. I am indebted to this essay for much of my discussion of Grosseteste.

33. The quotations are from his *De Lineis, Angulis, et Figuris* and his commentary on the *Posterior Analytics*; see Crombie, "Position," 107, 108.

34. See J. Loserth, *Johann von Wiclif und Robert Grosseteste* (Vienna, Alfred Hölder, 1918).

35. On Grosseteste's influence at Oxford see A. C. Crombie, *Robert Grosseteste and the Origins of Experimental Science* (Oxford, The Clarendon Press, 1953), Chs. 7–8. Also, J.A.W. Bennett, *Chaucer at Oxford and at Cambridge* (Toronto, University of Toronto Press, 1974), summarizes the intellectual picture at Oxford in Chaucer's lifetime.

36. See Ludwig Baur, "Der Einflus des Robert Grosseteste auf die Wissenschaftlishe Richtung des Roger Bacon," *Roger Bacon Essays*, ed. A. G. Little (Oxford, The Clarendon Press, 1914),

pp. 33–54, as well as the editor's introduction, "On Bacon's Life and Works."

37. *Opera quaedam hactenus inedita*, ed. J. S. Brewer (London, Longman, Green, Longman, and Roberts, 1859), I, 59.

38. *Opus Maius*, ed. John Henry Bridges (Oxford, The Clarendon Press, 1897), I, 2.

39. *Opus Tertium*, ed. Brewer, *Opera*, I, 73.

40. Ibid., 71.

41. *Opus Maius*, ed. Bridges, II, 167; English translation from A. C. Crombie, *Robert Grosseteste and the Origins of Experimental Science*, 141.

42. *Opus Maius*, II, 169–70.

43. See Hieronymus Wilms, *Albert the Great* (London, Burns, Oates, and Washbourne, 1933). The emphasis in these works is on detailed, precise, scientific observation and first-hand experience. Phrases such as "I saw," "I observed," "I could establish the fact" punctuate the texts. The scientific premise of Albertus's work is repeated again in his writings:

> We are not seeking a reason or explanation of the divine will but rather investigating natural causes which are as instruments through which God's will is manifested. It is not sufficient to know these things in a general sort of way; what we are looking for is the cause of each individual thing according to the nature belonging to it. This is the best and most perfect kind of knowledge. (*De causis proprietatum elementorum*, lib. I, tr. I, cap. 9)

> In this sixth book *De vegetabilibus* we satisfy the curiosity of our students rather than that of Philosophy itself. Therefore we will propose certain things more known to us and leave others out altogether. Of those which we shall treat, some we shall prove from our experience, whilst others we shall leave to the dicta of men who, as we have ascertained, do not say things lightly but base everything on experience. This method alone can give certainty in such things.
> (*De vegetabilibus*, lib. 6, tr. I, cap. i.)

From these and many such statements, it is clear that even the Seraphic Doctor could doff his scholastic cap when he chose and rely on experience, rejecting all authority that was not also thus responsibly established.

44. *Opera*, ed. Brewer, I, 397. I am grateful to Fr. Synan of the Pontifical Institute in Toronto for this and other references.

45. The idea, though not the vocabulary, may have come to Chaucer from the French, perhaps Jean de Meun. The ME *Romaunt* 4690 has Reason play on the contrast of "experience" and what is written, but the word translates "conoissance." The OF "experiment" performs the function of Chaucer's "experience" in *Roman* 7964, 8726, 12775, among others. Charles Muscatine, *Chaucer and the French Tradition* (Berkeley and Los Angeles, University of California Press, 1957), discusses the last passage, the speech of the Duenna, p. 83, and attributes the "increasing valuation of direct experience" to Averroism in particular, p. 77.

Poetic Fictions

1. As Derek Brewer has reminded us in "The Relationship of Chaucer to the English and European Traditions," *Chaucer and the Chaucerians* (University of Alabama Press, 1966), and P. M. Kean has reiterated in her introduction to *Chaucer and the Making of English Poetry* (London and Boston, Routledge and Kegan Paul, 1972).

2. See James Wimsatt, *Chaucer and the French Love Poets* (Chapel Hill, The University of North Carolina Press, 1968).

3. See Constance B. Hieatt, *The Realism of Dream Visions* (The Hague and Paris, Mouton and Co., 1967).

4. The observer, as P. M. Kean, *English Poetry*, II, 80, maintains, is "an essential part of the machinery of Chaucerian comedy." The literature on Chaucerian *persona* is vast and has been summarized by Robert M. Jordan, "Chaucerian Narrative," *Companion to Chaucer Studies*, ed. Beryl Rowland (London, Oxford University Press, 1968), esp. pp. 89–92, and most recently by Thomas J. Garbáty, "The Degradation of Chaucer's 'Geffrey'," *PMLA* 89 (1974), 97–104. Especially useful for the poems of this and the next section is Dorothy Bethurum, "Chaucer's Point of View as Narrator in the Love Poems," *PMLA* 74 (1959), 511–20. E. T. Donaldson's article, "Chaucer the Pilgrim," *PMLA* 79 (1954), 928–36, can now be appreciated as seminal, and though his position has been contested and qualified, it stands behind much of the best of modern Chaucerian criticism, as Jill Mann, *Estates Satire*, triumphantly confirms. For a larger view of this medieval

device, see Leo Spitzer, "Note on the Poetic and the Empirical 'I' in Medieval Authors," *Traditio*, 4 (1946), 414–22, and Alice Miskimin, *The Renaissance Chaucer* (New Haven, Yale University Press, 1975), Ch. III.

5. Wimsatt, *French Love Poets*, 85, points out that there is a precedent, however slight, for the inclusion of a "reading" in the dream-vision.

6. The problem was by no means a new one. Winthrop Wetherbee, *Platonism and Poetry in the Twelfth Century* (Princeton, New Jersey, Princeton University Press, 1972), analyzes the climate of thought in a period of undoubted transitional importance for Chaucer and other secular writers. In the hands of Bernardus Silvestris and Alain de Lille, poetry became a vehicle for philosophic speculation of a high order. Their poetic reformulation of Christian theology in terms of Platonic cosmology conferred a greater respectability on Nature and gave a new impetus to the creative expression of human psychology, which prepared the way for vernacular writers with more exclusively worldly themes. See also George D. Economou, *The Goddess Natura in Medieval Literature* (Cambridge, Mass., Harvard University Press, 1972), and E. R. Curtius, *European Literature*, Ch. 6, and Excursuses VII–XII.

7. For an excellent discussion of Chaucer's response to his audience and to the higher demands of morality, see Alfred David, "The Man of Law vs. Chaucer: A Case in Poetics," *PMLA* 82 (1967), 217–25.

I. The *Prologue* to the *Legend of Good Women*

1. *The Fall of Princes*, ed. Henry Bergen (London, Oxford University Press, 1924), Bk. I, Pro, 1. 330.

2. These lines are omitted in the G version, which was probably an attempt to salvage the *Prologue* after the death of Anne, in consideration of Richard's associations with the palaces mentioned. Other changes suggest a similar concern: the removal of much of the imagery drawn from the "religion of love," the incorporation of more of the action into the dream, the earlier identification of the queen as Alceste, all point to a desire to lower the intensity of the personal emotion and obscure the correlation of the experience in the poem with events outside it. I accept unabashedly the identi-

fication of Alceste with Anne, first suggested by Ten Brink in his *Studien* (1870) and vigorously expounded by J.S.P. Tatlock, *The Development and Chronology of Chaucer's Works* (Chaucer Society, 1907). Robinson's notes list the objections and alternative proposals offered since, but I remain convinced and trust that my analysis indicates the reasons for my support. The literal-minded quibbles of Kittredge, "Chaucer's Alceste," *MP* 6 (1909), 435–39, simply reflect an imperfect understanding of the flexibility of medieval allegory.

3. *Fall of Princes*, Bk. I, Pro., ll. 335–36.

4. Robert Worth Frank, Jr., *Chaucer and the Legend of Good Women* (Cambridge, Mass., Harvard University Press, 1972), has mounted a strong case for appreciating the necessary experimentation with narrative techniques at this point in Chaucer's career, but hesitates to claim more than occasional abiding literary merit.

5. (New Haven and London, Yale University Press, 1963).

6. John Gardner's analysis of the G text, "The Two Prologues to the *Legend of Good Women*," *JEGP* 67 (1968), 594–611, however, suggests that the changes made would accord with the emphases of this chapter—toward a more serious view of love, a more Christian "God of Love," and a neoplatonic implication that "human love typifies divine love" (611).

7. Delany, *House of Fame*, 23–25, takes these lines as an example of Chaucer's fideism, the "leap of faith" required when experience is unavailable and even authority seems to be in question, but the lines do not admit an interpretation of more than the common pious believer's willingness to accept on faith, authority of supernatural experiences.

8. Cf. esp. 53–54 and 84–96. The identification of the "Bernard, the Monk" by Skeat had been questioned but was further supported by Roland M. Smith, "The Limited Vision of St. Bernard," *MLN* 61 (1946), 38–44, and Marie P. Hamilton, "Bernard, the Monk: Postscript," *MLN* 62 (1947), 190–91. Smith's "evidence" is primarily a poem in the Vernon ms. called "Lamentations of St. Bernard," in which the Saint requests information of the Blessed Virgin on the celestial sights. That work, or the tradition behind it, may have served as a "source" not only for the ecstatic language addressed to the Lady in Chaucer's poem but also for the dramatic situation, in which the comic "limitations" of the poet-persona are played off against the queenly authority of the intercessor, Alceste.

9. He translated it in the *Prologue* to the *Second Nun's Tale*, revised it for the Prioress, and echoes it in Troilus's hymn (III, 1261ff.). See Robert A. Pratt, "Chaucer Borrowing from Himself," *MLQ* 7 (1946), 259–64.

10. As he does, translating from the *Legenda Aurea*, in the Legend of St. Cecilia, *Second Nun's Tale*, ll. 85ff. On "Etymology as a Category of Thought," see Curtius, *European Literature*, Excursus XIV.

11. *Commentary on the Dream of Scipio*, trans. W. H. Stahl (New York, Columbia University Press, 1952), p. 90.

12. See D. W. Robertson, Jr., "The Pearl as a Symbol," *MLN* 65 (1950), 155–61, for a four-level interpretation, and A. C. Spearing, *The Gawain Poet* (Cambridge, Cambridge University Press, 1970), for a more flexible reading.

13. See Charles S. Singleton, *Dante Studies 1, Commedia: Elements of Structure* (Cambridge, Mass., Harvard University Press, 1954).

14. She pleaded (on her knees) to Gloucester for Burley's life in 1388, was a "conciliatory influence" in Richard's quarrels with the Londoners in 1392, was well spoken of even in the Lancastrian chronicles as a "peace-lover and peace-maker," and called "illa benignissima domina" by Adam of Usk. See Harold F. Hutchinson, *The Hollow Crown* (London, Eyre and Spottiswoode, 1961), esp. pp. 120, 139, 144.

15. Perhaps reflecting Richard's almost pathological devotion to his Queen, exhibited in his forsaking of the royal residence of Shene at her death and ordering its destruction. See Gervase Mathew, *The Court of Richard II* (London, John Murray, 1968), pp. 17, 34.

II. The *House of Fame*

1. Except to Norman E. Eliason, *The Language of Chaucer's Poetry* (Copenhagen, Rosenkilde and Bagger, 1972), pp. 186–91, who proposes that the lack of the final "tiding" is part of a plan to squash the rumor of some scandal.

2. *Chaucer and The Tradition of Fame* (Princeton, New Jersey, Princeton University Press, 1966).

3. *Chaucer's Book of Fame* (Oxford, The Clarendon Press, 1968).

4. The phrases are all from Delany, *Chaucer's House of Fame*, 49.

5. James Winny, *Chaucer's Dream-Poems* (New York, Barnes and Noble, 1975), pp. 104–105, sees the imagination as the true subject of the poem, "the nature of literature and in particular the kind of creative activity which poetry involves."

6. Winter settings and barren landscapes are found in some of the French dream-visions, but their function is usually a pathetic response to the melancholy or mournful condition of the speaker, as in Henryson's "Ane doolie sessoun to ane cairfull dyte," *Testament of Cresseid*, l. 1.

7. Bennett, *Book of Fame*, 7.

8. The choice of the word "tidings," a verbal noun, rather than "tale" or "knowledge" reflects this interest in process.

9. An anticipation of Book III, 1214ff., and the external decorations of the House of Fame. On the medieval attitude to pagan authors, see Curtius, *European Literature*, Excursus VI.

10. Compare the *SNT*, 338–39, where "engyn" falls between "memorye" and "intellect" as one of man's three "sapiences." Winny, *Chaucer's Dream-Poems*, 33ff. and 86f., finds the passage as significant as I do, though he does not take into account the Italian, when he emphasizes the meaning of *wrot*, "created, wrought."

11. The physics of sound, like optics, fascinated the early scientific philosophers. Ockham shows the consequences of such "intuitive knowledge" by using the example of the vibrations of a long chord to infer the possibility with an infinity of cause and effect, thereby rejecting any possible demonstration of God's existence by means of a first cause. See Leff, *Medieval Thought*, 286–87.

12. Bennett, *Book of Fame*, 101.

III. The *Book of the Duchess*

1. Wimsatt, *French Love Poets*, p. 116, finds a similar pattern in Machaut's *Fonteinne Amoreuse*, where the lady "evidently was the Duke's wife in real life, but is portrayed poetically as a courtly mistress."

2. The allegorical interpretation of Bernard F. Huppé and D. W. Robertson, Jr., *Fruyt and Chaf* (Princeton, New Jersey, Princeton University Press, 1963).

3. As proposed by Bertrand H. Bronson, "*The Book of the Duchess* Ro-opened," *PMLA* 67 (1952), 863–81, esp. 870.

4. See Lynn Veach Sadler, "Chaucer's *The Book of the Duchess* and the 'Law of Kynde,'" *AnM* 11 (1970), 51–64, whose view of the "Law" is limited, however, to the operations of "'rowthe' or 'pitee'," and functional in this poem only in the experience of the dreamer.

5. For a summary of these systems, see Bundy, *The Theory of Imagination*, Ch. IX.

6. Boethius, *The Consolation of Philosophy* Bk. V, pr. 4, trans. Richard H. Green (Indianapolis and New York, Bobbs-Merrill, 1962), pp. 110–111.

7. Compare the similar experience of a "sely" old man in the *Miller's Tale*, 3612, 3834; but also *Troilus*, I. 365.

8. See Bundy, *Theory of Imagination*, p. 41.

9. Macrobius particularly defends the use of fables about Nature as used by philosophers to clothe that which Nature would otherwise have found distasteful if exposed to uncouth men. See his *Commentary on the Dream of Scipio*, trans. W. H. Stahl (New York, Columbia University Press, 1952), p. 86, and Economou, *The Goddess Natura*, p. 20.

10. As, for example, in the theory of symbolism of pseudo-Dionysius introduced into the West by John the Scot. For an excellent summary, see M.-D. Chenu, *Nature, Man and Society in the Twelfth Century*, trans. Jerome Taylor and Lester K. Little (Chicago and London, The University of Chicago Press, 1968) pp. 123ff.

11. As, for example, in the formulation of Gilbert of la Porrée summarized by Chenu, *Nature, Man and Society*, 40–41: "The relationship to God's creative work conferred a religious significance upon human productive activity; the relationship to the work of nature provided such activity with its earthly standard of truth." See also Curtius, *European Literature*, Excursus XXI.

12. See Economou, *The Goddess Natura*, 26–27, on the "three-fold division of creativity," reflected in a passage of the *Physician's Tale*: "Nature, who creates in the sublunary world by divine appointment of the principal creator of the universe, challenges the most famous of human artists to match her work. They cannot match it, of course, and were they to try, their vain attempt would be a presumption." See also Kean, *English Poetry*, II, 60.

13. Compare the living form given the sounds that arrive at the House of Fame.

14. *The Allegory of Love*, p. 169.

15. It is possible, I admit, to interpret the dreamer here as merely courteous and tactful, but I find this view less plausible dramatically and inconsistent with the persona Chaucer develops unmistakably in the later dream-visions and the *Troilus*. Either reading will suit my thesis in this chapter, however. The best known supporter of the "tactful" position is B. H. Bronson in the article cited in note 3; more recently Wolfgang Clemen, *Chaucer's Early Poetry*, trans. C.A.M. Syn (London, Methuen and Co. Ltd., 1965), pp. 49–50, and Kean, *English Poetry* I, 57–66, have been influential corroborators. For a contrary view and good bibliography of the periodical literature, see Martin Stevens, "Narrative Focus in the *Book of the Duchess*," *AnM* 7 (1966), 16–32.

16. That is, the literal level of the allegory, the kind of thing Lewis provides in Ch. III of the *Allegory of Love*.

17. An interesting gloss on this passage may be found in Maurice Valency's interpretation of the Narcissistic element in *fin amor, In Praise of Love* (New York, The Macmillan Co., 1958), p. 26.

18. Compare de Quincey, "On the Knocking at the Gate in *Macbeth*," *Literary Criticism*, ed. H. Darbishire (London, Henry Frowde, 1909), p. 149: "The pulses of life are beginning to beat again, and the re-establishment of the goings-on of this world in which we live, first makes us profoundly sensible of the awful parenthesis that has suspended them."

Philosophic Fictions

1. Usk and Hoccleve, respectively, cited by Caroline F. E. Spurgeon, *Five Hundred Years of Chaucer Criticism and Allusion* (Cambridge, The University Press, 1925), I, 8, 22.

2. The term may put off many scholars. Poetized philosophy, such as Pope's *Essay on Man*, for example, has not been a popular or critically accessible mode in this century. Recent theorists have tended to maintain that any narrative is susceptible to some kind of abstract interpretation—its "theme," if not the "underlying allegory" or "moral," *dianoia*, or most evasively, "what it is *about*." On the other hand, the philosophic content claimed for many poetic fictions is beneath the contempt of the true philosopher—

at its best, fodder for the historian of ideas; at its worst, conventional platitudes.

3. *Commentary on the Dream of Scipio*, trans. Stahl, p. 85.

4. The tradition has been well catalogued by D. S. Brewer in his edition, *The Parlement of Foulys* (London and Edinburgh, Thomas Nelson and Sons, Ltd., 1960), by J.A.W. Bennett in his "Interpretation," *The Parlement of Foules* (Oxford, The Clarendon Press, 1957), and George D. Economou, *The Goddess Natura*.

5. The following citations refer to Macrobius's prefered category, "the only type of fiction approved by the philosopher who is prudent in handling sacred matters," Stahl's trans., p. 85.

6. Kean, *English Poetry*, II, 42, similarly observes in this connection that Chaucer drew upon that "which would have its full share of what Lovejoy has aptly called 'philosophical pathos,' that is, which involves ideas with the power, within a given period, to exert a strong emotional effect on the audience. . . . In his handling of philosophical matter, it is always considerations of this kind which concern Chaucer: His aim is always to make structural use within his poem of the ideas he takes from the philosophers, not to explore and develop their meaning for its own sake."

7. See Paul G. Ruggiers, *The Art of the Canterbury Tales* (Madison and Milwaukee, The University of Wisconsin Press, 1965), pp. 152f.: "Although we cannot accuse Chaucer of being a philosopher, he is so sympathetic with the Boethian view that he adduces with considerable frequency attitudes and commentary of the more moral kind from the *Consolatio*. Not only were these views compatible with the religious views he held; artistically they were useful and provocative."

8. On the implications of the form, see R. H. Green in his introduction to the *Consolation*, p. xxxvi.

9. "What Chaucer Really Did to *Il Filostrato*," *Essays and Studies by Members of the English Association*, 17 (1932), 56–75.

10. See the chapter on "narrative structure" in Kean, *English Poetry*, II, Ch. 2, for some cogent remarks on Chaucer's use of epic and romance.

IV. The *Parliament of Fowls*

1. Most notably by those commentators mentioned in note 4 of the preceding section. Economou's "reading" of the poem, pp. 125–

50, is comprehensive, economical, and to my mind, at all points, convincing. Payne, *Key of Remembrance*, 139–44, is perceptive but somewhat skeptical about the structure in its relation to content.

2. Not, however, to F. W. Bateson, whose medieval obtuseness is spelled out in detail in *A Guide to English Literature* (2nd ed.; Garden City, New York, Anchor Books, 1968), pp. 18–19. Ian Robinson's rebuttal in *Chaucer and the English Tradition* (Cambridge, Cambridge University Press, 1972), Ch. 1, is one of his happier moments, and I trust he will understand my eagerness to work these stanzas over once again—along with D. S. Brewer, *Parlement*, 48ff.; H. S. Bennett, *Chaucer and the Fifteenth Century* (New York, Oxford University Press, 1947), pp. 89ff.; and Dorothy Everett, *Essays on Middle English Literature* (Oxford, The Clarendon Press, 1955), pp. 103ff., most of whom are primarily concerned with the presence of rhetoric in these stanzas rather than Chaucer's fascinating deviousness.

3. "Ars longa, vita brevis": The aphorism of Hippocrates is cited by Seneca in the first paragraph of his moral essay, *De Brevitate Vitae*. See, for another Middle English example, *The Cyrurgie of Guy de Chauliac*, ed. Margaret S. Ogden (London, Oxford University Press, 1971), p. 11: "The lyf is schort, þe craft forsoþe is long, experiment is deceyuable, dome is hard."

4. Brewer, *Parlement*, p. 49.

5. Kean, *English Poetry*, I, 67, comments on this "major" theme in the poem, and in her excellent discussion rivals Bennett with abundant documentation of its philosophic underpinnings.

6. The reflection of twelfth-century philosophers in the poem is strikingly suggested by the summary of their explanation of the *Timaeus* given by A.-J. Festugière, cited in Chenu, *Nature, Man and Society*, 21: "The world-intelligence contemplates the beauty of the ideal realm, and it is in virtue of this contemplation that it imposes upon the universe the ordered movement we see. In consequence, the world is truly an 'order,' a *kosmos*. To be sure, disorder is found within it, not, however, as an essentially evil thing but only as a lesser good. There could be no 'order' without a multiplicity of beings, each consequently limited; or without a diversity of beings, each consequently endowed with a greater or smaller share of goodness. If, therefore, one considers only a part of the whole, one necessarily discovers limits or privations of goodness, disorders. But this is precisely because one is looking only at

a part, not the whole. If one makes the effort to comprehend the whole in a single view, the disorder disappears; it becomes explicable within the whole and becomes absorbed in the total order. Always look to the whole—such will be the rule of this self-consciously optimistic philosophy."

7. Boethius, *The Consolation of Philosophy*, ed. G. K. Rand, Loeb Classical Library (Cambridge, Mass., Harvard University Press, 1953), p. 222.

8. *Consolation*, 356.

9. By the happy device of the bird assembly, Chaucer avoids the issue of "sacred marriage rites of chaste loves," raised in the Boethian metrum. In Martianus Capella's *De Nuptiis*, it is Hymen who, like Chaucer's Nature, is "conceived as a cosmic power which, 'constraining contentious particles with mysterious bonds, preserves union in discord by its divine embrace'," Wetherbee, *Platonism and Poetry*, 84, and he is the reconciler of opposites in the *De Planctu* of Alain de Lille as well. But Chaucer manages to suggest that the union of opposites defines natural life, without having to address himself to the question of marriage and its sacrament.

10. The speculations of the twelfth-century Platonists on sexuality form an important and insufficiently acknowledged foundation for late medieval thought. See esp. Winthrop Wetherbee's discussion, *Platonism and Poetry*, 183–85, of Bernardus Silvestris's highly suggestive imagery in the *De Mundi Universitate*; and Kean, *English Poetry*, II, 165–71.

11. See Economou's well-reasoned discussion, *The Goddess Natura*, 145ff. P. M. Kean, however, finds a significant and potentially pessimistic note in the differences between the order of birds: "Mankind, for whose dilemmas the noble birds stand, is left to grapple with the problems set them by an endowment which is not wholly Nature's and which, while it places heaven or hell within their reach, makes the simple happiness of the duck difficult to achieve," *English Poetry*, I, 84. Such hints, though far from dominant in the *Parliament*, anticipate the *Troilus* and recall Wetherbee's perception of a dark side to the *Consolation* and the tragic implications of Silvestris's celebration of human sexuality. See *Platonism and Poetry*, 77–82, 181–86.

12. Jill Mann, *Estates Satire*, 201, makes a similar observation about the *General Prologue*.

V. Palamon and Arcite

1. Perhaps the only point over which I would take serious issue with Economou; see *The Goddess Natura*, 143.

2. Muscatine, *French Tradition*, 181.

3. The number five, according to Martianus Capella in Book 7, *De Arithmetica* (ed. Dick, pp. 369–70), represents the cosmos. It is called a "recurrent" number, and astronomically that term refers to the return of a celestial body to the starting point of its orbit. Proclus (*Inst.* 199) uses it specifically to indicate the "return of the soul." Since Boethius seems to have conceived of his work as a kind of literary image of the cosmos and since the return of the *mens* to its proper home is its theme, the associations with the number may have influenced Boethius's division of his work into five books. (I am indebted for the above information to Myra L. Uhlfelder.) That Chaucer was influenced by Boethius's example to extend the number of books in the *Troilus* would be difficult to prove. Nevertheless, the "prohemium" to IV (exp. 26–28) suggests that the further book was a later thought, prompted perhaps by the additional bulk given the narrative by the Boethian passages and the piece from the *Teseida* which supplies a literal enactment of the "return of the soul." For other suggestions on the structural indebtedness to Boethius, see John P. McCall, "Five-Book Structure in Chaucer's Troilus," *MLQ* 23 (1962), 297–308.

4. *The Story of Troilus*, trans. R. K. Gordon (New York, E. P. Dutton & Co., Inc., 1964), p. 28. The Italian is "scudo verisimilmente del mio segreto e amoroso dolore," in the edition of Vittore Branca, *Tutte le Opera di Giovanni Boccaccio* (Mondadori, 1964), II, 21.

5. That the *Knight's Tale* antedates its Canterbury telling is attested by the catalogue of early works set into the *Legend of Good Women*, which includes "al the love of Palamon and Arcite / Of Thebes, thogh the storye ys known lite," (420–21). But what form the tale might have taken then is a matter of difficult conjecture. Had it been in rime-royal stanzas like the *Troilus*, the reworking to suit the voice of the Knight and the new dramatic situation is so thorough that the rhymed couplets have obscured all trace of a previous incarnation. Perhaps any chronological hypothesis is equally foolhardy, for though the *Tale* shares with the *Troilus* so

many thematic preoccupations as well as the combination of Boccaccian and Boethian sources, there is no guarantee that Chaucer's creative activities were as neatly compartmentalized as the literary historian would wish.

6. J.S.P. Tatlock, *The Development and Chronology of Chaucer's Works*, Chaucer Society Publications, 2nd Ser., No. 37 (London, 1907), pp. 231–33. The weakness of characterization, however, was noted as early as 1929 by J. R. Hulbert, "What was Chaucer's Aim in the *Knight's Tale?*" *SP* 26 (1929), 375–85, and the lack of significant distinction between the two cousins is assumed by most of the recent critics: Ruggiers, *Art*, 157f.; Robinson, *English Tradition*, 108; and Kean, *English Poetry*, II, 4.

7. Robert A. Pratt's summary of stanzas 49 and 50 of Book III, in *Sources and Analogues of Chaucer's Canterbury Tales*, ed. W. F. Bryan and Germaine Dempster (London, Routledge and Kegan Paul, Ltd., 1941), p. 95.

8. See Muscatine, *French Tradition*, 178ff.

9. See H. N. Fairchild, "Active Arcite, Contemplative Palamon," *JEGP* 26 (1927), 285–93, and the less extreme claim for significant differentiation in the important article of William Frost, "An Interpretation of Chaucer's *Knight's Tale*," *RES* 25 (1949), 290–304.

10. *French Tradition*, 178.

11. Dale Underwood, "The First of *The Canterbury Tales*" *ELH* 26 (1959), 455–69.

12. Many critics of the *Tale* have noted the symbolic importance of architecture as well as the act of construction itself: Robert M. Jordan, *Chaucer and The Shape of Creation* (Cambridge, Mass., Harvard University Press, 1967), p. 179, cites the concept of man as *homo faber*; while Kean, *English Poetry*, II, 22–25, reminds us of the literary and historical contexts for such a notion, and of Chaucer's tenure as Clerk of the Works.

13. See Richard Neuse, "The Knight: The First Mover in Chaucer's Human Comedy," *UTQ* 31 (1962), 299–315, esp. 303, and the discussion of Ian Robinson, *English Tradition*, 127ff. Kean's chapter on the *Knight's Tale*, which in my opinion supersedes most earlier discussions, especially in the subtlety and well-documented, original interpretations of some aspects of planetary deities, sees this aspect of Chaucer's narration as a return to the methods of Statius and Virgil (II, pp. 2 ff.).

14. See Walter Clyde Curry, *Chaucer and the Mediaeval Sciences* (rev. ed.; New York, Barns and Noble, Inc., 1960), pp. 119ff.

15. Following a tradition known as the "Children of the Planets," according to Kean, *English Poetry*, II, 25f.

16. Kean, 29ff., makes a case for a more complex understanding of Saturn's function: as a force for order (under Providence) and as a figure of Wisdom by virtue of his age (the "good" tradition of planetary influence found in Macrobius and Alexander Neckham, see p. 32) playing *theoretikon* to Jupiter's *vis agendi*, as Egeus does to Theseus in Part IV. Chaucer's reference to such traditions is certainly well hidden in the *Tale*, except in ll. 2443–49, but the argument is clearly worth pondering.

17. Kean, *English Poetry*, II, 48–52, more thoroughly than the many others before her, stresses the symbolic importance of marriage here: as a Boethian conjunction of opposites—male and female, death and love, sorrow and joy—and, as God's gift to man (Genesis 1:27–28), not at the mercy of Fortune. See her discussion of marriage in II, Ch. 4.

18. A similar point is made by Dale Underwood in the excellent article cited in note 11, and by Trevor Whittock, *A Reading of the Canterbury Tales* (Cambridge, Cambridge University Press, 1968), pp. 69ff. Underwood's argument is attacked by Jordan, *Shape of Creation*, 158f., but the difference resides, I believe, more in the theoretical terms used than in the particular critique. The question of the relation of form to content has been needlessly confused by the use of such ambivalent terms as "organic" and "gothic," each of which can mean both the rambling parataxis of natural growth and the perfectly conceived integration of part to whole, found in the cells of a living organism and the cruciform plan of a cathedral. The interrelationship of these terms and their semantic relativity has been explored by Arthur Lovejoy, "The First Gothic Revival and the Return to Nature," *MLN* 27 (1932), 414–46, which should have dispersed the confusion long ago.

19. The structure suggests, not only Boethius, but the dialectic of skepticism described by Delany, *House of Fame*, the discords of sublunary Fortune being resolved by Destiny in the person of Theseus, who acts throughout the poem as a force of union. As ruler he enforces a beneficent union of the martial and venusian; in both conquest and marriage, he comes to exemplify the ideal fusion of justice and mercy.

20. See, for example, the perverse discussion of Elizabeth Salter, *Chaucer: The Knight's Tale and the Clerk's Tale* (London, Edward Arnold, 1962).

21. Neuse, "The Knight," 312ff.

22. Kean, *English Poetry*, II, 11, refers Arcite's mention of "purveiaunce of God, or of Fortune" (1252) to IV, pr. vi, but only to illustrate his ignorance of the true distinction. Her analysis of Theseus's speech, pp. 41–48, contains, however, valuable documentation that adequately refutes the recent criticism of its logic.

23. Economou, *The Goddess Natura*, 29.

24. Underwood, for example, "The First of the *Canterbury Tales*," 462 and, more recently, Robinson, *English Tradition*, 118–21. Kean refutes this reading convincingly by her explication of Chaucer's use of the word, "conqueror" (*English Poetry*, II, 6–9), and analysis of Theseus's *magnanimitas* (II, 176). A still more unsympathetic view of the Duke is found in Henry J. Webb, "A Reinterpretation of Chaucer's Theseus," *RES* 23 (1947), 289–96.

25. Compare *Troilus*, III, 1282ff.

26. See, however, Robinson's useful discussion of the "tragic" aspects of the poem in *English Tradition*, 118–21.

VI. *Troilus and Criseyde*

1. Ed. Wilhelm Meyer, "Die Arundel Sammlung mittellateinischer Lieder," *Abhandlungen der kgl. Gesellschaft der Wissenschaften zu Göttingen*, 11 (1909), p. 22; see Wetherbee, *Platonism and Poetry*, 141–42.

2. The theme of Ida L. Gordon's sensitive but not entirely satisfactory analysis in *The Double Sorrow of Troilus* (Oxford, The Clarendon Press, 1970).

3. Compare Kean, *English Poetry*, II, 2: "While in the *Troilus*, in fact, Chaucer gives us a philosophical treatment of a love story, in the *Knight's Tale* a love story forms the pretext for a philosophical poem."

4. See for example Ian Robinson's chapter on the poem, *English Tradition*, 73ff., but note Kean's comment on the *Knight's Tale*: "We are not, in this tale, to be too closely involved with what Henry James likes to refer to as the victims bleeding in the arena—towards whom, too, he has much of Chaucer's attitude of com-

passionate, occasionally half-exasperated irony, and whom he also likes to view through the eyes of an observer only partially involved in the struggle," *English Poetry*, II, 15.

5. See Charles A. Owen, Jr., "The Significance of a Day in *Troilus and Criseyde*," *Med Stud* 22 (1960), 366–70, and Donald R. Howard, "Experience, Language, and Consciousness: *Troilus and Criseyde*, ll. 596–931," in *Medieval Literature and Folklore Studies: Essays in Honor of Francis Lee Utley*, ed. J. Mandel and B. A. Rosenberg (New Brunswick, N.J., Rutgers University Press, 1971). Jill Mann, *Estates Satire*, 199–200, offers a remarkably similar description of Criseyde's portrayal. (Her excellent book appeared after my chapter had been some time written.)

6. *The Book of Troilus and Criseyde*, ed. Robert K. Root (Princeton, Princeton University Press, 1945), p. lxxiii.

7. On the salvation of the "noble pagan," see *La Légende de Trajan*, by Gaston Paris, Bibliothèque de l'Ecole des Hautes Etudes, Fasc. 35 (1878); *St. Erkenwald*, ed. I. Gollancz (London, Oxford University Press, 1922), pp. xxxviii ff; and for Chaucer's familiarity with the possibility, *SqT*, 16–71.

8. The use of the historical setting is fully discussed by Donald R. Howard, *The Three Temptations* (Princeton, Princeton University Press, 1966), pp. 115ff.

9. Troilus's gain in eloquence in Book III (from the speechlessness of the opening scene to the concluding Boethian hymn) contrasted with Boccaccio's Troilo, who merely heats up his already overheated passion, nicely points up the fundamental alteration Chaucer has made in the values attached to the experience dramatized.

10. Compare the ending of Boccaccio's Canto III where the impending misfortune is explicitly included. Chaucer not only postpones this material to the next book, but also expands upon the narrator's satisfaction with the successful termination of this formal unit.

11. R. G. Collingwood, *The Idea of Nature* (New York, 1960), p. 88.

12. On the descent through the spheres, see Macrobius, I, xii, 13–14, cited by Kean, *English Poetry*, II, 31, and on the re-ascent, John M. Steadman, *Disembodied Laughter: Troilus and the Apotheosis Tradition* (Berkeley, University of California Press, 1972).

13. The term is borrowed from Muscatine's comment on the Envoy to the *Clerk's Tale, French Tradition*, p. 197.

14. See ibid., 165.

15. I use the term not in a technical, philosophic sense, but to refer to the fundamental and unalterable aspects of human life, "birth, copulation, and death," as T. S. Eliot put it.

16. Erich Fromm, *Man for Himself* (New York and Toronto, Rinehart and Co., Inc., 1947), p. 44.

17. Ibid.

18. Wetherbee, *Platonism and Poetry*, 82.

19. Ibid., 122.

20. Guillaume de Conches, *Philosophia*, i, 19, quoted in Reginald Lane Poole, *Illustrations of the History of Medieval Thought and Learning* (2nd ed.; New York, Dover Publications, Inc. 1960), p. 108.

VII. Patient Griselda

1. On the genre, see Dieter Mehl, *The Middle English Romances of the Thirteenth and Fourteenth Centuries* (London, Routledge and Kegan Paul, 1969), Ch. 5.

2. Chaucer even denies her "the gift of tongues" found in Trivet's heroine and calls attention with historical accuracy to the "maner Latyn corrupt" of her speech (519), a phrase that J. Burrow, *MAE* 30 (1961), 33–37, traces to Isadore's *Etymologiae*.

3. The generic situation is delicate and complex: while the Greek romance requires a "comic" resolution of the narrative in earthly terms, the hagiographic element permits terrestrial suffering and even martyrdom, if the focus is on otherworldly values. The historical adaption places the emphasis on continuity within time, but Chaucer's excerption of the tale from the chronicle deliberately removes such a possibility (see 1121–27) and emphasizes the generic incongruity. Apologists for the *Tale* such as Kean (*English Poetry*, II, 117) have been forced to give undue consideration to the narrator's assumed intentions, found in the interpolated rhetorical passages but not in the conduct of the narrative. Morton Bloomfield, "The Man of Law's Tale: A Tragedy of Victimization and a Christian Comedy," *PMLA*, 87 (1972), 384–90, ignores the text in calling the end of the *Tale* comic and

citing only "Joye after wo" in the penultimate line of the poem, the formulaic benediction.

4. Ruggiers, *Art*, 170. For a thorough examination of the alterations from the source, see Edward A. Block, "Originality, Controlling Purpose and Craftsmanship in Chaucer's *Man of Law's Tale*," *PMLA* 68 (1953), 572–616, who finds an "irreconcilable dualism of purpose."

5. See John A. Yunck, "Religious Elements in Chaucer's *Man of Law's Tale*," *ELH* 27 (1960), 249–61, and Paull F. Baum, "*The Man of Law's Tale*," *MLN* 64 (1949), 180–93.

6. See Robert T. Farrell, "Chaucer's Use of the Theme of the Help of God in the *Man of Law's Tale*," *NM* 71 (1970), 239–43.

7. Bloomfield's argument in "Tragedy of Victimization" fails where his treatment of the *Troilus* does not, because of this lack of an unambiguously defined narrator. Compare "Distance and Predestination in *Troilus and Criseyde*," *PMLA* 72 (1957), 14–26.

8. See Robert Enzer Lewis, "Chaucer's Artistic Use of Pope Innocent III's *De miseria humane conditionis* in the Man of Law's Prologue and Tale," *PMLA* 81 (1966), 485–92, who raises the possibility of unflattering characterization in the *MLP*; Alfred David, "The Man of Law vs. Chaucer: A Case in Poetics," *PMLA* 82 (1967), 217–25, who describes the Man of Law as a "fool and perhaps also something of a knave" (219); and Rodney Delasanta, "And of Great Reverence: Chaucer's Man of Law," *ChauR* 5 (1970), 288–310, who takes the matter even farther, pointing out factual errors in the Man of Law's "rhetorical excess" and connecting his "religious exhibitionism" with the "medley of unnamed legalists" in the Gospels and with Lollard denunciations.

9. *French Tradition*, p. 191.

10. See James Sledd, "*The Clerk's Tale*: The Monsters and the Critics," *MP* 51 (1953–54), 73–82, for a survey of these attitudes and an anticipation of some aspects of the interpretation offered here.

11. An example of "late medieval sensibility," according to Kean, *English Poetry*, II, 128, who finds that the story "suffers in part from an excess of meaning, in part from the very urbanity which makes it impossible for Chaucer to come down emphatically on one side or the other, and which ensures his success in so

many other works," a judgment that echoes Elizabeth Salter's in her pamphlet on this and the *Knight's Tale*, but is surprising from one who writes so well on the Knight's performance.

12. The translation is from James H. Robinson and Henry W. Rolfe, *Petrarch* (New York and London, G. P. Putnam, 1898), pp. 195–96, and was cited by A. S. Cook, "The First Two Readers of Petrarch's Tale of Griselda," *MP* 15 (1918), 633–43. The Latin text may be found in *Originals and Analogues of some of Chaucer's Canterbury Tales*, ed. F. S. Furnivall, et al., Chaucer Society, 2nd Ser., v. 10 (London, Oxford University Press, repr. 1928).

13. Particularly that of Griselda, whose patience he believes impossible, though Petrarch concludes the letter by citing classical models of virtue who were nonetheless historical.

14. J. Burke Severs includes a discussion of "Chaucer's Treatment of His Sources" in Ch. IV of *The Literary Relationships of Chaucer's Clerkes Tale* (New Haven, Yale University Press, 1942).

15. See esp. ll. 359ff. and 650–51, not discussed by Severs.

16. "The Clerk admits the opposition purposely, so willingly and extravagantly as to make safe from vulgar questioning the finer matter that has gone before," *French Tradition*, 197. See also Jordan, *Shape of Creation*, p. 207: "The Clerk's envoi forms a concentric ring of wit around the tale."

17. See Barbara Bartholomew, *Fortuna and Natura* (The Hague, Mouton and Co., 1966), pp. 58–63.

18. Robinson, *English Tradition*, 164–71, makes a similar claim "that the greatness of *The Clerk's Tale* is in its profound exploration of patience, and that that is the kind of achievement that is paid for at great cost, demanded of more than the intellect!" (though he regrets the "happy ending").

Psychological Fictions

1. It will be obvious to all Chaucerians that I am reviving here the infamous "dramatic propriety" theory—which G. L. Kittredge, *Chaucer and His Poetry* (Cambridge, Mass., Harvard University Press, 1915), has been blamed for originating, and R. M. Lumiansky, *Of Sondry Folk* (Austin, University of Texas Press, 1955), for driving into the ground. This thesis has taken much battering of late from all sides—from the radical allegorists of the Robert-

sonian school, from the "middle-of-the-roaders" such as Bronson and Jordan, and even from the right-wing, "plain common-sense" types such as Eliason. These attacks have proved to be a necessary corrective to the over-zealousness of ingenious students, especially those required to publish. But with the desirable modifications and qualifications made in response to these critiques, it remains, I believe, the underlying assumption of many of the best modern critics—Muscatine, Donaldson, Owen, Lawlor. See, for example, Kean's statement that, in the most complex figures of the *Canterbury Tales*, Chaucer "explores and exploits more fully than had ever been done before all the opportunities for the development of character afforded by the device of the series of tales within a frame," *English Poetry*, II, 156.

2. See M.L.S. Lossing, "The Order of the Canterbury Tales: a Fresh Relation between A and B Types of MSS.," *JEGP* 37 (1938), 153–63.

3. See Muscatine, *French Tradition*, 216–17, and Bruce A. Rosenberg, "The Contrary Tales of the Second Nun and the Canon's Yeoman," *ChauR* 2 (1968), 278–91.

4. See Raymond Preston's comment: "The only thing I find in Chaucer's version of the tale that obviously fits the reputation of a physician is the professionally brisk manner of piling the corpses." *Chaucer* (London and New York, Sheed and Ward, 1952), p. 228.

5. Stephen A. Barney, "An Evaluation of the *Pardoner's Tale*," *Twentieth Century Interpretations of the Pardoner's Tale*, ed. Dewey R. Faulkner (Englewood Cliffs, Prentice-Hall, 1973), pp. 83–95, calls such performances "anti-tales" and gives the most perceptive analysis to date of the formal and thematic interrelationships among these opening pairs.

6. R. G. Collingwood, *Idea of History*, 231.

VIII. The Canterbury Experiment

1. For example: in the homely simile covering Chaucer's abridgement, 886–87; in the passage on "gereful" lovers, 1531ff.; and on the serious consequences of romantic games, 2714 ("for they wolde hir lymes have") and 2759–60.

2. See E. T. Donaldson, "Idiom of Popular Poetry in the Miller's Tale," *Eng. Inst. Essays*, 1950, ed. Alan S. Downer, pp. 116–40,

and the numerous subsequent articles listed by Ruggiers in his note, *Art*, p. 57.

3. The final pages of William Frost's article, "An Interpretation of Chaucer's *Knight's Tale*," *RES* 25 (1949), 290–304, suggest that the *Miller's Tale* provides a dramatic context and "a certain artistic distance to its predecessor." See also William C. Stokoe, Jr., "Structure and Intention in the First Fragment of the *Canterbury Tales*," *UTQ* 21 (1952), 120–27, and Charles A. Owen, Jr., "Chaucer's *Canterbury Tales*: Aesthetic Design in Stories of the First Day," *ES* 25 (1955), 49–56, who find the parallelism and paradox of the *Knight's Tale*, carried into the pairing of the next tales with each other. For more recent comments, see Ruggiers, *Art*, 55–56, and Kean, *English Poetry*, II, 94–95.

4. See Muscatine, *French Tradition*, pp. 224–26.

5. Robinson, *English Tradition*, 97–98, alone (to my knowledge) among the critics, finds the *Tale* "wholly consistent" with the Miller's character and extends the "poetic justice" even to Alison, whose "reward" is to have a tale of "farting and hairiness" attached to her.

6. Paul A. Olson, "Poetic Justice in the *Miller's Tale*," *MLQ* 24 (1963), 227–36, justifies the use of the fabliau by its implied moral purpose, in this case, the exposure of the sins of lechery, avarice, and pride, exemplified in its three male characters, but equally embodied in the teller himself.

7. See Ruggiers, *Art*, 66n., for a summary of the pertinent bibliography and a comparison with the *Miller's Tale*, p. 71 and n. Though he also finds in the *Tale* a response of the teller's personality (pp. 57, 67, 79), Ruggiers discusses the *Prologue* as a significant extension of the *General Prologue* portrait, but questions its integration to the *Tale* (pp. 67–70).

8. Jill Mann, *Estates Satire*, 163, chides Curry for not quoting the whole of the description of the choleric man, yet fails to mention Chaucer's ironic use of impulsive, wrathful, and lecherous characteristics of the type in the Reeve's *Prologue*.

9. See Muscatine, *French Tradition*, 200, and M. Copland, "The Reeve's Tale: Harlotrie or Sermonyng?" *MÆ* 31 (1961), 14–32, who also finds "psychological duplicity behind the Reeve's cultivation of a priestly appearance," but defends the fabliau with a sophisticated argument that allows a measure of true moral objection to remain in the Reeve's not "wholly irresponsible carica-

ture" of the Miller in Symkyn. He finds in the "superior 'realism' " of the *Reeve's Tale* a critique of the Miller's "aesthetic vision of life supplied by Chaucer that is the equivalent in the realm of art to the life-attitudes embodied in the behaviour of the 'real-life' Miller" (30–31). Paul Olson, "The Reeve's Tale: Chaucer's Measure for Measure," *SP* 59 (1962), 1–17, uncovers a moral purpose in the exposure of the Reeve's assumption of the role of "merciless judge" in a tale whose principle of justice is based on a logical measure of punishment proportional, not to specific sins as in the *Miller's Tale*, but "to the will to do evil" exhibited by Symkyn.

10. See esp. A. H. MacLaine, "Chaucer's Wine-Cask Image: Word Play in the Reeve's Prologue," *MÆ* 31 (1962), 129–31.

11. Robinson's note to line 3876 suggesting Luke 7:32 provides a source too slight to be noticed, if indeed it is not simply proverbial as in *TC*, II, 1107.

12. Walter Benjamin, "The Storyteller: Reflections on the Works of Nikolai Leskov," *Illuminations*, ed. Hannah Arendt (New York, Harcourt, Brace and World, Inc., 1955) pp. 83–110, has some pertinent remarks on the relationship between the storyteller and his audience, and the changes that occurred with the shift to a solitary, novel-reading audience.

13. See esp. 1322–23 and the justly famous 1354.

14. Aspects of this verbal pattern are also spelled out by Richard H. Passon, " 'Entente' in Chaucer's *Friar's Tale*," *ChauR* 2 (1968), 166–71. Aquinas singled out intention, the *finis operantis*, as the most important "formal" element of morality; see Dom O. Lottin, *Psychologie et Morale aux xiie et xiiie siècles* (Louvain, Abbaye du Mont César, 1942–60), IV, 517. Most of the early literature on the *Friar's* and *Summoner's Tales* merely belabors the obvious dramatic ironies and has been subsumed in more recent full-scale treatments of the *Canterbury Tales*, of which Ruggiers's is perhaps closest to mine.

15. The term alludes to W. K. Wimsatt's discussion, "One Relation of Rhyme to Reason," *The Verbal Icon* (New York, Noonday Press, 1958), pp. 153–168.

16. The echo of some of the portrait's rhymes in the *Tale* is no doubt more than an audience might be expected to pick up, but suggests a concentration of intent on Chaucer's part.

17. The ironies of the Tale have been repeatedly explored; see

Earle Birney, "Structural Irony Within the *Summoner's Tale*," *Anglia*, 78 (1960), 204–18 and John F. Adams, "The Structure of Irony in *The Summoner's Tale*," *EIC* 12 (1962), 126–32.

18. On "Chaucer's Puns," see Paull Baum, *PMLA* 71 (1956), 225–46, and 73 (1958), 167–70, as well as Helge Kökeritz, "Rhetorical Word Play in Chaucer," *PMLA* 69 (1954), 937–52.

19. See *Inferno*, xxi, 139. Marie Borroff has called my attention to a passage in II Corinthians, which, as its proximity to the famous text perverted by the friar in 1794 ("lettre sleeth") confirms, lies behind this image. Paul is speaking of the true preachers of the Word: "Quia Christi bonus odor sumus Deo in iis qui salvi fiunt," 2:15.

20. See John V. Fleming, "The Summoner's Prologue: An Iconographic Adjustment," *ChauR* 2 (1967), 95–107.

21. See Kean, *English Poetry*, II, 89.

22. "The Parody of Pentecost in Chaucer's *Summoner's Tale*," *UTQ* 40 (1971), 236–46.

23. As do Paul E. Beichner, "Baiting the Summoner," *MLQ* 22 (1961), 367–76, and Paul N. Zeitlow, "In Defense of the Summoner," *ChauR*, 1 (1966), 4–19.

24. Jill Mann, *Estates Satire*, stresses the importance to Chaucer's satiric method of the "lack of systematically expressed values," particularly the confusion of moral and aesthetic appreciations by the narrator in the *General Prologue*; see esp. the discussions of these two figures and pp. 192ff.

25. It is difficult to understand Robertson's refusal, *Preface to Chaucer* (Princeton, Princeton University Press, 1962), to allow that moral evaluation was intimately allied with psychological process in the high Middle Ages. One need only glance at the six volumes of Dom O. Lottin, *Psychologie et Morale aux xii⁰ et xiii⁰ siècles* for theological support, and the innumerable works on the iconography of the vices and virtues which art and literary historians have supplied us with during the past fifty years.

26. In Walter Benjamin's terms, Chaucer combines the role of the secularized storyteller with the fiction of the chronicler or history-teller in the posture taken by the narrator of the framing story, thus implicitly providing an eschatologically determined perspective to the enclosed tales. See "The Storyteller," *Illuminations*, esp. pp. 95–97.

IX. The Pardoner and the Canon's Yeoman

1. George L. Kittredge, *Chaucer and His Poetry*, 211ff.

2. G. G. Sedgewick, "The Progress of Chaucer's Pardoner, 1880–1940," *MLQ* 1 (1940), 431–58.

3. R. M. Lumiansky, "A Conjecture Concerning Chaucer's Pardoner," *Tulane Studies in English*, 1 (1949), 1–29.

4. John Halverson, "Chaucer's Pardoner and the Progress of Criticism," *ChauR* 4 (1970), 184–202.

5. The recent collection of essays edited by Dewey R. Faulkner, *Twentieth Century Interpretations of Chaucer's 'Pardoner's Tale'* (Englewood Cliffs, Prentice-Hall, 1973) provides a bibliographical summary as well as choice excerpts and new material.

6. On the allegorical antecedents of the Pardoner, see Kean's discussion of Chaucer's use of Faux Semblant, *English Poetry*, II, 87–108, and Rosemond Tuve, *Allegorical Imagery: Some Medieval Books and Their Posterity* (Princeton, Princeton University Press, 1966), pp. 176–77.

7. The effectiveness of the *Tale* was assumed by Kittredge for generations after him. Only recently have the causes been seriously explored; see Ian Bishop, "The Narrative Art of the Pardoner's Tale," *MÆ* 36 (1967), 15–24; David V. Harrington, "Narrative Speed in the *Pardoner's Tale*," *ChauR*, 3 (1968), 50–59; and Stephen A. Barney, "An Evaluation of the *Pardoner's Tale*," in Faulkner's *TCI* collection, pp. 83–95, who contrasts its eloquence with the failure of the *Physician's Tale* and relates its famous dramatic ironies to the intelligence as well as the self-deception of the teller.

8. Charles Mitchell has explored the implications of the Pardoner's "truth," in "The Moral Superiority of Chaucer's Pardoner," *CE* 27 (1966), 437–44.

9. The most recent and comprehensive discussion of this generic problem is by Nancy H. Owen, "The Pardoner's Introduction, Prologue, and Tale: Sermon and *Fabliau*," *JEGP* 66 (1967), 541–49.

10. For the exegetical background of this concept, see Robert P. Miller, "Chaucer's Pardoner, the Scriptural Eunuch, and the *Pardoner's Tale*," *Spec* 30 (1955), 180–99.

11. On this relationship, see the notes on *GP* 163, by D. Biggins, *NQ* 6 (1959), 435–36, and B.D.H. Miller, *NQ* 7 (1960), 404–406.

12. From Maximian, as first pointed out by Kittredge, *AJP*, 9 (1888), 84f. Portions of the first Elegy were excerpted as early as the 11th century by Aimeric in his *Ars Lectoria*; see Edmond Faral, *Les arts poétiques du XIIᵉ et XIIIᵉ siècle* (Paris, Champion, 1958), p. 80.

13. For a summary of these interpretations, see John M. Steadman, "Old Age and *Contemptus Mundi* in the *Pardoner's Tale*," *MÆ* 33 (1964), 121–30, who finds that Chaucer takes us to "the frontiers of allegory but does not cross"; the old man belongs to a *memento mori* tradition as a type-figure, introducing into the *Tale* such antitheses as "youth and age, folly and wisdom, avarice and contemptus mundi" (130). See also Alfred David, "Criticism and the Old Man in Chaucer's Pardoner's Tale," *CE*, 27 (1965), 39–44, who considers him an archetype, like the Wandering Jew, but existing only within the *Tale* and exerting an influence on the pilgrim audience, correlative with the evil of the Pardoner, but "telling us something about the frustration, the suffering, the self-destructiveness of evil" (42).

14. This theme has been well delineated in terms of the Pardoner's eucharistic image of turning "substaunce into accident" (539) in the two original essays of Faulkner's *TCI* collection by Barney, "An Evaluation," and Janet Adelman, " 'That We May Leere Som Wit,' " pp. 96–106.

15. *On Christian Doctrine*, trans. D. W. Robertson, Jr. (Indianapolis and New York, Bobbs-Merrill, 1968), p. 84.

16. The implications of the Pardoner's performance for the fictive process have been discussed by G. D. Josipovici, "Fiction and Game in *The Canterbury Tales*," *CritQ* 7 (1965), 185–97, as well as by Barney and Adelman in the Faulkner *TCI*.

17. On the inversion of inner value and outward worthlessness expected of a symbol, see Stephen A. Khinoy, "Inside Chaucer's Pardoner?" *ChauR* 6 (1972), 255–67.

18. This reading of the *Prologue*, first offered by Kittredge, "The Canon's Yeoman's Prologue and Tale," *Trans Royal Soc of Lit* 30 (1910), 87, has since been challenged: by R. G. Baldwin, "The Yeoman's Canons: A Conjecture," *JEGP* 61 (1962), 232–43, who takes the Yeoman's statements about the Canon as ironical, indicating his readiness to break away; by John Reidy, "Chaucer's Canon and the Unity of *The Canon's Yeoman's Tale*," *PMLA* 80 (1965), 31–37, who points out that had they come to swindle the

pilgrims, the Yeoman had ready answers to the Host's remarks on their poverty (in the tradition of deceiving alchemists that extends into the Renaissance); and by John Gardner, "*The Canon's Yeoman's Prologue and Tale*: An Interpretation," *PQ* 46 (1967), 1–17, who finds the Yeoman intelligent and capable of subtle metaphysical intuitions, though comically unable to articulate them on his own.

19. *French Tradition*, pp. 213–221. His description of alchemy as a "universe of technology" that promotes a "complacent faith in science" is perhaps too specifically a reaction of the "atomic age" in spite of his support from Dante; it leads to some liberal pieties which distort the Yeoman's peroration. For a similar objection, see Bruce L. Greenberg, "*The Canon's Yeoman's Tale*: Boethian Wisdom and the Alchemists," *ChauR* 1 (1966), 37–54. But Muscatine's reading is for the most part superbly developed— a pioneer exegesis of a performance whose technical vocabulary and apparent inconsistencies had long frightened off the critics.

20. On the linguistic and symbolic ambiguities of this episode, see Joseph Edward Grennen, "The Canon's Yeoman and the Cosmic Furnace: Language and Meaning in the *Canon's Yeoman's Tale*," *Crit* 4 (1962), 225–40, and "Chaucer's Characterization of the Canon and His Yeoman," *JHI* 25 (1964), 279–84.

21. Significantly Plato is substituted for Solomon in the "book Senior" exemplum, perhaps to avoid association of the wise king, who "prophesied" the coming of Christ, with a "pagan" religion that inverted the symbols and theology of Christianity. See Gardner, "An Interpretation," 16–17.

22. Paull F. Baum, "The Canon's Yeoman's Tale," *MLN* 40 (1925), 152–54, notes the technical information required to understand the experiments alone.

23. Baldwin, for example, "The Yeoman's Canons."

24. See Reidy, "Unity," for a sympathetic reconstruction of the Canon's pathetic downfall.

25. The debate over the significance of this final passage began as early as 1477 with Norton's inclusion of the *Tale* in a book of alchemical lore. Ashmole embraced Chaucer as a fellow initiate, "one that fully knew the *Mistery*," but Tyrwhitt in his edition of 1775 considered the work an anti-alchemical statement, which anticipated the statutes against "multiplying" of 1403, and his position was not challenged until S. Foster Damon, "Chaucer and

Alchemy," *PMLA* 39 (1924). Two recent articles of great erudition have set the facts of the tradition, its theory and terminology, as straight as can be expected: Edgar H. Duncan, "The Literature of Alchemy and Chaucer's *Canon's Yeoman's Tale*: Framework, Theme, and Characters," *Spec* 43 (1968), 633–56, and Dorothee Finkelstein, "The Code of Chaucer's 'Secree of Secrees' ": Arabic Alchemical Terminology in *The Canon's Yeoman's Tale*," *Archiv* 207 (1970), 260–76.

26. John Holmyard, *Alchemy* (Penguin Books, 1957), pp. 72–73 cites the phrase as part of the title of Arnold's work *The Rosary of the Philosophers*, itself a borrowing from Al-razi (824–929). But Karl Young, "The 'Secree of Secrees' of Chaucer's Canon's Yeoman," *MLN* 58 (1943), 98–105, considered it a "generic term" for the alchemists' secret and Joseph E. Grennen, "Chaucer's 'Secree of Secrees': An Alchemical 'Topic,' " *PQ* 42 (1963), 562–66, has called it an ironic *topos*.

27. Muscatine's view that it is Chaucer who steps forward at the conclusion of the *Tale* has been accepted by several critics. Gardner ("An Interpretation,") finds it necessary that the Yeoman's "wisdom" be narrated by another, and Judith Scherer Herz (*"The Canon's Yeoman's Prologue and Tale*," *MP* 58 [1961], 231–37), who interprets the ending as the achievement of "social reconciliation" by joining the pilgrimage for one who has "little moral imagination, but a strong sense of himself, which enables him to change during his performance," nonetheless considers the final lines to be imposed from without.

X. The Monk and the Prioress

1. Jill Mann (*Estates Satire*) extends brilliantly the relevance of the "victim" throughout her discussion of the pilgrims—from the "victimless" misdoer to those who prey upon the innocent, and others, like the Reeve and Summoner, whose victims are equally corrupt.

2. I suspect that the majority of the collected tragedies do belong to an early period, but the four "modern instances" must belong to a time after 1385, the year in which Bernabó Visconti "fell," by which time we assume Chaucer had arrived at the maturity of his poetic powers. The insertion of these four tragedies between the least well-paired of the other exempla, Zenobia and Nero, may

have been on Chaucer's mind when he has the Monk comment on his imperfect chronological memory (1984-90). A similar self-consciousness about the accommodation of old material to the Canterbury format may have resulted in the remarks of the pilgrim Chaucer on his translation of the *Melibeus* with its extra padding of proverbs (VII, 943ff., esp. 955-58).

3. Kean, *English Poetry*, II, 130, comments on the "complacent, pounding beat of the verse."

4. See John F. Mahoney, "Chaucerian Tragedy and the Christian Tradition," *AnM* 3 (1962), 81-99, who attempts to salvage the Monk's definition by extending it: "the fall of a man from high degree, but as a representation of life whereby the unpleasant and frail about man and his postlapsarian world are reconciled with the Divine Plan of Providence, by which the tragic, gaining no more attractiveness and pleasantness, gains a certain economy in the work of God in the Christian view" (94). The article also contains a useful corrective to Robertson's emphasis on Troilus' "wrong" love by reference to a comparable instance in the *Purgatorio* 17.

5. The classic discussion of this matter is Howard R. Patch, *The Goddess Fortuna in Medieval Literature* (Cambridge, Mass., Harvard University Press, 1927), whose crediting of Boccaccio as Chaucer's inspiration has been corrected by R. W. Babcock, "The Medieval Setting of Chaucer's 'Monk's Tale,'" *PMLA* 46 (1931), 205-13, who quotes F.N. Robinson in a classroom lecture as claiming that Chaucer's work "grew out of the *Roman*." Edward M. Socola, "Chaucer's Development of Fortune in the Monk's Tale," *JEGP* 49 (1950), 159-71, finds the "increasing personification" of Fortune the unifying factor in the *Tale*.

6. R. E. Kaske, "The Knight's Interruption of the *Monk's Tale*," *ELH* 24 (1957), 249-68, believes the Monk to be a grotesque parody of the Knight and his tale, an attempt at imitation that misfires.

7. Florence H. Ridley, *The Prioress and the Critics* (Berkeley, University of California Press, 1965), gives an excellent survey and assessment of the criticism of the portrait in the *General Prologue* as well as fine reading of the *Tale*. A splendid analysis of the complexity of Chaucerian irony may be found in U. C. Knoepflmacher, "Irony Through Scriptural Allusion: A Note on Chaucer's Prioresse," *ChauR* 4 (1970), 181-83, who maintains that

"even if the Prioresse's sentimentality is faulty, her ability to feel separates her from the unfeeling Pardoner who may be sending others to their death" (183).

8. "Echoes of Childermas in the Tale of the Prioress," *MLR* 34 (1939), 1–8. Ruggiers, *Art*, 181, also attributes the "unifying embellishment," which contributes to and heightens the *Tale's* "religious meaning," to the Mass and liturgy for the Feast of the Holy Innocents. See also J. C. Wenk, "On the Sources of the *Prioress's Tale*," *Med Stud* 17 (1955), 214–19, on this and other liturgical influences, and especially the sensitive and sympathetic essay of G. H. Russell, "Chaucer: The Prioress's Tale," *Medieval Literature and Civilization*, ed. D. A. Pearsall and R. A. Waldron (London, The Athlone Press, 1969), pp. 211–27, which anticipates many of the points in this chapter.

9. Ruggiers, *Art*, 179, also comments on the dignity in the Prioress's character which "gives us witness to the devotion and conscience which are the better parts of her personality."

10. To put it in other terms: by having "prevented" (in the archaic and etymological sense) the descent of the Holy Spirit, she has made herself a vehicle for "Prevenient Grace," a term Kean (*English Poetry*, II, 209) applies to the ensuing tale as well.

11. A comparison with the *Prologue* to the *Second Nun's Tale* is instructive. Much of the "Invocacio ad Mariam" (esp. ll. 54–56) reads like a rough draft of the *Prioress's Prologue*, but it is diffuse, eclectic, and unfocused upon what is to follow. Furthermore, it is placed between the disquisition on "ydelnesse" and the etymologizing of "Cecilie," an excess of pious information which is thoroughly unshapely and undramatic. In contrast, the work of the Prioress is both discrete and elegant.

12. As evidenced by the large number of analogues printed by Carleton Brown in *Sources and Analogues*.

13. Raymond Preston, *Chaucer* (London and New York, Sheed and Ward, 1952), p. 207.

14. One is reminded of Wordsworth's statement: "The mode in which the story is told amply atones for the extravagance of the miracle," *Selections from Chaucer Modernized*.

15. See Raymond Preston's cogent summary of the contemporary situation, "Chaucer, His Prioress, the Jews, and Professor Robinson," *NQ* 8 (1961), 7–8. The concluding lines on Hugh of Lincoln point to the source of this fantastic tradition of ritual

murder, which has been convincingly attributed to John of Lexington's influence on Henry III in an important article by Gavin I. Langmuir, "The Knight's Tale of Young Hugh of Lincoln," *Spec* 47 (1972), 459–82.

16. John Speirs, *Chaucer the Maker* (London, Faber and Faber, 1951), p. 180.

17. Erich Auerbach's comments on the "figural tradition" are pertinent here: "The various phases of the story of the hero or the traitor or the saint are concretized in gestures to such an extent that the pictured scenes, in the impression they produce, closely approach the character of symbols or figures, even in cases where it is not possible to trace any symbolic or figural signification," *Mimesis*, trans. Willard Trask (New York, Anchor Books, 1957), p. 101.

18. See Northrop Frye, *The Anatomy of Criticism* (Princeton, Princeton University Press, 1957), p. 144.

19. See, for example, the contemporary illuminations in Psalters and Books of Hours, the kind of art with which the Prioress would have been familiar in her professional life, reproduced in Eric G. Millar, *English Illuminated Manuscripts of the XIVth and XV Centuries* (Paris and Brussels, G. van Oest, 1928).

20. *The Discarded Image* (Cambridge, Cambridge University Press, 1964), p. 101.

21. Edward H. Kelly, "By Mouth of Innocentz: The Prioress Vindicated," *PLL* 5 (1969), 362–74, refers the style of the *Tale* to "Augustine's *granditer* category," a grand manner that is by definition "unreasoned" and cannot be long sustained, yet nonetheless has the power to move its audience to tears. Kelly's thesis is confirmed by the pilgrim's response to the Prioress's performance as well as by centuries of critical comment on Chaucer's characteristic pathos.

22. See Albert B. Friedman, "The *Prioress's Tale* and Chaucer's Anti-Semitism," *ChauR* 9 (1974), 118–29, and Robert W. Frank, Jr. in a forthcoming paper, "The Sentimental Anti-Semite." It must be admitted that the Prioress is a victim of our present sensitivity to this above other intolerances. Equally, the "new criticism" of the same era, by making a whipping-boy of "sentimentality," has made it very difficult to define the limits of pathos.

23. *English Poetry*, II, 193, 197.

24. For a definition of the term "illuminated," applied to the rhetorical practice admired in Chaucer by Lydgate and others, see ibid., 233: "to make expressive, capable of being used for the laying-out and organizing of a poet's subject-matter."

25. Jill Mann (*Estates Satire*, 128–37) demonstrates that the portrait of the Prioress is wrapped up in the ambiguities of "curteisie." Medieval devotional manuals encouraged nuns to think of their vocation in the imagery of an aristocratic, courtly "manere": in the *Ancrene Wisse*, for example, "the author associates beautiful scents, jewels and so on, with heavenly values" (p. 193). The Prioress of the *General Prologue* returns such spiritual metaphors to their literal, worldly meaning. What I suggest here is that, in her *Tale*, Chaucer reverses the process, as the effort to "countrefete cheere / Of court" is reinvested with a spiritual direction, if not its most profound values.

26. Compare the similar but unidentified judgment in the final note to Ruggiers chapter on the Prioress, *Art*, 183.

XI. The Franklin and the Merchant

1. See William L. Sullivan, "Chaucer's Man of Law as a Literary Critic," *MLN* 68 (1953), 1–8.

2. For the prehistory of the *Tale*, see Margaret Schlauch, *Chaucer's Constance and Accused Queens* (New York State Library, 1927).

3. For a fully annotated statement of this interpretation of the Franklin, see my article, "The Art of Chaucer's Franklin," *Neophil* 51 (1967), 55–71, reprinted with minor corrections in J. J. Anderson, ed., *Chaucer: The Canterbury Tales* (London, Macmillan Casebook Series, 1974), pp. 183–208. Some of the more recent publications will be cited in the notes below. The first volume of the *Chaucer Review* (1966) alone contains many articles of varying persuasions; see esp. Harry Berger, Jr., "The F-Fragment of the *Canterbury Tales*," 88–102, 135–56, and Russell A. Peck, "Sovereignty and the Two Worlds of the *Franklin's Tale*," 253–71.

4. The value of the Squire's rhetorical accomplishments has been subjected to considerable scholarly analysis. See Gardner Stillwell, "Chaucer in Tartary," *RES* 24 (1948), 177–88; D. A. Pearsall, "The Squire as Story-Teller," *UTQ* 24 (1964), 82–92;

and Robert S. Haller, "Chaucer's *Squire's Tale* and the Uses of Rhetoric," *MP* 62 (1964-65), 285-295. All of these critics take the Squire's performance as dramatically appropriate to the youthful aristocrat whose command of rhetoric is superficial and ostentatiously exhibited as a testimony to his social status. Haller (p. 294) concludes his essay with an estimate of the Franklin that is similar to mine: "The Squire is 'gentil' by blood and presumably may outgrow his ideas of the meaning of his degree; but in the meantime he has fed the pretensions of a man whose only qualification for gentillesse is self-indulgence."

5. See Charles F. Duncan, Jr., " 'Straw for Youre Gentilesse': The Gentle Franklin's Interruption of the Squire," *ChauR* 5 (1970), 161-64, and John W. Clark, "*Does* the Franklin Interrupt the Squire?" *ChauR* 7 (1972), 160-61.

6. *Chaucer and His Poetry*, 205, Donald R. Howard, "The Conclusion of the Marriage Group: Chaucer and the Human Condition," *MP* 17 (1959-60), 223-32, has cogently dissented from Kittredge's identification of Chaucer with the Franklin's "Solution" to the Marriage Question.

7. Robert K. Root, *The Poetry of Chaucer* (Cambridge, Mass., Houghton, 1906), p. 273.

8. Raymond Preston, *Chaucer*, 274.

9. See *Sources and Analogues*, 377-97, where Germaine Dempster and J.S.P. Tatlock offer as a "highly probable" source the story of Menedon in Boccaccio's *Filocolo*.

10. "Chaucer and the Breton Lays of the Auchinleck MS," *SP* 38 (1941), 14-33; see esp. pp. 16-17.

11. By Kathryn Hume, "Why Chaucer Calls the *Franklin's Tale* a Breton Lai," *PQ* 51 (1972), 365-79.

12. For this translation, see Robinson's note on l. 689. The Franklin's own rhetoric has been categorized by Benjamin S. Harrison, "The Rhetorical Inconsistency of Chaucer's Franklin," *SP* 32 (1935), 55-61, and sympathetically analyzed by Stephen Knight, "Rhetoric and Poetry in the Franklin's Tale," *ChauR* 4 (1970), 14-30.

13. On this *topos* of "affected modesty," see Curtius, *European Literature*, 83ff.

14. "Chaucer and the Rhetoricians, *Warton Lecture on English Poetry XVII* (Oxford, 1926), p. 20.

15. *The Text of the Canterbury Tales* (Chicago, 1940), II, 315.

16. "Chaucer at Work on the Complaint in the Franklin's Tale," *MLN* 52 (1937), 22. See also James Sledd, "Dorigen's Complaint," *SP* 45 (1947), 35–45. Robert A. Pratt, "St. Jerome in Jankyn's Book of Wikked Wyves," *Crit* 5 (1963), 316–22, suggests that the Franklin intends Dorigen as a foil for the Wife of Bath and that the additional virtuous exempla in her complaint are a critique of the Wife's conduct. Donald C. Baker, "A Crux in Chaucer's Franklin's Tale: Dorigen's Complaint," *JEGP* 60 (1961), 56–64, argues that the sequence of exempla reflects changes in Dorigen's attitude toward her situation.

17. For a similar evaluation of Arveragus, see D. W. Robertson, Jr., *A Preface*, 470–72.

18. For a contrary view, see Kean, *English Poetry*, II, 93, who considers the *Tale* "perhaps not entirely serious," but "a gracious story, graciously told," and "to see it as a parody of courtliness is to underrate it grossly." On the theme of "gentillesse," see Alfred David, "Sentimental Comedy in the *Franklin's Tale*," *AnM* 6 (1965), 19–27, and Alan T. Gaylord, "The Promises in The *Franklin's Tale*," *ELH* 31 (1964), 331–65, who distinguish, on generic and casuistic grounds respectively, the teller from the poet, and Lindsay A. Mann, " 'Gentilesse' and the Franklin's Tale," *SP* 63 (1966), 10–29, who does not.

19. R. M. Lumiansky, in his article, "The Character and the Performance of Chaucer's Franklin," *UTQ* 20 (1951), 344–56, reproduced in *Of Sondry Folk*, pp. 180–93, finds a discrepancy between the sophisticated, aristocratic ideal of courtly love and the practical bourgeois insistence upon a perfect, happy marriage. So, too, C. Hugh Holman, "Courtly Love in the Merchant's and Franklin's Tales," *ELH* 18 (1952), 241–52. But see Kean's refutation of this view on the basis of its source in the *Roman, English Poetry*, II, 141ff., and Gervase Mathew, "Marriage and *Amour Courtois* in Late-Fourteenth-Century England," *Essays Presented to Charles Williams*, ed. C. S. Lewis (Oxford, Oxford University Press, 1947), pp. 128–35. Two recent articles propose a qualification of the "ideal marriage" by the characterization of the participants in the *Tale*: See A. M. Kearney, "Truth and Illusion in the *Franklin's Tale*," *EIC* 19 (1969), 245–53, and Malcolm Golding, "The Importance of Keeping 'Trouthe' in *The Franklin's Tale*," *MÆ* 39 (1970), 306–12.

20. Compare Kean, *English Poetry*, II, 146: "In this predica-
ment, Arveragus is steadfast in keeping the vows he made to his
wife on their marriage. He approaches the problem as it affects
her as an individual, not as a wife whose identity is not separate
from his own or who is thought of as his possession. This is the
generosity in which his 'gentilesse' consists, and it is so remark-
able that it triggers off all the subsequent acts of *gentilesse* which
ensure the happy ending."

21. See, for example, Kean's excellent comments on the struc-
ture of the *Knight's Tale, English Poetry*, II, 66–70. Paul E. Gray,
"Synthesis and the Double Standard in the *Franklin's Tale*," *TSLL*
7 (1965), 213–24, offers a sophisticated discussion of the actual
patterns in the *Tale*.

22. Kean, *English Poetry*, II, 147, concurs at least in accusing
Dorigen of the lack of patience, as do Gray and Kearney in the
articles mentioned above. On the philosophical implications of
the *Tale*, see Edwin B. Benjamin, "The Concept of Order in the
Franklin's Tale," *PQ* 38 (1950), 119–24, and Gerhard Joseph,
"*The Franklin's Tale*: Chaucer's Theodicy," *ChauR* 1 (1966),
20–32.

23. Compare Mann's perceptive reading of the ironic implica-
tions of the portrait in the *General Prologue*: "We are invited to
admire the means, the superlative way in which the Franklin pur-
sues a life-style, rather than the ends towards which it is directed
. . . Chaucer transforms what for other writers are the burdensome
preparations, the loading of the stomach, the selfish guzzling, the
restless search for titillating variety, into a hymn to 'pleyn delit',"
Estates Satire, 158–59.

24. There are indications, however, that the flurry will be a
brief one. See Norman T. Harrington, "Chaucer's Merchant's
Tale: Another Swing of the Pendulum," *PMLA* 86 (1971), 25–
31, for a summary of the early views and a bibliography. Robert J.
Blanch has edited a collection of the important articles, *Geoffrey
Chaucer: Merchant's Tale*, Merrill Casebooks (Columbus, Ohio,
Charles E. Merrill, 1970).

25. The text is not found in all the MSS. See Tatlock, *Develop-
ment and Chronology*, 200–201, and J. M. Manly and Edith
Rickert, *The Text of the Canterbury Tales* (Chicago, University
of Chicago Press, 1940), II, 266.

26. This view has been thoroughly explored by Tatlock and

Sedgewick (in Blanch's anthology) and more recently by Rug-
giers's chapter in the *Art*, Donaldson's commentary in *Chaucer's
Poetry*, and others who at best wish to salvage something of the
fabliau tone. The contrary position is the work of Bertrand H.
Bronson, "Afterthoughts on the Merchant's Tale," *SP* 58 (1961),
583–96, and Robert M. Jordan, "The Non-Dramatic Disunity of
the Merchant's Tale," *PMLA* 78 (1963), 293–99, both of whom
over-react, I believe, to Kittredge's characterization of the tone as
a "frenzy of contempt and hatred." Another recent attempt to
deny the self-revelation of the teller is Martin Stevens, "'And
Venus Laugheth': An Interpretation of the Merchant's Tale,"
ChauR 7 (1972), 117–31.

27. Mary C. Schroeder, "Fantasy in the Merchant's Tale," *Crit*
12 (1970), 167–79, extending the ideas of Donaldson and Owen,
offers a valuable discussion of the mirror image.

28. "The Crucial Passages in Five of *The Canterbury Tales:
A Study in Irony and Symbol*," *JEGP*, 52 (1953), 294–311.

29. See, for example, Owen, "Crucial Passages," 297–301,
though I find his description of January as an idealist misleading.

30. The enclosed garden, a traditional figure for the Virgin
and her immaculate womb, is also savagely parodied by May's
plans for sexual fulfillment, invisible to her Joseph–January, in a
place where her vehement professions of obedience constitute an
ironic inversion of Griselda's behavior.

31. See John S.P. Tatlock, "The Marriage Service in Chaucer's
Merchant's Tale," *MLN* 32 (1917), 373–74.

32. On this episode, see Mortimer J. Donovan, "The Image of
Pluto and Proserpine in *The Merchant's Tale*," *PQ* 36 (1957),
49–60, and Karl P. Wentersdorf, "Theme and Structure in *The
Merchant's Tale*: The Function of the Pluto Episode," *PMLA* 80
(1965), 522–27.

33. See Germaine Dempster's chapter in *Sources and Analogues*.

34. Which may have been the motive described by the merchant
of the *Shipman's Tale* to "kepen oure estaat in pryvetee," ll.
230–34. "Concealment is the key to the Merchant's character," ac-
cording to John H. Elliott, Jr., "The Two Tellers of *The Mer-
chant's Tale*," *TSL* 9 (1964), 11–17.

35. G. L. Kittredge, "Chaucer's Discussion of Marriage," *MP*
9 (1912), 435–67.

36. Owen, "Crucial Passages," 301.

XII. The Wife of Bath and The Nun's Priest

1. The approaches of Curry, *Mediaeval Sciences*, 91–118, and Frederick Tupper, "Chaucer and the Seven Deadly Sins," *PMLA* 29 (1914), 93–128, as well as H. R. Patch, "Characters in Medieval Literature," *MLN* 40 (1925), 1–14.

2. The views, respectively, of D. W. Robertson, Jr., *Preface*, esp. pp. 380–82, and David Holbrook, *The Quest for Love* (University, Alabama, The University of Alabama Press, 1965), pp. 91–126. For a cross-section of recent opinions, see *ChauR* 4 (1970), No. 2.

3. Robert A. Pratt, "The Development of the Wife of Bath," *Studies in Medieval Literature*, ed. MacEdward Leach (Philadelphia, University of Pennsylvania Press, 1961), pp. 45–79.

4. On the medieval English and Scots tradition, see Francis Lee Utley, *The Crooked Rib* (Columbus, The Ohio State University, 1944). The tradition is also discussed by Mann, *Estates Satire*, 121–27, and the adaptation of Jean de Meun's La Vieille, by Kean, *English Poetry*, II, 148–56.

5. The most perceptive study of this section of the Prologue I know is by Anne Mendelson (Iger), "Some Uses of the Bible and Biblical Authority in the Wife of Bath's Prologue and Tale" (unpublished Ph.D. dissertation, Bryn Mawr College, 1972).

6. This observation is supported by Mann, *Estates Satire*, 121f.

7. On the possibility of a single source for this material, though with a very different interpretation, see Robert A. Pratt, "Chaucer and the Hand that Fed Him," *Spec* 41 (1966), 619–42. On "Jankyn's Book," see note 3 above and Pratt's numerous other articles.

8. An interesting modern survival occurs in Muriel Spark's *The Comforters*, where the heroine hears a typewriter and voices recounting the events she is in the process of enacting.

9. *French Tradition*, 132–33. The term is borrowed from S. L. Bethell's *Shakespeare and the Popular Dramatic Tradition* (London, 1944), pp. 26–29.

10. C. S. Lewis, "Imagination and Thought in the Middle Ages," *Studies in Medieval and Renaissance Literature*, coll. by Walter Hooper (Cambridge, The University Press, 1966), p. 54, an attractive pair of lectures that complement his *Discarded Image* (Cambridge, 1964).

11. On the *Tale* as a reply to the Monk, see Kean, *English Poetry*, II, 133–39.

12. *Mediaeval Sciences,* 195–240.

13. *Chaucer's Poetry* (New York, Ronald Press, 1958), p. 941. See also the important study of the narrative voice in the *Tale* and its genre by R. T. Leneghan, "The Nun's Priest's Fable." *PMLA* 78 (1963), 300–307.

14. *Chaucer's Poetry,* 943.

15. See E. T. Donaldson, *Speaking of Chaucer* (London, The Athlone Press, 1970), p. 88.

16. "The Road of Excess," *Myth and Symbol,* ed. Bernice Slote (Lincoln, University of Nebraska Press, 1963), p. 14.

17. On the ancient association of story-telling with "something useful," a moral, practical advice, a proverb or maxim, see Walter Benjamin, "The Story Teller," sect. iv.

The Uses of Fiction

1. *A Preface,* 342.

2. See J. B. Friedman, *Orpheus in the Middle Ages* (Cambridge, Mass., Harvard University Press, 1970), p. 130.

3. See Delany, *House of Fame,* pp. 3–4, citing Trevisa's englishing of the *Polychronicon.*

4. *A Preface,* p. 335.

5. See James D. Gordon, "Chaucer's Retraction: A Review of Opinion," *Studies in Medieval Literature,* ed. MacEdward Leach (Philadelphia, University of Pennsylvania Press, 1961), pp. 81–96.

6. *Boccaccio on Poetry,* trans. Charles G. Osgood (Indianapolis, Bobbs-Merrill Co., 1956), Ch. 14.

7. *The Complaint of Nature,* trans. Douglas M. Moffat (New Haven, Yale University Press, 1908), p. 40. See also Curtius, *European Literature,* Chs. 11 and 12.

8. A New Family Instructor (1727), pp. 51–53, cited by Alan D. McKillop, *The Early Masters of English Fiction* (Lawrence, University of Kansas Press, 1962), p. 5.

9. Harold C. Goddard, "Chaucer's Legend of Good Women," *JEGP* 7 (1908), 87–129; 8 (1909), 47–112.

10. See Gilson on "Love and Its Object," *The Spirit of Mediaeval Philosophy,* trans. A.H.C. Downes (New York, Charles Scribner's Sons, 1936).

11. "An Evaluation of the *Pardoner's Tale,*" p. 84.

12. I use Barney's terms, ibid., p. 88, though this study was completed to this point before his excellent essay appeared.

INDEX
OF AUTHORS AND
WORKS CITED

287

Library of Congress Cataloging in Publication Data

Burlin, Robert B.
   Chaucerian fiction.

   Includes bibliographical references and index.
   1. Chaucer, Geoffrey, d. 1400—Criticism and interpretation.   I. Title.
PR1924.B78   821'.1   76-45892
ISBN 0-691-06322-2